DISCARD

Unaffordable

Unaffordable

*American Healthcare
from Johnson to Trump*

Jonathan Engel

THE UNIVERSITY OF WISCONSIN PRESS

The University of Wisconsin Press
1930 Monroe Street, 3rd Floor
Madison, Wisconsin 53711-2059
uwpress.wisc.edu

3 Henrietta Street, Covent Garden
London WC2E 8LU, United Kingdom
eurospanbookstore.com

Printed in the United States of America

This book may be available in a digital edition.

Library of Congress Cataloging-in-Publication Data
Names: Engel, Jonathan, author.
Title: Unaffordable: American healthcare from Johnson to Trump /
   Jonathan Engel.
Description: Madison, Wisconsin: The University of Wisconsin Press,
   [2018] | Includes bibliographical references and index.
Identifiers: LCCN 2017015526 | ISBN 9780299314101 (cloth: alk. paper)
Subjects: LCSH: Medical policy—United States—History—20th century
   | Medical policy—United States—History—21st century. | Medical
   care—United States—History—20th century. | Medical care—United
   States—History—21st century.
Classification: LCC RA395.A3 E546 2018 | DDC 368.38/200973—dc23
LC record available at https://lccn.loc.gov/2017015526

aided with a grant from

Figure Foundation

in search of the increment of healing

For

Andrew and Samuel

הִנֵּה מַה טּוֹב וּמַה נָּעִים שֶׁבֶת אַחִים גַּם יָחַד.

How good and pleasant it is for brothers to dwell together.

Psalm 133:1

Contents

Timeline of Major Federal Legislation Affecting Healthcare Delivery

1964–66   Congress creates Model Cities and the Office of Economic Opportunity, leading to funding of Neighborhood Health Centers

1966   Medicare and Medicaid launched

1972   National Advisory Committee on Health, Science, and Society created for considering ethical parameters of care

1972   Beginning of Professional Standards Review Organizations to monitor quality of physicians and hospital services

1973   Health Professions Education Act passed to augment medical education budgets

1973   HMO Act passed to direct grants and start-up loans to HMOs

1974   Creation of Health Systems Agencies through the Health Planning Act

1978   Adoption of DRG payment scheme by New Jersey Medicaid

1978   Consumer Choice Health Plan proposed by Alain Enthoven

1983   Medicare adopts the DRG payment scheme

1985   Medicare offers risk contracting for all beneficiaries to enroll in HMOs

1988   Catastrophic Care Act passed to expand Medicare coverage
            (repealed later that year)
1989   Beginning of Agency for Healthcare Quality and Research
1992   Medicare reforms DRG levels using the RBRVS
1992   Project 3000 by 2000 proposed to increase numbers of mi-
            nority physicians
1994   President Clinton proposes the Health Security Act based
            on the principles of managed competition (fails to pass
            Congress)
1997   The Food and Drug Administration allows direct-to-
            consumer TV ads for prescription drugs
1997   Balanced Budget Act passed, creates Medicare+Choice
2003   Medicare Prescription Drug, Improvement and Moderniza-
            tion Act (Medicare Part D) passed
2010   Patient Protection and Affordable Care Act (ACA, "Obama-
            care") passed, creates universal mandate and health pur-
            chasing exchanges and expands Medicaid
2012   Supreme Court rules universal mandate constitutional but
            removes mandate for Medicaid expansion
2013   Universal mandate begins under the terms of the ACA

Unaffordable

Introduction

A 1971 editorial in the *New Republic*, the small but highly influential magazine of political commentary, announced that the US health system was "staggering towards a breakdown." With hospital care having climbed from $48.15 a day in 1966 to $74 a day (a 53 percent increase), the system had been recently profiled as "Our Ailing Medical System" on the cover of a national business magazine. "We think this can't go on," wrote the editors.[1] Writing concurrently, Rashi Fein, professor of healthcare economics at Harvard, declared simply, "It is a mess."[2]

A mess, indeed.

This is fundamentally a book about *system*, or lack thereof. In theory, a healthcare system exists as a coordinated network of public and private providers spread throughout the country to provide care where care is needed while not overproviding care where it is not. Individuals should be able to turn to insurers to make certain that their total financial obligations to that system do not become crushingly high, while using the same insurers to distribute, or perhaps redistribute, assets so that all citizens have access to at least some care. Ideally all of this should be done as inexpensively as possible such that individuals and nations do not purchase services and products that provide little benefit.

This is a tall order, to say the least, and no country in the world does this perfectly. The nations that routinely top lists of healthcare, such as France, Germany, and Switzerland, spend enormous amounts of money each year keeping their citizens well. Wealthy people in many nations, notably in the United Kingdom, spend additional funds to purchase higher-grade care outside of the general system in which healthcare is produced and delivered. Complaints abound, with each system falling short in different areas—extraordinarily short doctor-patient interactions in Japan, lengthy waits for elective surgery in Canada and the United Kingdom, a moribund biomedical research enterprise in Germany, and bureaucratic barriers to over-the-counter medications in France. No country delivers healthcare perfectly or seam-lessly, and a careful analyst can find room for improvement wherever she looks.

But the US health system is uniquely dysfunctional among industrial-ized nations. Spending nearly a third more per capita on healthcare compared with other leading nations, while producing outcomes that place it near the bottom of industrialized economies, US healthcare is uncoordinated, excessive, laden with profit-taking, and overcapitalized. The United States invests more in hospital infrastructure and physician training than does any other country, yet finds itself unable to provide primary and prenatal care to large numbers of its citizens. The profound changes in the system implemented under the Affordable Care Act ("Obamacare") have, if anything, concretized long-standing systemic problems. Prices continue to rise quickly, administrative overhead and costs grow ever more Byzantine, and young physicians find the cost of training so daunting that careers in primary care medicine are closed to all but the wealthiest or most idealistic.

Some of the roots of this dysfunction can be traced to decisions made in the early twentieth century not to pursue a unified single-payer model, but much of the dysfunction has grown incrementally over the past half century.[3] At many junctures individuals or institutions have made decisions that may have been rational for a person but produced broad effects that were ultimately inimical to the health of the popula-tion or to the fiscal health of the healthcare system. Hospitals that chose to invest in unnecessary equipment and redundant beds grew larger and stronger but heaped unnecessary capital into local markets, the cost of which would need to be recouped through higher billings. Physi-cians who chose to pursue specialty and subspecialty training increased their expected lifetime earnings but created a shortage of primary care physicians whose ranks could only be filled by importing doctors from abroad or by promoting advanced practice nurses into roles as primary care physicians. Pharmaceutical companies, which produced new drugs of dubious utility, larded the system with products aggressively promoted by armies of sales representatives.

Healthcare is a complicated product insofar as we are ambivalent about its publicness. In economic terms, a public good is a good people benefit from regardless of whether they help pay for it. The classic examples are lighthouses and police forces. We generally produce public goods in the public sector and distribute the costs over the population through the tax system. Public goods may benefit individuals and the broader society; education falls into this category. We each benefit from the education we receive, and we accrue benefits from others' education by living in a wealthier society with better services and better employment opportunities. There is not much point in being well educated if nobody around you is.

Healthcare is similar to education. We benefit individually from access to healthcare and from our neighbors having access to healthcare. In part this is because good healthcare prevents or limits the spread of infectious disease, and in part we benefit from living in a society where those around us are healthy and vigorous; firms are more productive, the military and police force are stronger, our children's friends are more robust. Precisely this tension between the public and private benefits of healthcare have made us so ambivalent about pursuing a clear and unified system of healthcare delivery. If healthcare is a public good, like the highways, then it behooves us to plan carefully and only produce and deliver the exact care we all need to consume to stay healthy. But if healthcare is a private good, we are interested in being able to peruse wares in a diversified and competitive private marketplace where we can shop and consume as much as we wish. Such is the tension.

Adding to this problem is the fact that markets fail in various ways when healthcare is produced and consumed. Competitive markets require transparency, good information, and for consumers to know their own utility, and this is most certainly not true for healthcare. Few among us know what we really need when purchasing healthcare (which is why we consult with trained doctors). In times of acute need we do not have the time to comparison shop and thus cannot exert normal consumer pressure on the market to produce high-quality goods at competitive prices. Moreover, doctors exist in a state of moral compromise in that they make money on the therapeutic interventions they recommend for us. "Never ask a barber if you need a haircut," goes an old saw, yet we frequently ask surgeons if we need surgery, endoscopists if we need endoscopy, and radiologists if we need X-rays. As far back as 1973, Paul Ellwood argued for a radical new organizational structure— the health maintenance organization (HMO)—by pointing out that a sick person was a financial liability to an HMO but a financial asset to a provider of conventional fee-for-service care.[4]

As we examine the evolution of the US healthcare system over the past half century, we find other market flaws. Black Americans prefer to get their care from black doctors, yet gifted black undergraduates tend to eschew careers in medicine at unusually high rates. Most of us prefer to consume care close to where we live, yet most doctors prefer to live and work in narrow bands of upper-middle-class suburbs surrounding a handful of great cities. Most care needs to be provided at a generalist level, yet most US-trained physicians prefer to practice medicine within very narrow and highly specialized boundaries. The healthiest people are those who take care of themselves through healthy living and eating and seek wellness care long before problems grow acute. Yet doctors make the most money off of treating advanced, acute cases of a variety of illnesses and syndromes. The poorest citizens are generally the sickest, but the poorest are most likely to be insured through Medicaid, which many physicians refuse to take as payment. Rashi Fein once wrote of the healthcare market: "The invisible hand of the market in health is all thumbs."[5]

Perhaps the greatest market flaw is in the insurance markets. Insurance is a product predicated on distributing random risk across broad groups of people. But insurance cannot work in distributing healthcare costs, where risk and pathology are highly predictable based on age, past health history, family history, and occupation. The only way to bring most Americans into insurance markets is by forcing them into mandatory groupings, be they work-based, place-based, trade-based, or something else entirely. This need for a mandate to create workable insurance pools has been clear since Otto von Bismarck forced his entire population to purchase state-based sickness insurance at the end of the nineteenth century, yet we still resist the concept.[6] Even as the Affordable Care Act was being argued in front of the Supreme Court, a justice asked if the government could compel citizens to buy a product they might never need, such as broccoli. US Solicitor General Donald Verrilli Jr. replied that in this case it was okay, as all citizens would someday need healthcare, whereas not all people would need broccoli.[7] Verrilli was wrong, however. The government mandates that people buy insurance not because we will all need it someday, but because we know to a large extent who will need it and who will not, and thus private insurance markets cannot work.

Last, healthcare usage correlates closely with age; we use little when we are young and a lot more when we are old. This usage patterns make sense, given the increasing frailty of our bodies as we age. The proper way to distribute the cost of our life's usage is to overpay when we are young so that we can underpay when we are old. We have mandated this pattern of payment to some degree since 1965 when we increased the FICA payroll tax on all earned dollars up to a cap to pay for part of the cost of Medicare Part A. But Medicare does not become available until we are 65, and many of us will begin consuming a lot of healthcare before then. One response might have been to expand Medicare to people of younger ages, but that proved politically unpopular. An alternative solution has been to require that people join private insurance pools through the terms of the Affordable Care Act. It is difficult to understand why people resist the essential actuarial soundness of the requirement.

These market failures lead one to consider discarding market-based solutions altogether and turning to a tightly controlled government model of care. This is what most other countries have done, whether through nationalization of hospitals and insurance or tight regulatory controls on capital investment and training. The United States continues to resist these sorts of strictures and allows instead medical entrepreneurs to build hospitals, open practices, found clinics, and expand operations where they choose to, rather than where they are needed. Market failures dictate that normal market constraints—falling demand and price sensitivity—do not work to limit supplies as we would expect them to. In fact, we have long known of the odd phenomenon of induced demand in medicine: the ability of a doctor to raise demand for her products or services, demand that did not exist prior to her availability. Numerous studies, many conducted by the Dartmouth Institute for Health Policy and Clinical Practice, have shown that the frequency of many procedures is much better predicted by the number of doctors present who do the procedure, rather than by any objective assessment of the demand for the procedure.[8] Induced demand renders most market mechanisms irrelevant.

The story becomes more complicated when we venture into murky ethical areas. Since 1968, medicine has periodically exceeded our ability to clearly evaluate life and health. Through such landmark cases as those involving Karen Ann Quinlan, Nancy Cruzan, and Baby Doe (from the 1980s), we have come to recognize that there are times when our physicians and hospitals should sagely refrain from treating and let nature take its course. We see now that more life is not necessarily better life, and that more medicine may actually lead to diminished utility. Decisions in such extreme cases, in which we must grapple with fundamental definitions of when life begins, when death occurs, and when life is simply not worth prolonging are made even harder by financial concerns. When we spend hundreds of thousands of dollars treating patients who are unlikely to improve, we effectively decide not to treat others who might improve but who cannot afford high-quality care. As one bioethicist asks, "What are we *not* doing with that money?"[9]

Underlying the story of US healthcare since 1968 is a pattern of ever-rising prices. In every year in the past fifty, healthcare prices have risen faster than the Consumer Price Index—sometimes much faster. In two years alone, to take one example, the cost of tuition for a year at Georgetown University Medical School rose from $5,000 to $10,000.[10] The Congressional Budget Office predicted that without strong cost control measures, total spending on healthcare would rise from 16 percent of gross domestic product (GDP) in 2007 to 25 percent in 2025 and 49 percent in 2082. The costs of Medicare and Medicaid alone would rise from 4 percent of GDP to 20 percent during the same time.[11]

Rising prices have forced health insurers—private and public—to shift a growing portion of all healthcare costs onto their policy holders through higher premiums, co-payments, annual deductibles, and out-of-network costs. Purchasers of bronze-tier policies on the federal exchanges, which began operating in 2013, found that their policies required them to pay the first $9,000 of health costs they incurred each year out of pocket.[12] Medicare patients similarly were responsible for 20 percent of all hospital costs up to 150 days of care a year: a sum that could easily total tens of thousands of dollars for a lengthy stay.[13] Patients have responded by eschewing necessary care, self-medicating, seeking care from alternative healers, or going abroad for tests and procedures. When Atul Gawande, a physician and medical columnist, asked several colleagues if they had treated patients whose health had been adversely affected by lack of insurance, one responded, "This falls under the 'too numerous to count' section."[14]

This book has no simple take-away message. Certain themes are constant, including specialization, overexpansion, inflation, and profiteering. But other themes are not so easy to digest, including the stubborn disparities in health status in the United States between rich and poor, black and white, and city and country. Underneath most of the questions are more ethereal considerations of mission, purpose, and morality. What claim do we have on life, and to what extent can we ask others to shoulder our debts? Does life have a price, and does that price fluctuate with the quality of our experiences? What claim on our public funds do we allocate to the young, the old, the not-yet-born, and the permanently incapacitated? How do we balance our lust for miracles with the mundane demands of prophylactic care?

1

A System Run Amok

Rising Costs

In 1969, rising healthcare costs were gaining prominence as one of the nation's foremost domestic challenges. Over the previous decade, average annual medical costs for a family of four had risen from $408 to $676: a rate of increase roughly three times that of general inflation. Some psychiatrists were charging a "dollar a minute" for therapy, while hospital beds were topping $160 a day.[1] The substantial injection of funds provided by the four-year-old Medicare and Medicaid programs were acting as an accelerant on this trend. Cost overruns in both programs promised to be "spectacular."[2] In July of that year, President Richard Nixon deemed the rising costs, along with growing opposition to Medicaid commitments from state governors, a "massive crisis."[3]

Hospitals led the sector, constituting 40 percent of all health expenditures by 1970.[4] Their costs rose in part because of a tendency of board members and administrators to overinvest in technology and capacity. An arms-race mentality had seized many of the institutions after Medicare had come into being in 1966, with easy money facilitating irresponsible investments in machines, operating rooms, and specialty units. By 1971, the typical general hospital was equipped for far more specialized tests and procedures than local demand warranted—777 US hospitals were equipped with heart surgery suites, for example, but nearly 30 percent performed no procedures. Stuart Altman, a deputy assistant secretary at the Department of Health, Education, and Welfare (HEW), feared that endlessly rising hospital costs had "the potential to blow our system right out of the water."[5] One critic wrote, "The result of this Cadillac-only syndrome is that we pay Cadillac prices when we, or most of us, might be willing to settle, or might be sensible to settle, for Chevrolet."[6]

It was not just cost increases, however, that threatened the integrity of the nation's medical system. Even for those who could afford the bills, shortages of physicians—or more accurately misdistribution of physicians—threatened to bar sick citizens from obtaining care. The problem seemed to be not so much that the number of physicians and other healthcare workers had declined, but that the new sort of high-tech medicine the nation was embracing required greater numbers of highly trained professionals to deliver the care. In the greater Washington, DC, area, for example, the number of hospital beds had increased by 25 percent since 1960, but the number of hospital employees had increased by 75 percent during the same period. Open heart surgery might require a dozen people in the operating room, with multiple surgeons, interns, nurses, anesthesiologists, and technicians all participating in the operating team in an effort to produce a surgical miracle. New dialysis and radiation units opening in urology and oncology divisions promised new hope for patients, but at the cost of intensive use of highly trained clinicians. Walter McNerney, president of the Blue Cross Association, sagely noted that the new technology was generally additive: "Rarely does it substitute for a significant number of simpler procedures preceding it," he wrote.[7]

Nobody in the tripod of hospital leadership—doctors, board members, administrators—was inclined to rein in these excesses. Board members, drawn largely from the local business community, tended to equate hospital expansion with prestige. Doctors viewed increased capacity as an invitation to admit more patients, perform more tests, and attempt newer procedures.[8] Administrators wedded their own professional success to the approval of board members and the medical staff. Three business analysts studying the management model in 1973 noted that to administrators, "it appears that neither the trustees nor the medical staff really want to control costs."[9] Not surprisingly, they did not.

Fueling the irrational expansion was a torrent of easy Medicare and Medicaid money which by 1973 had displaced local philanthropy as the major source of investment capital for hospital building. The operating budget of many community hospitals now came largely from government sources.[10] Philanthropy's contribution to the annual budget, meanwhile, had dwindled to 3 percent, making many "private" hospitals essentially extensions of state and federal governmental programs.[11] Given the provisions embedded in the original Medicare legislation, which failed to cap the program and committed the federal government to making endlessly larger commitments to the growing hospital sector, Congress had effectively given private hospitals the "power to tax."[12]

Unsurprisingly, all of this construction produced many empty beds. Some of the new capacity was absorbed by physicians attempting new procedures on sicker patients, but much was left fallow. By 1971, 20 percent of hospital beds on any given day were empty—roughly five times the vacancy rate for hospital beds in other industrialized nations. Although the admissions rate for new patients actually increased by 2 percent that year, it was offset by declining lengths of stay. Hospitals were becoming places of concentrated procedures and quick discharges, rather than oases of respite. Week-long postoperative recoveries were now endured mostly at home, or at best in an affiliated nursing facility. The new model was reflected in rising staff ratios, with recommended employees per patient rising by 3 percent in one year.[13] The building spree had not only been irresponsible. In failing to take into account new models of hospital practice, it was turning out to be anachronistic.

Undergirding the huge hospital expansion lay Medicare, the pathbreaking national health insurance program for the elderly adopted in 1965. The program seemed almost designed to be inflationary, with its legislative preamble expressly prohibiting any governmental oversight over medical practice.[14] Almost alone, Medicare had doubled the portion of healthcare paid for by government, going from 13 percent in 1966 to 26 percent in 1972.[15] Indeed, of all federal funds spent purchasing healthcare, through the Veterans Administration, Department of Defense, federal hospitals, Indian Health Service, and Medicaid, nearly three fourths ($16 billion) was funneled through Medicare by 1972.[16]

Medicare was actually two programs: a mandatory program of hospital insurance funded through payroll taxes (Part A) and an optional program of physician insurance funded through general taxes, monthly premiums, and relatively extensive deductibles and co-payments (Part B). Part A was the more consequential of the two programs—a form of socialized insurance that underwrote the majority of healthcare risk in the nation's elderly population. Part A was highly inflationary, however, in that it allowed hospitals to roll debt service into their patient billings and pass these costs back to the federal government as part of the "reasonable charges" allowed by law. Thus, not only did Medicare fail to rein in the inflationary impulse in hospitals, it significantly exacerbated it.[17]

Moreover, Medicare was as susceptible as any government program to political influence. Hospital, doctors, and patient advocacy groups aggressively lobbied for greater benefits and reimbursement budgets, with little opposition to offset them. From the program's inception, members of Congress and federal oversight agencies faced enormous pressure from patient lobbies to expand coverage into long-term care, new drugs, experimental procedures, and expensive tests. By 1973, for example, parents of children whose kidneys had failed and who required thrice weekly dialysis treatment at an annual cost of $50,000 persuaded Medicare's masters to cover the treatment. Despite the fact that dialysis and kidney transplants were inimical to the original vision of Medicare—a program of social insurance for the nation's elderly—the Health Care Financing Administration (HCFA) agreed to cover the procedures for thirteen thousand eligible patients that year. The initial cost of $250 million was slated to rise to $1 billion by 1978, even as HEW attempted to control the financial damage by limiting dialysis reimbursement to 750 institutions.[18]

Medicare expansion along multiple axes—volume, treatments, patients, drugs, services, tests—drove costs up rapidly. The 2.27 percent payroll tax used to fund the Part A program was originally applied to only the first $6,600 of wage earners' pay; within three years, Congress was forced to raise the taxable wage cap to $7,800. In planning the program, the federal budget office had estimated the 1970 cost of the program to be $3.1 billion. But when 1970 arrived, the cost of the program already exceeded $5.8 billion. In a frantic effort to control costs, HEW raised Part A deductibles from $40 in 1966 to $44 in 1969, and then again to $52 in 1970. Even so, analysts working for the Senate Finance Committee predicted that Part A alone would cost taxpayers $131 billion over the next twenty-five years.[19]

As fast as Medicare had been increasing, Medicaid had been growing even more quickly. Conceived as a sort of poverty add-on to the 1965 Medicare legislation, Medicaid was a series of state-level programs that states adopted voluntarily in an effort to garner federal matching funds. But just as Medicare was practically designed to be inflationary, so was Medicaid. The enabling legislation demanded that states continually expand their poverty medical programs to cover every medically indigent resident by 1975, forcing states into poverty care programs far more expansive and generous than most had previously deemed necessary. Thus, by 1969, state and federal poverty care programs throughout the country were spending $5.5 billion annually—nearly four times the $1.5 billion they had spent in 1965.[20] California, for example, had increased its spending on the poor from $186 million in 1964 (through its Public Assistance Medical Care program) to just over $1 billion by 1971 (through the state's Medi-Cal program).[21]

Such rapidly escalating Medicaid bills caused panic among governors. Most state governments simply could not afford to cover the bills. New Mexico went as far as threatening to end its Medicaid program entirely if relief was not forthcoming. In response, Congress agreed to extend the timeline for program expansion to 1977, although several prominent liberals, such as Ted Kennedy (D-MA) and Abraham Ribicoff (D-CT) called the move "regressive" and a "potentially significant step backward."[22]

With so much money coursing through the system, physicians were seduced. The "customary and prevailing fee" language in the Medicare legislation meant that doctors had every incentive to push the boundaries of previously acceptable fees while inflating the volume of visits. Unethical doctors resorted to "gang visits" of nursing homes and hospitals, unnecessarily visiting all of their patients in a facility—forty to fifty patients a day—all of which could be billed to Medicare through a Blue Shield intermediary. Some surgeons began to parse their pre- and postoperative care such that these visits constituted separate billable events from the surgery.[23]

The billing guidelines ceased to make sense. One study of physician billing rates conducted in 1974 showed prices ranging from $280 to $1,200 for a mastectomy; $226 to $1,075 for a leg amputation; $168 to $610 for an appendectomy; and $147 to $650 for a basic hernia repair.[24] In response, Blue Shield plans disallowed some of the more exorbitant charges but provoked the ire of the American Medical Association, which claimed there was "no such thing as overcharge, only fees that vary from low to high."[25]

High reimbursement rates seemed to embolden many physicians to provide more intensive services that could be billed at higher rates but were of questionable utility. A "wait-and-see" attitude among surgeons gave way to an aggressive practice ethos, in which more invasive procedures became routine.[26] The perverted financial incentives were in evidence in the disparate rates of surgery among US and British patients, with Americans opting for surgery at nearly double the rate of their British counterparts.[27] A hospital administrator described the medical staff of his hospital as behaving "like fighter pilots" as they strongly resisted his cost-cutting efforts.[28]

The problem went beyond greed. The system seemed designed to inflate costs, built on the founding "cost reimbursement" principles of the Blue Cross plans. The earliest of these, founded in Dallas, Texas, in 1929, seemed benign enough: nurses and teachers paid 50 cents a month into a fund to prepay up to twenty-one days of hospitalization each year. The plan contained a hidden poison pill at its genesis, however: the program would reimburse hospitals at their declared costs rather than on a prearranged fee schedule. The system of Blue Cross plans emanating from the Dallas experiment grew rapidly after World War II, increasing from six million members in 1940 to seventy-eight million by 1971. Other private health insurers followed the cost-reimbursement model and also grew quickly. By 1971 the Prudential Insurance Company, the nation's largest for-profit health insurance company, had forty-eight million policy holders.[29]

Opaque medical pricing exacerbated the problem. Physicians and hospitals fiercely resisted posting fees or even discussing them. The two most powerful provider groups—the American Medical Association and the American Hospital Association—rejected all efforts at organized price controls and price transparency proposed by the federal government: "It will create hostility and make the waiting room look like a barbershop," explained the president of the Washington Medical Society.[30] At the same time, nonclinicians working in the sector hurried to claim a piece of the inflated revenues, with unionized orderlies and nurses negotiating aggressively for wages based on the profitability of their nonprofit employers. One senior hospital administrator, facing a prolonged negotiating battle with the local union, predicted a "gruesome year, an impossible year."[31]

Few industry observers or participants produced workable solutions. One conservative critic posited doing away with the nonprofit status of many of the hospitals, in the hope that the discipline of the market would work its magic.[32] The suggestion ignored the huge efforts in charity care, research, teaching, community education, and outreach that many community and academic hospitals made in pursuit of their charitable missions. Another thoughtful observer suggested shifting the whole system of inpatient care to a more home-intensive model, citing research that showed that up to one in eight hospital patients could be adequately treated at home. Given that home care cost only $16 a day in 1973, compared to nearly $100 a day for hospital care, the suggestion seemed reasonable.[33] Market forces prevented implementation, however. Home treatment might save $84 a day, but to the well-insured patient, the savings would be all but invisible, while the hospital and doctor had substantial incentives to maintain the status quo. Unless third-party payers could more aggressively pursue their own interests, trends would continue unchecked.

Poor People's Challenges

The poor trailed the rest of the nation by almost every indicator of health status in 1968. They suffered at higher rates from gastrointestinal infection, tuberculosis, sexually transmitted disease, speech disorders, and emotional ailments. They had more dental disease, mental disorders, and joint disease. They got pregnant at younger ages, gave birth to premature babies at greater frequencies, and experienced birth complications in higher numbers. Their children were less likely to be immunized, examined, monitored, and treated, and poor adults suffered the ill effects of harsher employment and poorer lifetime nutrition. Throughout life they were shorter, sicker, more congested, more allergenic, and more asthmatic (particularly the urban poor). They suffered disproportionately from malnutrition and vitamin deficiencies.[34] George James, the health commissioner of New York City, declared that "poverty is the third leading cause of death in New York City."[35]

Even when the poor survived their working years, they suffered through them disproportionately. Men of working age who earned under $2,000 a year in the late 1960s claimed fifty days of disability a year, whereas men of the same age earning more than $7,000 a year claimed only 14.3 days. The poor spent 10 days a year in the hospital, while the wealthier spent just 7. Racial effects heightened the disparities. Four times as many nonwhite mothers died in childbirth as did white mothers, and twice as many nonwhite babies died in infancy as did white babies. Hubert Humphrey, the nation's vice president wrote, "The shadow of poverty and the shadow of avoidable disease and early death are the same shadow. They beshroud the same land and the same people."[36]

Poor people had a harder time accessing healthcare at every point. Even when free clinics and services were available, patients faced long lines, indifferent staff, chaotic administration, and disjointed care. One impoverished young mother related her experience at a neighborhood clinic in New York: "I went there at 9:00 like they said. About 12:30 I saw the doctor and he said I was in the wrong clinic. I went to the other clinic and waited until 2:00 and there were still people in front of me. The kids get out of school at 2:30, so I had to leave. That's just the way it is if you're poor."[37] Kenneth Clement, a Cleveland physician and keynote speaker at a conference at Howard University Medical School, echoed the young mother's point. Poverty care, he noted, was delivered in ways that were "depersonalized and lacking in continuity." It was fragmented, "rendered without care for the family unit," and often inaccessible. The poor person's "desire for privacy [was] consistently ignored and his dignity in many ways degraded."[38]

Poverty was a fluid category when it came to healthcare. Working-class families without good insurance could descend into poverty as a result of an accident or serious illness. Divorce, violent crime, and natural disasters pushed people into poverty regardless of their personal fortitude. The growing scourge of unemployment in the early 1970s (the infamous "stagflation" of the Nixon years) nearly always cost laid-off workers their health insurance, pushing them into the world of poverty medicine. One study showed that 80 percent of all laid-off people lost health coverage within ninety days.[39] Once unemployed, most people could ill-afford a private insurance policy; typical unemployment benefits were $65 a week, while the cost of a family insurance policy for nongroup coverage ran from $50 to $90 a month.

The nation struggled to serve this population in a hodgepodge of venues using funding and manpower from a variety of local, state, and federal sources. Some of the venues—dispensaries, public hospitals, community chest clinics—had been around for decades or even centuries. But much was changing in the world of charity healthcare in 1970.

In 1964, Congress passed the Economic Opportunity Act, giving rise to the Office of Economic Opportunity (OEO) and concomitant grants starting in 1965. These grants, coupled with lesser grants from the Model Cities program of 1966, flowed out to municipalities, universities, and nonprofits, which used the grants to create Neighborhood Health Centers (NHCs). Although public community clinics and health centers had existed since the nineteenth century, OEO grants spurred the

establishment of many new ones over the succeeding decade. Nearly
sixty new centers were established between 1966 and 1969, such that by
1971 more than 130 were in operation around the country.[40]

NHCs took many different forms, so it is difficult to offer a simple
description of what they were. All had staff nurses and counselors and
contract relationships with primary care physicians. A few had dentists
on contract. Many attracted rotating groups of medical students and
interns, particularly when they were affiliated with medical schools.
Some were free-standing, whereas others were affiliated with hospitals and medical schools. Most were started under a nonprofit aegis,
but a few were founded and owned by the municipality in which they
were located. Funding came from OEO grants but also from grants from
the US Children's Bureau (through Project CHILD), the Public Health
Service, the Model Cities program, and private foundations. Patients
might pay no fees at all or modest co-payments of 50 cents a visit. As
poor people began to qualify for the newly established state Medicaid
programs (more below), many of the centers began to bill the Medicaid
programs for their services. To take one example, the Eastside Neighborhood Health Center in Denver, Colorado, accommodated three thousand patients a week staffed with a family physician, two pediatricians,
an obstetrician, a variety of public health and pediatric nurses, a social
worker, a nutritionist, and half a dozen administrative and clerical
staff. In 1968 the center received $3.5 million from the OEO, $1.3 million
from Project CHILD, $1 million from the Children's Bureau's Bureau of
Maternity and Infant Care, $700,000 from the Public Health Service,
and an additional $1 million from state agencies.[41]

Of note was the emphasis the NHCs placed on treating illnesses
and problems with a cultural or social component. Almost all centers
provided birth control counseling, mental health counseling, and group
therapy. Many offered nutrition counseling, hygiene education, and
outreach programs to the local schools. Most devoted substantial efforts
to treating sexually transmitted diseases, alcohol and narcotics abuse,
and general social maladjustments. Notably, many served ethnic populations chronically underserved by the mainstream medical system,
including Hispanic populations in Texas and African American populations in many states.[42]

Much of the expansion of poverty care, whether through NHCs,
Model Cities, or public hospitals, was underwritten by Medicaid
funds. Technically there was no one Medicaid program, but fifty separate ones, each established by its home state and designed to meet

specific standards set by HCFA to qualify for federal matching funds. Medicaid had been added to the more substantial Medicare legislation of 1965; the two programs constituted Titles XVIII and XIX of the Social Security Act and worked in tandem to extend health insurance to the elderly (Medicare) and poor adult women and children who met federal poverty cut-offs (Medicaid). Notably, Medicaid did not cover able-bodied adult men who were poor, although it did provide health insurance to the permanently disabled and to impoverished elderly in nursing homes.

Medicaid was structured such that the federal government matched state investments in the program based on the per capita earnings of the state: the wealthiest states could shift 50 percent of the cost of the programs onto the federal government, while the poorest states could shift 80 percent. States also had the latitude to set Medicaid reimbursement rates, although they were required to cover a comprehensive array of services and tests. Reimbursement rates ranged from laughably low to relatively generous. In New York, for example, Medicaid reimbursement rates were high enough that they actually exceeded Medicare reimbursement rates for a number of procedures and made the state's Medicaid patients quite attractive to physicians and hospitals.

Medicaid was largely responsible for closing the gap between the volume of health services consumed by rich and poor between 1966 and 1976. At the beginning of the program, wealthy children saw physicians 65 percent more frequently than did poor children; a decade later the two groups visited physicians at identical rates. During that decade pre- and postnatal visits, immunization rates, prophylactic pediatric visits, and annual gynecological visits for the poor all increased substantially.[43] Death rates for young children from poor households declined by 14 percent during this time, largely due to reductions in pneumonia, flu, and malignant neoplasms.

Unexpectedly, the cost of the Medicaid programs rose dramatically in their first decade. In part this was due to higher penetration than had been predicted—the program grew from nine million people covered at the end of its first year to twenty-three million a decade later. At the same time, the high rates of medical inflation borne by the private payer markets drew on the Medicaid budgets. Medicaid payments totaled $3.45 billion in 1968, $6.35 billion in 1971, and $12 billion in 1976. By that time the program represented only 2 percent of most state expenditures, but the sharp rate of increase alarmed many governors and state budget directors.[44]

Notably, Medicaid did not wholly negate racial disparities in medical care access. Some of the poorest states, largely in the deep south, ran the most miserly Medicaid programs with the tightest eligibility requirements and least generous payments. While nationwide about two-thirds of all poor people were covered by Medicaid in 1975, in Alabama, Arkansas, Louisiana, Mississippi, South Carolina, and Texas only one-tenth were covered. In seven additional states—Florida, Idaho, Indiana, Montana, New Mexico, and the Dakotas—coverage was more inclusive but still left two-thirds of the poor residents uninsured.[45] In addition, poor people in rural areas generally had worse benefits than those in urban areas. Together these trends tended to depress benefits for African Americans, whose Medicaid benefits nationwide averaged only two-thirds of those to white recipients.

The physician community extended the efforts of the NHCs by opening opportunities in community and social medicine. NHCs and small community hospitals created residency programs in social medicine aimed at training general practice physicians with expertise in caring for patients in underserved communities. The training aimed to sensitize young physicians to the unique needs of patients from immigrant and minority backgrounds and give them the skills to work in collaborative health teams alongside physician assistants, social workers, and pediatric nurses.[46] Medical schools created departments of community medicine that drew on physicians across the curriculum who were particularly interested in the needs of the underserved communities. Mount Sinai Medical School in New York was particularly aggressive in directing students and residents into its community medicine program, requiring participation of first- and third-year medical students and inviting residents and independent physicians to participate in summer internships.[47] The programs worked closely with established physicians groups, prepaid practice groups, and NHCs.

Urban hospitals began to foment for more generous treatment of their poorest patients. Montefiore Hospital, in the Bronx, New York, teamed up with the Martin Luther King, Jr., Health Center to move community medicine into healthcare advocacy. Integrating volunteer law students and lawyers into their efforts (funded through the VISTA program), Montefiore moved beyond patient care into legal advocacy for community groups, consumers, the mentally ill, and tenants.[48] The center focused its efforts particularly on lead paint poisoning in public and subsidized housing, where effective solutions needed to address both medical and legal challenges. Lawyers associated with the program brought suit against landlords and the city to force them to remediate the problems, even as the NHC treated affected children for lead poisoning and educated their parents about appropriately protecting their children from environmental hazards.[49] In this model, the Public Health Service worked with Model Cities to create fourteen Pilot Neighborhood Service Centers around the country committed to improving urban living situations through pest control, water filtration, garbage removal, nutrition and hygiene education, mental health counseling, and pediatric immunizations and screening.[50]

These efforts, inevitably, drew largely on youth. Many of the most eager entrants to community medicine were medical students or residents who had been politically active in college and took their activist mind-set and liberal politics into the medical schools. Building on an expanded notion of health and a newly enlarged purview of sociomedicine, medical students demanded curricular changes to accommodate their politics and their more expansive professional goals. Michael Michaelson, a graduate student pursuing degrees in both medicine and sociology at the University of Pennsylvania, wrote in 1969 that students "have begun to resent their roles as automatons, to question the models and methods of their profession, and to abandon passivity for immediate social action."[51] Around the country, medical students lobbied for curricular change, engagement in community clinics, and more liberal admissions standards to raise enrollments of African American students in the medical school programs.

It is important to note, however, that although a certain portion of mostly young and idealistic physicians and medical students committed themselves to medical activism, most physicians did not. The profession had been rooted in a narrowly defined physiological and biomedical approach to health and disease for over a century, and social activism was inconsistent with the training and orientation of the profession. Most doctors dismissed the activists' efforts as quixotic, and some actively lobbied against them, finding them a distraction from the essential work of the profession and suggesting that physicians were not particularly well suited to the task of political engagement. Michael Halberstam, a physician in private practice in Washington, wrote: "A medical school dean, confronted by an applicant who says his goal in life is to end the misery of the slums, might well steer the applicant into law, city planning, politics, or dozen other equally fine professions." He went on, "I would guess and hope that my black patients care less about my social and political feelings than my ability to diagnose chest pain and my availability on a Sunday afternoon."[52]

Racial Disparities

The impulse to more socially active medicine was directed most en-thusiastically at the stubborn health disparities between white and nonwhite populations in the country. By almost every measure, the health of black Americans trailed that of whites. They gave birth to low-birthweight babies at nearly double the rate of whites (13.6 percent versus 7.1 percent), and their infant mortality rate was 60 percent higher (23.2 death per 1,000 births versus 14.8 deaths).[53] For American Indians and Native Alaskans (Eskimos) the disparities were even more stark. Indian life expectancy at birth was twenty-five years less than that for white Americans, due in part to infant death rates nearly 50 percent higher than those for whites. Indian mothers had nearly twice as many children as white mothers, frequently spacing them so close together as to be forced to wean them too early.[54] Native children died at double the rate as white children between ages one and fourteen, suffering par-ticularly from pneumonia, tuberculosis, dysentery, and fatal accidents.[55]

Indian and black children were born sicker and poorer; were less likely to live close to a doctor, clinic, or hospital; and were substantially less likely to have private health insurance. One study of school-aged children in New York showed that while 80 percent of white Protes-tant children and 83 percent of white Catholic children were receiving regular dental care, only 58 percent of Puerto Rican children and 56 per-cent of black children were getting the same care. These disparate rates partly reflected disparities in family income, but the racial disparities seemed to persist beyond what income alone would have predicted. A mixture of gaps in access, culture, health knowledge, and income ex-plained the poor outcomes. Jewish children, for example, used dentists at the highest rates (over 90 percent) even when coming from families with low levels of parental education. Mata Nikias, a researcher studying the phenomenon, concluded that the odd utilization rates reflected "the complexity of dental health behavior and of its culture-connected patterns."[56]

Patients tended to seek care from physicians with whom they were culturally akin. One study of this phenomenon conducted in 1974 by the Office of Health Resource Opportunity found that black patients made up 87 percent of the visits to black doctors but only 7 percent of the visits to white doctors, suggesting that the nation's physicians needed to roughly reflect the racial mix of the general population. In that year, only 2.1 percent of all US physicians were black, whereas nearly 13 percent of the general population was. Even this statistic understated the seriousness of the shortage of black doctors in rural areas, where only 4 percent of all black doctors practiced. Not a single black physician in the state of Michigan practiced outside of a metropolitan area, for example. To put this in context, at the time just under one-third of all visits (of all races) to physicians took place outside of metropolitan areas.[57]

The shortage of Native American physicians was even more acute. In 1973 there were only forty Native American physicians and one dentist in the entire country to serve a Native population of 435,000. The government countered this particular problem through its century-old Indian Health Service (IHS), which provided free medical care to all Indians resident on reservations with 500 physicians and 180 dentists. Almost all IHS physicians were white, and schools had little success in recruiting qualified Native students.[58]

Aggressive efforts by the medical schools to recruit black and Native American students could not solve the problem. The pipeline of well-prepared minority graduates produced inadequate numbers of qualified medical school applicants. Moreover, many of the brightest black college students chose to enter other competitive professions—law, finance, accounting, and business—at greater rates than did their white counterparts. In response, medical schools lowered their entrance standards for black candidates, in the hope that intensive training could compensate for any weaknesses in their backgrounds. But affirmative action for racial minorities for medical schools alarmed some of the profession's leaders, with a professor at Harvard Medical School questioning whether "we have been properly balancing our obligation to promote social justice with our primary obligation to protect the public interest."[59] The dean of Harvard Medical School disagreed, asserting that it was impossible to "distinguish between minority and non-minority students on the basis of their records."[60]

Fifteen years later, half of all black physicians in the United States were graduates of just two historically black medical schools—Howard and Meharry—and a quarter of all black medical students continued to enroll in those schools and two newer black medical schools, Drew and

Morehouse. Although the remainder of the nation's 127 medical schools continued to make efforts to increase enrollment of black students, they were only modestly successful. During this time, the portion of all US physicians who were black had increased only half of a percentage point, and the numbers of black medical students in most private medical schools declined.[61]

There was no obvious solution. New York State considered establishing an urban medical school aimed at disproportionately admitting black students but found that it could not practically do so.[62] Private medical schools continued to put weight on applicants' ethnicity in the admissions process, but could not easily compensate for the poor premedical training many black undergraduates had received. The ultimate answer needed to be far more comprehensive and would need to include more intensive exposure to sciences for black students at much younger ages.

Missing Doctors

Poor distribution of physicians exacerbated many problems in the health system. In 1972 the United States had 147 nonmilitary physicians per 100,000 people. This ratio appeared adequate (policy experts placed the healthy threshold at 100 per 100,000 for industrialized nations), but it was undermined by regional inequities. South Dakota, for example, had only 76 doctors per 100,000 people, while New York had 234. Nationwide, urban areas had 175 doctors per 100,000, and rural areas had only 80. The problem was getting worse. A decade before, New York had had 2.75 times the doctors (per capita) as South Dakota; now it had over three times as many.[63]

Increasingly, rural areas lacked physicians entirely. Four counties in the state of Florida had none, as did 134 counties nationwide. Over a quarter of the US population (55 million people) lived in areas where healthcare was essentially nonexistent.[64] Again, the problem was growing worse. Nearly half of the counties in Kansas had lost physicians in the previous decade, such that by 1970, in twenty counties, more than half of the physicians were over age sixty.[65] The town of Jackman, Maine, put up a sign on the highway on the way into town reading, "Drive Carefully, There's No Doctor in Town."[66] Roger Egeberg, the assistant secretary for Health and Scientific Affairs in HEW asserted, "The Number 1 problem is the distribution of health care."[67]

Although health planners at state and federal levels understood the problem, they were unable to produce a remedy. Federal funds made available in the 1960s increased medical school enrollment nationwide by 60 percent, yet few of these new doctors chose to practice in rural areas.[68] Solutions ranged from towns offering bonuses for young doctors to take over practices from aging physicians to a federal mandate to conscript young doctors into rural service for a set number of years.[69] A few medical schools began to skew their recruitment toward young men and women from small towns, theorizing that they would be more like to return and set up a practice.[70]

Paradoxically, urban areas also lacked for physicians. The growing ghettoization of many inner-city neighborhoods had compelled doctors to desert their old practices and establish new ones in the suburbs. The trend increased with suburbanization and white flight in the 1950s, and increased again after the riots that plagued many cities following the assassination of Martin Luther King Jr. in 1968. By 1974, Chattanooga, Tennessee, had only two physicians (out of three hundred in the metropolitan area) serving its central neighborhoods, and whole areas of the south side of Chicago and the Bronx lacked physicians entirely. A study conducted by the US Public Health Service that year found more physicians in one medical office building in the Lincoln Park neighborhood of Chicago than were located in the entire West Side (an area with 300,000 residents). Similarly, the South Bronx had one physician per twelve thousand residents, while urban black neighborhoods around the country usually had few more.[71]

A reasonable response was simply to produce more doctors. Although the general pool of physicians for the US population appeared to be adequate at 147 per 100,000 people, it was substantially lower than that of industrialized nations such as Israel (244 per 100,000), Russia (217), Czechoslovakia (185), and Scotland (156).[72] The only two ways to increase the number of doctors were to train new ones at home or import doctors who had been trained abroad. In 1971 President Richard Nixon signed the Comprehensive Health Manpower Training Act into law, freeing up grants to schools of medicine, osteopathy, and dentistry at $2,500 to $4,000 per student per year.[73] While these grants were awarded to institutions rather than individuals, federal planners hoped that they would induce schools to expand class size and start additional campuses.[74] The new law, building upon the Health Professions Education Act of 1973 (which had provided construction funds to teaching institutions) and the Allied Health Professions Act of 1966 (funding non-doctoral level clinical study) spurred universities around the nation to create new medical schools or expand existing ones.[75]

By 1973, five new medical schools were in operation with eight additional schools in planning stages.[76] That year, 114 US medical schools produced eleven thousand graduates: a 50 percent increase in the number that had graduated a decade before.[77] At the same time, schools were experimenting with new ways of accelerating training, including shortening medical school to three years, combining BA and MD degrees into a single six-year program, doing away with the required postgraduate internship year, and shortening residency training programs in primary care. Not all such efforts were equally successful. While Northwestern University's six-year program, begun in 1961, produced competent young physicians (drawn from an extraordinarily accomplished applicant pool), Stanford University's all-elective MD curriculum, tailored precisely to the unique academic preparation of each incoming student, was quickly abandoned. The American Association of Medical Colleges experimented with collapsing the rotating internship into the fourth year of medical school, but insisted that even primary care required a minimum of two years of postgraduate residency training.[78]

The ability of the nation to produce new physicians was limited by the extraordinarily high standards to which the profession held itself. The AMA Council on Medical Education maintained strict standards governing almost every aspect of a medical school's activities. Although these standards had grown out of nineteenth-century medical school abuses and had produced a physician workforce with training unparalleled in the world, they had become a "straightjacket" on growth in training opportunities.[79] Nonphysician clinicians took up some of the slack in the labor pool, but distorted the historic role of physicians in providing care. In 1900, for example, physicians constituted 35 percent of all healthcare workers; by 1971 they constituted only 9 percent.[80]

The overall shortage of doctors was only part of the problem. For forty years doctors had been migrating away from primary care toward the medical and surgical specialties. In 1930, 70 percent of all doctors in the United States had been general practitioners (GPs); by 1970 only 20 percent were.[81] The raw numbers of GPs had declined in that period from 112,000 to 52,330, even as the nation's population had grown by 50 percent, and GPs were retiring or dying at the rate of two thousand a year.[82] A survey conducted in 1969 by the journal *Medical Economics* found that two-thirds of all GPs in the nation reported that they could not take on any additional patients without "seriously affecting the quality of patient care."[83]

Doctors turned away from general practice for a variety of reasons. Certainly the higher fees to be earned in the specialties were part of the reason, but so was the emphasis on specialty care in the nation's medical schools. Both "undergraduate" medical training (the years spent in medical school earning the MD) and postgraduate training (the years spent in internship and residency immediately following graduation from medical school) were conducted in hospitals, often highly special-ized teaching hospitals. During these years, students and residents tended to see some of the sickest patients with the most complex condi-tions, seeking relief in some of the most sophisticated institutions in the country. One medical observer wrote of young doctors' "intense pre-occupation" with only those patients who had sought care at the highest levels of medicine.[84] Such experiences distorted young doctors' views of medical practice and impelled them toward specialty training. In a sobering reflection of this trend, the three medical schools in Boston in 1968 (Tufts, Boston University, and Harvard) produced not even a single graduate intending to enter general practice.[85]

Schools began to make some efforts to address the problem in the early 1970s. A dozen medical schools, along with 170 hospitals, started informal residency programs in family medicine. (Before this, young physicians wishing to enter primary care often simply completed a one-year rotating internship and went into practice.)[86] At the same time, $3.7 billion of federal funds were made available to establish five new medical schools and expand training opportunities at existing schools, in hopes that new slots might be designated for students declaring interest in primary care.

Expanding capacity in medical schools was not the only solution. By 1970 the United States was importing substantial numbers of doctors who were trained abroad. These foreign medical graduates (FMGs) made up over half of all young physicians admitted to residency training programs (10,540 in 1971 versus 8,974 graduates of US schools), staffed just under one-third of all hospital-based physician staff positions, and made up a total of 20 percent of the entire US physician workforce. They came from Europe, India, Korea, the Philippines, and, increasingly after 1972, Mexico and Italy.[87] (Graduates of Canadian medical schools, although technically considered FMGs, were usually not counted in these statistics given the close ties between the academic medical com-munities of the United States and Canada.)[88] At this rate, FMGs would make up over 30 percent of all practicing US physicians by 1980. Although the FMGs might conceivably help alleviate the shortage of physicians in rural areas, they tended to stay in urban practices (often in poorer urban communities). Only one-ninth of all FMGs took on practices in communities with under fifty thousand people after completing their residencies.[89]

A number of public health leaders expressed concerns over the trend. Leaders of US medicine questioned the quality of the training that the students had received abroad, their mastery of spoken English, and their ability to relate culturally to US patients. Congressman William Roy of Kansas, himself a physician, questioned their ability to understand the "subtle nuances of American culture."[90] One study found evidence suggesting not so much that most FMGs were incompetent but that "many FMGs were . . . insufficiently competent."[91]

More troubling was the underlying ethical issue raised by the practice. Almost every country from which the United States was drawing physicians had greater need than the United States for their services. In the Philippines, India, and Korea—all suppliers of substantial numbers of doctors to the United States—physician shortages were acute. More Thai doctors were practicing medicine in New York City (population eight million) than were practicing in all of rural Thailand (population twenty-eight million).[92] The United States was, in effect, the recipient of "reverse foreign aid," in the words of one public health scholar.[93] That is, the United States was effectively accepting subsidies from the poor nations which had invested in medical training for their citizens, only to see that training flee to US medical practices, taking with them $100 million worth of training as they departed their countries.

A different and potentially more promising approach to the physician shortfall was nonphysician clinicians. These "Medex" professionals (later "physician's assistants") grew out of discharged army medical corpsmen returning from Vietnam—some thirty thousand a year by 1970. The corpsmen had been trained in basic diagnosis, critical care, battlefield surgery, and pharmacology. In Vietnam they had often performed fairly complex procedures, stepping in as both physician and surgeon in difficult situations. Back home in the United States, their army training counted for little in the civilian medical sector.

In 1965, Duke University created the first university-based program in physician's assistant (PA) training. The program drew initially from discharged corpsmen, but quickly expanded to bring in students from the general population. It required twenty-four months to complete and set a high initial standard for rigor and comprehensiveness.[94] In the five years following the establishment of the Duke program, schools of medicine, nursing, and pharmacy as well as independent hospitals established programs. By 1969 there were nine programs; two years later there were thirty-two.[95] Programs varied in quality, rigor, and competitiveness. In 1970 the Board of Medicine of the National Academy of Sciences (today's Institute of Medicine) attempted to impose some order and standards on the new profession with its report, "New Members of the Physician's Health Team: Physician's Assistants," which proposed a tiered structure for the new profession; the best-trained practitioners would have the most professional independence and would be called physician's associates.[96]

Although the medical profession eyed the new PAs skeptically, the public often welcomed the new clinicians, particularly in areas where physicians had been scarce. In 1971, for example, a community clinic in rural Gilchrist County, Florida, recruited two PAs after failing to recruit a single full-time physician. The clinic was able to treat 1,500 patients a week with the PAs, either through direct intervention or referral. The clinic's offerings were "comparable to conventional ambulatory care settings in terms of acceptance, cost, quality, accessibility, impact, and population's attitudes," according to a study.[97] In Cheney, Washington, a physician who hired Bob Woodruff, a discharged Green Beret and newly certified PA, initially asked permission from his patients before letting Woodruff examine them. The physician stopped being so apologetic when one of his patents responded, "I trusted somebody like your Medex with the life of my son [in Vietnam]."[98]

Other categories of nonphysician clinicians also helped alleviate the physician shortage. Midwives—the ancient profession which had been largely superseded in the United States by obstetricians in the twentieth century—aided substantial numbers of Mexican American, black, and American Indian women in their deliveries. The majority received little formal training, learning "by doing" from more senior midwives, but their patients claimed to be satisfied with their work.[99] The midwives operated exclusively in home settings (lacking hospital admitting privileges), and despite the dangers inherent in nonhospital births (the midwives had no means to stop maternal bleeding, for example), their patients claimed to prefer the less medicalized approach to childbirth. One patient interviewed in a study of the practice said of her hospital experience "I got so lonesome—couldn't speak English—husband couldn't visit—nobody to stay with the kids. It was scary in the hospital."[100]

Midwifery was a good fit for the nursing profession, which had long prided itself on being more empathetic and "patient-focused" than its medical counterpart. Johns Hopkins University's School of Nursing launched a "nurse-midwife" program in 1961 for holder's of the BA or BSN degree who were already registered nurses. In the decade following, Kings County Hospital (Brooklyn), the University of Mississippi, and the Kentucky Frontier Nurse Service began similar programs.[101] Lacking MD degrees, many nurses at the time had little outlet for clinical skills and insights gained over years of bedside nursing. One nursing professor wrote of the traditional "fetch and carry role" that even senior nurses were often relegated to, making them a vast "untapped resource."[102] Nurse midwifery offered a path to independence and professional advancement.

Nonphysician clinicians faced substantial regulatory barriers. Virtually every state in the United States prohibited practicing medicine without a license, and laws were slow to change.[103] The licensing laws, enacted at the beginning of the twentieth century to protect patients from inept practitioners, were proving to be overly restrictive and ultimately harmful to the population. Such laws impeded clinical advancement by people with unorthodox backgrounds.[104] Medical practice acts in most states continued to criminalize independent clinical work, and even as states began to revise their statutes in an effort to accommodate the growing ranks of PAs, the new laws continued to demand close supervision of PAs by licensed doctors.[105]

Poor Health Indicators

High costs and barriers to access depressed national health statistics. Although the nation proudly pointed to its extraordinary success in basic sciences research (US scientists regularly garnered the preponderance of Nobel Prizes in the sciences), and the pathbreaking capabilities and procedures displayed in its academic hospitals, its vital statistics exposed anemic national health. By 1970 the nation ranked tenth in life expectancy for ten-year-old boys and thirteenth for newborns.[106] Its infant mortality rate of twenty-five deaths per one thousand live births was nearly double that of Sweden and the Netherlands (and only barely ahead of the Soviet Union's), placing the country alongside developing Singapore and impoverished Ireland.[107]

Of course, such disheartening news needed to be seen in the context of the steadily improving circumstances of the previous century. The great infectious and parasitic scourges of smallpox, tuberculosis, hookworm, malaria, yellow fever, and cholera had been all but wiped out in most of the United States. Life expectancy was at an all-time high, and once a child made it past infancy his chance of reaching old age was nearly certain. Eric Cassell, a physician in New York, noted that the death of young adults was so improbable in 1969 that "it must be removed from the realistic possibilities of young life."[108] Measles, long a feared childhood killer, was now little more than an inconvenience for most citizens. While the 14,000 cases of measles in 1964 in Egypt and Syria had killed 8,000, the 458,000 cases in the United States during the same period had killed only 451.[109] A hospital administrator, defending his industry and his calling, pointed to the ever-rising levels of professionalism in the sector. He wrote, "Hospitals not very long ago were places to go to die. Today, we go to live."[110]

Moreover, the challenges healthcare faced in 1970 were changing rapidly, as infectious and congenital diseases gave way to ones born of human foible and excess. Rising incidence of heart disease, stroke, cancer, liver disease, and traumatic injury resulted from higher rates of obesity, smoking, drinking, and driving. Cancer rates rose because people now lived long enough to actually develop it. The old sciences of pharmacology, anatomy, and physiology were being displaced by the newer populational sciences of epidemiology, biostatistics, and sociology—all tools to better understand human beings' folly.[111] At the same time, the medical profession was still largely devoted to treatment and intervention, rather than prevention and education. Cutting-edge transplant surgery continued to excite the public's imagination, while governmental warnings of the risks of smoking and saturated fats were largely ignored.[112]

Underlying the entire morass were large holes in the system of payment and insurance which the nation had reluctantly adopted piecemeal after World War II. Although the majority of Americans had hospital insurance by 1970, few had policies that covered ambulatory care, physician and pharmaceutical fees, and basic tests and imaging. Hospital insurance policies often contained mandates for co-payments and deductibles and capped annual and lifetime benefits. Even well-insured people were at risk of financial ruin when faced with a catastrophic health event, which was a "virtual impossibility" in most Western

European countries.[113] The lack of ambulatory coverage meant that many patients (as high as one-fourth, by one estimate) purposely admitted themselves to hospitals for nonnecessary care in an effort to avoid paying out of pocket. The Committee for National Health Insurance, composed of leaders from organized labor, foundations, think tanks, and the progressive physician community, decried the absence of a national health program for the country, calling the existing system "an unacceptable second-rate health service—disorganized, disjointed, and obsolete."[114]

❧

Regardless of how good US medicine was in 1975, stubborn holes in coverage denied many Americans the benefits of the system. Whether poor, geographically isolated, or members of a racial minority group, large numbers of people simply could not easily get to a doctor. A number of federal initiatives implemented at the time, including Medicaid, the Neighborhood Health Center Program, and the Health Manpower Training Act weakened some of these barriers to care, but the problems persisted.

The answer seemed to lie partially in recruiting different sorts of persons to medical school programs. College graduates from small towns who indicated a willingness to return to those areas to practice medicine were attractive candidates for state medical schools wishing to better serve rural populations. Black college students with particular interest in or aptitude for science and medicine were aggressively wooed by both public and private medical schools in an effort to increase minority ranks in the profession. Physicians trained abroad were eager to join primary care residency programs in the United States, and stay after to serve in underserved areas.

More promising still were the young professions of physician's assistant and nurse practitioner. These physician "extenders"—non-MD clinicians with skills in primary care diagnosis and treatment—were cheap to train and easy to recruit. Both physician societies and state licensing boards were skeptical of their competency in the 1970s, but early results were promising. If US doctors were unwilling to go to where the patients were, non-MD clinicians could be trained to fill in the gaps.

2

![black bar]

Medical Free Markets

Managing the Entrepreneurs

American healthcare in the early 1970s was ill, but the ailment was not readily apparent. The rising costs, misdistribution of doctors, over-capitalization of hospitals, poor public health outcomes, overspecialization of physicians, and general shortage of good preventive care were all symptoms of a broader malaise: disorganization. Unlike healthcare in many other industrialized countries, the United States lacked a governing system to allocate appropriate resources and manpower to where they were most needed. In the words of the president of the American Association of Medical Colleges, it was "the last of the cottage industries."[1]

American medicine was loosely based on an entrepreneurial model, in which individual physicians or physician groups located their practices where they wanted to practice; community organizations founded hospitals where and when they wished to; and public health agencies were detached from the private sector clinicians and agencies that served patients. For-profit, nonprofit, and government agencies and firms resisted joint planning, failed to coordinate their efforts, and generally viewed each other as private sector competitors chasing finite patient revenues.

33

Unlike in the true private sector, however, neither consumers nor providers in the medical sector responded to price signals. The growing predominance of third-party payers—private health insurance, Medicare, and Medicaid—meant that neither patients nor doctors followed the normal strictures of supply and demand. For a well-insured patient, hospital care was largely free and mundane preventive care was substantially more expensive, as many private insurance plans failed to reimburse for outpatient preventive care. Drugs administered as part of hospital treatment were free, but those taken at home were quite costly. Anything reimbursable by insurance was heavily discounted, and thus overconsumed, to the detriment of sound preventive care. One hospital president quipped, "The system puts a premium on being a horizontal rather than a vertical patient."[2]

The predominant health insurance product of 1970 was an indemnity policy, which reimbursed patients for covered services consumed at the market price. The system, often called "fee-for-service," impelled doctors and hospitals to sell greater volumes of indemnified services than they might judge optimal for a patient. Tests, injections, probes, screens, surgeries, transfusions, and images all became potential sources of revenue in this system, while preventive, outpatient cogitative medicine produced little. By the odd logic of the prevailing system, sickness actually became a revenue generator for physicians, whereas wellness had a deadening effect. Many physicians cleaved to the ethical mandate of doing no harm and placing the patient's interests first, but even the most saintly physician could be tempted to run additional tests in the interest of safety and revenue. One physician at the time admitted, "There is no doubt that fee-for-service tempts the greedy physician to provide unneeded services."[3]

American medicine's entrepreneurial quality and lack of systemization produced care that was overly specialized, overly capitalized, and overly oriented toward treatment rather than prevention. By the odd mores of 1970 US medicine, a sick patient was an asset rather than a liability. "The doctor with an empty waiting room, the hospital with empty beds, is soon bankrupt," observed one administrator.[4] Although public health agencies maintained their century-old mission of preventing the spread of infectious disease within a community, they had little impulse to help people care for themselves and maintain good health. No agency in state or federal government was committed to coordinating the efforts of the many providers of care, planning strategically for the demands of the future, or seeding institutions where they were needed.

Starting in the early 1970s, a number of scholars and medical leaders conceptualized an alternative medical care delivery system that would turn healthy people into assets and sick people into liabilities. Such a system would impel doctors to try to prevent illness from happening rather than treat it after the fact. Moreover, a more rational system would train clinicians with the skills demanded by the community while placing them where they were most needed. Private doctors would coordinate their efforts with preventive agencies and community hospitals to produce a rationalized system of care that emphasized prevention, primary care, minimally invasive hospitalizations, hygiene, and public health.

These thinkers did not have to create a conceptual model from scratch. Instead, they seized on an existing but somewhat scarce model of healthcare delivery known as the prepaid group practice. Prepaid group practices were groups of primary care and specialist physicians who were salaried by the practice and charged patients annual fees regardless of how heavily the patients used their services. This capitation model reversed the logic of healthcare consumption. Because the fees were paid up front, every test, service, procedure, or clinical intervention actually became a financial liability for the practice. The group had a financial incentive to prevent illness rather than merely treat it and to push patients to the least sophisticated treatment possible. The model emphasized primary care over specialty care, prevention over treatment, and outpatient care over inpatient care. Moreover, it invited cooperation between a patient's several doctors, ending some of the worst Balkanizing instincts of the fee-for-service system. It negated the overspecialization syndrome in medicine in which (in the words of a New York neurologist) "the patient's left-toe specialist doesn't know what the right-toe specialist is up to."[5]

Prepaid group practices were not a new idea. Logging companies had experimented with the idea in the late nineteenth century in an effort to care for their lumberjacks in medically inaccessible forests. A number of nonindustrial plans were started in the late 1920s and early 1930s, including the Ross-Loos Clinic in Los Angeles, the Group Health Association in Washington, the Health Insurance Plan of Greater New York, the Group Health Cooperative of Puget Sound in Seattle, and the most successful of all, the Kaiser Health Plan in California. Over the succeeding half century these plans became a small but important component of the US health insurance net. By 1970 there were twenty-five such plans in the country enrolling two million members. By 1970, as well, the prepaid group practices had a new name: health maintenance organizations (HMOs).[6]

By 1970 HMOs took on a number of forms. All had relationships with doctors; some employed doctors outright while others had contractual relationships with independent physicians. Some (such as Kaiser) owned their own hospital or system of hospitals, and others made arrangements with independent nonprofit hospitals. All HMOs emphasized capitation, cooperation, and prevention in an effort to minimize superfluous tests and procedures, maintain patient health, and reduce costs. They also limited choice for patients. Members who went outside of the HMO's physician network risked having to bear all or most of the cost of their treatment themselves. The mantra of the system was coordination, which presupposed exclusion.

President Richard Nixon, acting on the advice of Paul Ellwood, a neurologist long interested in the economics of healthcare delivery, supported increasing the presence of HMOs as one response to the health "crisis" he trumpeted in 1971.[7] Ellwood, the originator of the term *health maintenance organization* and founder of the healthcare consulting group Interstudy, encouraged the administration to promote the organizations. The resulting HMO Act of 1973 laid the ground for creating new HMOs by extending feasibility and development grants and start-up loans. The act required firms with twenty-five or more full-time employees to offer membership in an HMO to employees as one choice in their array of health benefits, provided such an option was available. The new law, coupled with a new federal HMO Service within the Department of Health, Education, and Welfare (HEW), and Ellwood's almost zealous marketing efforts, resulted in the rapid expansion in the number and size of HMOs in the nation. By 1975, more than two hundred were in operation with membership approaching eight million.[8]

Although the HMO Act provides a convenient jumping-off point for the genesis of modern managed care, careful analysis suggests that the law accomplished less than it might have. Underfunded and overly demanding in the restrictions it placed on "qualifying" HMOs, the program funneled only several tens of millions of dollars in start-up grants in its first few years, despite having been initially budgeted at $5 billion over three years. Many of the HMOs started between 1970 and 1975 had already been in formation before the law's passage, and the feasibility grants were so modest as to be insignificant. The law required qualifying HMOs to price premiums on a community rather than experience basis placing them at a significant price disadvantage to indemnity insurance plans. Last, the law required that qualifying HMOs offer home health services, mental health, dental care, alcohol and drug treatment services—a substantial challenge for new organizations. Paul Starr, a health policy scholar, judged the law an "experiment designed to fail" and thought its provisions so rigid as to actively discourage the development of new health plans.[9]

HMOs faced an odd assortment of hurdles. Besides general public suspicion of a new payment and delivery mechanism, many doctors aggressively opposed the new model. Although those who worked for HMOs generally liked the experience (Kaiser experienced only 2 percent annual turnover in its medical staff), most doctors viewed the arrangement as inherently coercive and professionally degrading.[10] HMOs seemed to turn doctors into mere employees of large corporate entities: a direct rebuke to the proud tradition of professional independence that doctors valued. Moreover, the whole notion of being "managed" implied that doctors needed managing—again, a rebuke to their sense of professional pride. One doctor wrote that salaried practice, "tempts the lazy physician to prolonged coffee breaks and extra reasons for not operating on the weekend."[11]

Broader governmental systems unexpectedly worked against the model. Medicare, for example, reimbursed on a "reasonable cost" basis, meaning that physicians had little incentive to hold down their own charges. But when HMOs tried to bill Medicare at prevailing rates, and keep the difference between those rates and their actual costs as profit, the Health Care Financing Administration (HCFA) refused, penalizing organizations for their own efficiency. James Cavanaugh, deputy assistant secretary of HEW overseeing Medicare reimbursement, admitted that although his agency was aware of and even excited by the potential of the new organizations, there had "never been a move in that direction."[12] Most private insurance companies followed HCFA's lead and failed to build appropriate profit margins into their reimbursement to network-model HMOs.

The legislation had required larger employers to offer a qualifying HMO as a choice, but it had demanded that all employers offer employees the ability to switch in and out of plans for one month each year during "open enrollment" season, meaning that patients felt little need to truly commit themselves to the new model.[13] Moreover, HMOs hardly sold themselves as conduits to better health. Many were aggressively profit-oriented, with little grounding in professional mores of medical behavior. One skeptic of many new HMOs noted, "They offer fried chicken to anyone who joins the group. And they send solicitors around door to door, and pay them three dollars a head for every patient they sign up."[14]

Despite the challenges facing the organizations as they expanded in the early 1970s, and despite the limited federal funds the HMO Act injected into the sector, HMOs worked. They held costs down, kept patients out of the hospital, and more successfully maintained their members' health. Most posted costs per patient 25 percent lower than typical fee-for-service insurers.[15] HMOs used two hospital beds per one thousand enrollees, compared to 4.5 for typical insurers. They posted between eighty and ninety hospital admissions annually for each one thousand enrollees; Blue Cross/Blue Shield posted 123. Patients hospitalized by HMOs accrued between four hundred and six hundred days of hospitalization a year; those hospitalized by the Blues accrued 864.[16] Members of HMOs were almost 50 percent more likely to get an annual check-up than conventionally insured patients, 12 percent less like to give birth to underweight or premature infants, and about 11 percent less likely to lose their babies in the first eighteen months.[17]

All of these statistics might have been influenced by bias in self-selection, however. HMO members may have been, and in fact probably were, unusually young and healthy and certainly more proactive in taking responsibility for their own health. The mere act of signing up for an HMO required new members to take above-average interest in health insurance and educate themselves on the advantages and disadvantages of competing insurance products. HMO members who became ill with unusual diseases or conditions had a strong incentive to transfer out of the HMO into a conventional insurance program at the first available open enrollment, thus preserving greater control over their own treatment. The vaunted collaboration HMOs promoted among their physicians was largely absent in practice. Although proponents championed potential interactions (physicians could "pool their skills for the patient's benefit" and be "mutually responsible to their patients and to each other") few careful studies or even anecdotes supported these claims by 1975.[18] Certainly the model seemed plausible. But most doctors were annealed in a professional cauldron of independence and self-sufficiency. Historically, doctors had not been team players, and little evidence supported the idea that changing payment schemes could rapidly shift that culture.

Health Planning

Nixon's efforts at reform were part of a broader movement toward planning. The Great Society programs of the 1960s were largely predicated on the idea that the nation had adequate resources to defeat poverty, if only those resources were effectively marshaled and optimally coordinated. Great Society planners wished to see all social service systems planned well, and the ethos was particularly applicable to healthcare with its large capital investments and localized means of production.[19]

Health planners of the 1960s situated themselves in a dizzying array of new federal health agencies. In addition to the long-established Public Health Service, these new agencies included the National Institute of Mental Health, the Community Health Service, the Health Facilities Planning and Construction Service, and the National Information Center on Health Services Research. Many of these agencies were staffed with optimistic new graduates of expanding public health schools, which were generally committed to social change and health education efforts.[20] These young graduates spoke of "action planning," "community-wide planning," and planning that was "continuous in nature, comprehensive in scope, all inclusive in design, coordinative in function, and adequately staffed."[21]

Planners were remarkably opaque about what precisely would be planned. Clearly the nation had redundant capacity in some areas and inadequate distribution in others, but even central state planning (such as could be found in the Soviet Union and Cuba) would not be able to eliminate these problems. Doctors congregated in wealthy cities and suburbs not through lack of understanding but because they were aware that these areas hosted the best markets for their services. Similarly, hospitals had grown up around ethnic and religious communities that had proactively established communal institutions over the course of a century or longer. Central planning could hardly persuade a small Lutheran community in Seattle to establish its hospital where it was better needed—such as in Spokane.

On the other hand, planners were on firmer ground when they turned their attention to quality and coordination. As Medicare and

Medicaid became sources of increasingly large healthcare payments after 1965, federal and state governments could rightly claim an interest in overseeing healthcare quality and delivery. Planners aspired to cut costs and ensure strong outcomes by excising weak or redundant facilities, limiting capital investment, and creating relationships between primary and tertiary hospitals. They focused particularly on superfluous surgery suites accredited to perform complex operations but rarely used. Of the 776 hospitals certified to perform open heart surgery in in 1969, only 210 performed more than one such procedure, and 330 performed none. Planners viewed these sites as poor investments that seemed almost guaranteed to produce poor outcomes.[22]

Moreover, when planners looked at healthcare as part of a broader panoply of social services, the need for coordination, if not long-range planning, became apparent. In a stirring speech in 1973, HEW Undersecretary Frank Carlucci described the complexity of the challenge: "For instance, a disadvantaged teenage girl who gets pregnant needs at least ten services—prenatal medical care, nutrition guidance, guidance on being a parent, continuation of her regular high school education, obstetric and pediatric care when her baby is born, vocational education, job placement assistance, day care for her child so she can work, family planning help to avoid unwanted future pregnancies. . . . We have calculated the odds of a person getting all the services that he needs, and those odds come out to a flat zero."[23]

Health planning dated to before 1965. Congress, working with Franklin Roosevelt, had repurposed the existing Marine Hospital Service (dating to 1798) into the modern uniformed Public Health Service in two laws passed in 1943 and 1944. The service expanded rapidly during the war years and took on the control of malaria, typhus, and sexually transmistted diseases, in addition to applying itself to industrial hygiene. Harry Truman amended the laws to allow the Surgeon General (the head of the Public Health Service) to expand the National Institutes of Health and create additional research institutes.[24] At roughly the same time, the Hill-Burton Act enabled the federal government to fund, through grants or loans, small rural hospital construction through much of the country. Over the following thirty years, the Hill-Burton program provided nearly $4 billion in construction funds for seven thousand new, renovated, or expanded hospital projects with the simple requirement that the hospitals serve their communities with a "reasonable volume" of free care.[25]

Working in combination, the Public Health Service, the Hill-Burton grants, and the Indian Health Service (which dated to the nineteenth century) effectively distributed healthcare into pockets of the country that had previously lacked it. But such efforts were hardly the panacea health planners had envisioned. Many people, as detailed in the previous chapter, continued to lack access to care or at least to appropriate care, wherreras many hospitals were underutilized and understaffed. Research in the 1970s indicated that many of the Hill-Burton hospitals routinely failed to provide substantial amounts of free care or community outreach; of those that did, many lacked well-trained specialists with which to staff their operating rooms.

Congress made two more attempts to plan and coordinate healthcare delivery with the establishment in 1972 of Professional Standards Review Organizations (PSROs) and in 1974 of Health Systems Agencies (HSAs). PSROs and HSAs were created as community watchdog organizations—the PSROs would be dominated by physicians and monitor quality of physician services and overprovision of medical care, whereas the HSAs would be consumer dominated and would work to direct health planning and construction in such as way as to control communal costs and rationally distribute resources. Both groups met with fierce criticism due in part to the fact that they effectively worked against each other. (Ensuring medical care quality was philosophically at odds with cost control.)[26] More important, they were designed with unrealistic goals. In using physicians as monitors, the PSROs were the classic "fox watching the henhouse," whereas the HSAs had little authority to implement an ambitious agenda. One noted healthcare scholar observed, "It would take an evangelist to believe that the quality of health care would be significantly improved by the establishment of PSROs."[27] The American Medical Association (AMA) as usual responded to the relatively toothless development with hyperbole: "The next breath of hot air from Washington will bring with it the clank of prison chains," said one member of the AMA's House of Delegates.[28]

Of the two groups, the HSAs were the more ambitious, charged with collecting and interpreting health data, creating strategic plans and lists of priorities for community construction, and creating an annual health system plan for the state, while incorporating viewpoints from academics, consumers, providers, nonprofit and government leaders, and payers.[29] In theory, the impulse behind the HSAs was reasonable: reining in unwise spending and distributing health resources where they most needed through a collaborative and inclusive process. In reality, however, the agencies operated at odds with the entrepreneurial zeitgeist of US healthcare. Doctors practiced where they chose to practice; communities established hospitals where they chose to establish hospitals; insurers produced policies they felt they could sell; and consumers purchased health services, goods, and drugs they chose to purchase. Government played little role in decisions at any juncture, outside of paying roughly one third of all costs accrued nationally.

Physician Culture

The greatest obstacle HMOs faced was physicians, or perhaps more accurately, physician culture. At the time of the passage of the federal HMO Act (1973), US physicians were inheritors of a proud tradition of autonomy, professional discretion, and patient focus. Fiercely antagonistic toward third-party payers since the 1930s, and to a governmental role in healthcare payment since national health insurance proposals in the 1910s, most US physicians had opposed health reform proposals from Presidents Roosevelt, Truman, and Nixon.[30] They had forced President Lyndon B. Johnson to cede control of Medicare billings to the point where they exercised near total control over their fees and practice decisions for which they billed the federal government billions annually. They now generally opposed HMOs.

Most doctors were skeptical that a nonphysician could play a constructive role in the physician–patient relationship. While nurses had a role, it was very much one of subordinate assistant, with clear boundaries regarding autonomy, discretion, and relationship with the patient. Although physician's assistants might play a more active assisting role sometime in the future, in 1972 over half of doctors felt uncomfortable with the idea of a nonphysician performing even a preliminary physical exam on a patient, and a third felt that a nonphysician might be able to competently prescribe a therapeutic regimen.[31]

But far worse than a nonphysician clinician was a nonphysician administrator exercising authority over physician performance, whether that administrator was a private health insurer, an HMO manager, or a civil servant in a government agency. Most physicians were extraordinarily resistant to the idea of being managed, all the more so when the manager worked for the government. The AMA routinely demonized government bureaucrats and government health planning not only as inimical to high-quality medical care but as essentially un-American. In response to Nixon's efforts at health reform, for example, one prominent physician in California issued a screed on the "healthocrats" who would socialize doctors and hospitals, undermine patient care, and generally degrade the profession. The bureaucrats would inject themselves into the doctor–patient relationship and corrupt it. The movement, he wrote, "would be *disastrous*. Patient care will *not* be improved . . . it will deteriorate."[32] Another doctor wrote of the "great bureaucratic monster in Washington loose to do as it pleased with our medical system."[33]

HMOs threatened the established order of many physicians. On many levels, the ways the HMOs promised to improve medical care were built on disempowering physicians. The collegial interactions implicit in the group nature of the HMOs quashed doctors' independence and judgment. Capitation meant that physicians needed to consider the cost of performing an additional test or procedure. In-network restrictions meant they could not refer patients to some of their most trusted friends and colleagues. Although initial studies showed that none of these restrictions appeared to undermine patient outcomes and satisfaction, all undermined doctors' sense of professional dignity. One scholar of physician culture wrote at the time of the profession's "anti-intellectualism," "pre-occupation with medical economics" (which placed a premium on billings), and "resistance to change."[34] Another observer of physician mores, himself a doctor, recognized that practice at the time was antithetical to concern for the public's health, which was "an abstraction that was difficult for the physician to grasp."[35] Arguing for HMOs as a constructive response to weaknesses in the healthcare delivery system simply failed to resonate with most physicians.

The fact that HMOs were growing in part due to federal action made them all the less credible. Doctors viewed virtually all federal legislation and regulation concerning healthcare delivery as potentially destructive, and the HMO Act was no exception. Doctors resisted health insurance proposals, insurance regulation, Medicare, Medicaid, hospital oversight, licensure, government accreditation, and continuing education requirements. They opposed toothless legislation creating community boards to oversee hospital charges and capital expansion. After the passage of a modest 1974 law creating local hospital oversight agencies, James Sammons, executive vice president of the AMA, said, "Of all the

bills they've ever passed short of declaring war, this is the most danger-
ous. It vests decision-making power in the hands of totally unprepared
people."[36]

Notably, physician attitudes had not stayed wholly stagnant. Doctors
coming of age in the early 1970s were generally more receptive to new
forms of organization, greater empowerment of patients, and expanded
roles for government and nonphysician clinicians. Younger physicians
were far more likely than their older colleagues to share clinical decision
making with the patient (in 1961 only 10 percent of a group of surveyed
physicians regularly shared a cancer diagnosis with a patient).[37] When
the federal government created the PSROs in 1972, 55 percent of physicians under age 45 approved of the measure, while only 33 percent of
older physicians did so.[38]

Physicians were generally ambivalent about transferring authority
from doctor to patient. While many professed to enjoy their work, even
finding it compelling and meaningful, most were aware of the price
the profession extracted. Patients were a needy lot and respected few
boundaries. Many doctors were on call at all hours, and those in small
practices had little ability to limit their practice hours. Treating a patient
could be rewarding, but it could be frustrating if the patient refused to
take responsibility for his or her health or failed to comply with a physician's recommendations. One study of physicians' attitudes in 1970
concluded that many doctors viewed their patients as "a self-indulgent
lot" who created their own ill health.[39] Doctors complained about ir-
regular hours, "unreasonable" patients, and the challenges of "maintaining a family life."[40] One fed-up doctor wrote, "How often is it the
person who increases his need for health care by smoking three packs
of cigarettes a day at a cost of $450 a year who shouts the loudest about
health care costs!"[41]

The stress of practice took its toll. Nearly half of doctors at midcareer
were either divorced or described their marriages as unhappy.[42] One
study conducted by the AMA found narcotic addiction rates among
physicians at thirty times the rate of the general population.[43] Suicides
were unusually frequent. Fear of malpractice litigation haunted the
profession, leading doctors to overtest, overprescribe, and overtreat. One
writer, exploring the dimensions of US healthcare in 1971, called malpractice a "plague" that caused physicians to be "increasingly fearful."[44]
Even if some of the malaise could be attributed to external factors—
availability of prescription narcotics, self-selection of particularly driven
people into the profession—the nature of practice created a siege

mentality among doctors. Nonphysicians attempting to displace physicians' authority threatened the integrity of a professional brotherhood annealed in uniquely hard experiences.

At the same time, medicine was changing dramatically. From a cottage industry of solo practitioners plying a general trade in small towns, medicine had become increasingly specialized and infused with sophisticated technology. Young doctors were liable to be academically accomplished but interpersonally challenged. Overspecialized medical school faculty tended to overemphasize technical diagnosis over humane treatment.[45] As early as 1963, a report on medical education in New York expressed concern that medical care not become "increasingly an episodic, impersonal and even haphazard matter of a patient's shopping in bewilderment from specialist to specialist."[46] Guardians of the profession pleaded for the continued concern of the "*whole* patient . . . his dignity, his self respect," and one bitter rural practitioner complained of a system "that has seen the degradation of the family practitioner to a level of a mid-wife."[47]

Specialization, mechanization, grueling hours, and rising litigiousness all worked to harden doctors against their patients and the public. The academically demanding nature of the classroom years and the outrageous hourly demands on medical interns and residents all contributed to a culture of callousness and later arrogance. Doctors looked down on the many planners, administrators, and legislators who claimed to work on behalf of the health system in part because they felt that none of these people had experienced hardships comparable to those experienced during medical training. One doctor told an anecdote about an undergraduate premedical chemistry class: "The professor told everyone to 'look to your left and look to your right because two of the three of you won't be here at the end. It's my job to make sure you flunk.'" The narrator admitted that the experience "doesn't reward you for being helpful . . . that process just continues through medical school."[48]

In 1973 the profession faced a series of troubling philosophical questions. Was a physician an applied scientist—an engineer of the human body—or a healer with the holistic dimensions that term implied? Did a good doctor need to be more than technically proficient? Did the patient even exist outside of a series of interlocking systems of biochemical reactions and mechanical forces? Certainly some doctors abhorred the direction they saw medicine taking. Small groups of physicians worked to establish "medical humanities" curricula in medical schools with required ethics courses and public health experiences for young doctors.[49] Similarly, some doctors questioned the utility of focusing exclusively on organ systems and chemical reactions divorced from the broader societal pathologies of violence, poverty, and insalubrious environments. Even so, many vociferously rejected these soft concerns and celebrated the extraordinary accomplishment wrought by molecular biology, genetics, and biochemistry over the previous decades. One strident doctor refused to "ride shotgun for human rights" and defended his profession's essential aloofness. "You cannot legislate morals, or coerce a physician's love of people who aren't all that lovable."[50]

Underlying these arguments about professional identity lay ambivalence about money. Generalists and specialists alike needed to be paid, and in the past they had the most success in boosting their incomes by charging on a piecemeal basis. Procedures, tests, and office visits were all itemizable and billable in a way that general health maintenance was not. HMOs threatened to disrupt a stable revenue stream, even if they seemed to promise greater individual and societal health. Doctors defended themselves against accusations of conflicted interests and mercenary behavior, but the essential conundrum of the healing profession remained. One pithy retired surgeon, tired of the hypocrisy of his profession, recalled George Bernard Shaw's *Doctor's Dilemma* in offering his critique: "What other men dare to pretend to be impartial where they have a strong pecuniary interest on one side?"[51] The rising prominence of HMOs threatened to focus the country's attention on precisely that question.

Greed

Doctors had long made a respectable living, but given the natural constraints of patients' ability to pay, had subordinated the importance of income to professional standing, prestige, and philanthropy. Men and women had been drawn to medicine not because of high pay but because of the intrinsic satisfaction garnered from applying specialized knowledge in the service of humanity. Doctors who were particularly cerebral had added a strong dose of research to their professional mix; those who found serving patients tedious could try their hand in administration, teaching, or public health.

Third-party payments changed the mix. Although health insurance had begun to permeate the population in the years after World War II, it was initially aimed primarily at hospital reimbursement, with physician reimbursement limited to certain cases and procedures. Medicare had pushed physician reimbursement to a more comprehensive model with doctors charging back to Medicare's primary intermediary, Blue Shield, for almost all tests and procedures they could conduct. Blue Shield, in turn, adopted Medicare's "customary" reimbursement schedule (repaying the fees at 75 percent of the "usual" communal standard); other private insurers tended to follow Blue Shield's lead.[52]

Growing third-party reimbursement sowed the seeds of greed in the profession and increased the allure of specialization. Although specialty training had always produced a modest lifelong return on the initial investment of time, third-party payment increased the return to a point difficult for young physicians to resist. Suddenly, neuro and cardiothoracic surgeons, gynecologists, anesthesiologists, radiologists, and oncologists were not merely well-off; they could become genuinely rich if they worked hard. Primary care physicians, with little to bill for besides well and sick patient visits, vaccinations, quick lab tests, and annual physical exams fell increasingly far behind.

Reimbursement policy pulled doctors firmly toward specialization. The essence of primary care was cogitative—teasing out a patient's medical narrative from his or her complex life history, symptoms, complaints, and vital signs. The thinking was time consuming and critical, but difficult to place a value on. Specialists who performed tests and procedures could easily bill for discrete tasks, but generalists had to bill for their time and judgment, both of which tended to be discounted by private patients and third-party insurers. Physician leaders and policy makers understood the problem but could devise no concrete solution that would appeal to payers (never eager to pay for services whose value could not be easily discerned) and patients. Two Yale Medical School professors pondered the dilemma: "What would be the effect on career choices if the reimbursement for medical care were restructured to reward cognitive skills equally with technical skills?"[53]

The procedure that exemplified the trend was the coronary artery bypass. This modestly risky procedure, in which a surgeon transplanted a piece of healthy arterial tissue (usually from a patient's leg) to the patient's heart to compensate for vessels clogged with arterial plaque, routinely saved lives. Millions of patients who would have died in their fifties and sixties from cardiac infarction ("heart attack") could be saved and gain decades of life. By 1980 the nation's cardiac surgeons were performing 125,000 bypass procedures annually, at a typical surgeon pay rate of $3,800. Efforts from an anesthesiologist, ICU physician, cardiologist, and pump perfusionist added $3,000 per case, and hospital charges added an additional $9,000. The nation's total bill for the procedure that year was $1.5 billion. For the seven hundred cardiac surgeons who performed nearly all of the procedures, this one operation yielded roughly $350,000 per surgeon per year. Additional cardiac procedures brought the average income of a cardiac surgeon above $500,000. These numbers are conservative. Elite surgeons on the coasts might charge $4,000 to $6,000 for the procedure, which generally took three to four hours to perform.[54]

Money at this level distorted professional norms. All professionals work for pay, but the essence of professionalism dictates subordinating purely monetary concerns to standards of professional practice.[55] The opportunity to garner hundreds of thousands of dollars in fees, however, overrode medical judgment. Most doctors cleaved to the Hippocratic dictum to "do no harm," but many were lured to perform procedures or prescribe tests and medications that were at best only marginally beneficial to the patient and, at worse, scarcely outweighed the risks they imposed. Even internists, generally buffered from greed by the limits of their own earning ability, were subject to corrupting pressure by pharmaceutical firms who sought to buy their loyalty with gifts, trips, and meals.[56]

Third-party money corrupted hospitals, too. While the dominant model of US hospital organization for two centuries had been the nonprofit sectarian model—community-based, private, and charitable in intent—a new for-profit model was ascendant in the early 1970s.[57] Humana, American Medicorp, Hospital Corporation of America (HCA), and American Medical International (AMI) were all growing rapidly by 1975, taking ever increasing revenues from their more traditional nonprofit competitors.[58] These hospitals carefully parsed their revenue streams to discover which services were (or were not) profitable and then discontinued the unprofitable services. This was antithetical to the historical model of a hospital, which provided a broad array of inpatient and outpatient services for the community and used the more profitable ones to subsidize the less so. Some 350 for-profits were in operation by 1975, housing thirty-five thousand beds in thirty states, and representing 5 percent of all nonfederal hospital beds nationwide.[59]

Contrary to received wisdom, for-profit hospitals did not necessarily provide lower-grade care than did nonprofit hospitals. Rather, they were organized to respond to market conditions, aggressively expand into underserved markets, sell profitable services, and cut unprofitable ones when possible. (Nonprofitable services, like the emergency room, were frequently maintained as loss leaders to induce patients to check themselves in.) Although the hospitals may not have delivered low-grade care, their management ethos lay at odds with the charitable impulse of traditional hospitals. Jack Massey, president of HCA (with forty hospitals and over five thousand beds), exclaimed that the chain's growth potential was "even better than Kentucky Fried Chicken."[60] (He had formerly served as president of that restaurant chain.) Similarly, Uranus Appel, founder of AMI in 1959 (and a former hotelier), noted, "In hotels the profit center is in bars. In hospitals it's in ancillary medical services."[61]

Managers of for-profit hospitals voiced concerns over similar matters as managers of nonprofit hospitals—staff ratios, nonpayment of bills, bad debts, supply costs—but unlike nonprofit managers, they were not bound by a broader mission of community service. For-profit managers were businesspersons first, and healthcare providers second. They charged higher prices per day, moved patients through their institutions more quickly, imposed greater numbers of tests and procedures, and rapidly transferred unprofitable patients to public facilities. One for-profit hospital encouraged its medical staff to maintain privileges at the local nonprofit hospital so that they could "dump" financially unattractive patients more rapidly.[62] The hotelier-turned–hospital manager explained his management insight thus: "Both are basically service oriented. Face it, you go into a hospital and the surgery could be terrible, but you'll probably never know. But what you do know and care about are the same things that matter to the hotel guest: good food, clean floors, and a big color TV."[63]

For-profit hospitals operated at odds with HMOs, too. HMOs were predicated on capitation, in which providers had a vested interest in keeping patients healthy (that is, by avoiding treatment), but for-profit hospitals produced revenues by selling services—that is, by admitting sick people. A community of healthy people taking responsibility for its own well-being through prophylaxis and good living spelled doom for the for-profits, which tended to locate in the Southern states, where HMOs had lower rates of penetration. Moreover, while HMOs tended to seek less capital-intensive modes of treatment, for-profit hospitals were known for their intensive construction budgets, which could be leveraged for higher billings. Humana Corporation, for example, built thirty-nine new hospitals over just seven years starting in 1969.[64] While

Humana was actually operating its facilities at a deficit by 1977, it hoped that careful patient mix, coupled with new federal Medicare reimbursement guidelines, would soon bring it to profitability.

By 1980, Humana and HCA each owned roughly seventeen thousand hospital beds, producing revenues of roughly $1.5 billion. Humana's stock price had risen from $8 in 1968 to $336 in 1980, and its two co-founders were each worth $40 million. The firm built and acquired hospitals aggressively and frequently sued planning boards in an effort to avoid limitations on expansion imposed through the certificate-of-need process. When it acquired forty hospitals owned by rival American Medicorp in 1978, it dismissed redundant workers, rewrote third-party payment agreements, renegotiated supply contracts, and increased profitability at the new hospitals.

For-profit hospitals negated some of the impetus in the early 1970s toward systematization and coordination. If HMOs represented a somewhat idealistic impulse in health planning, profit-seeking institutions demonstrated that medicine had been and continued to be in part a business. Although the sector had long prided itself in balancing a business ethos with a commitment to care and quality, the business aspect of medicine could not easily be rooted out. The business of medicine, like all businesses, promoted creativity, industriousness, and entre-preneurialism, while rewarding productivity and customer service. These attributes were hardly perfectly aligned with the utopian impulse in health planning in 1975.

Greed was natural, but so was the impulse for consumers to check it. When markets worked, suppliers charged what the market would bear, but consumers imposed downward pressure on prices. Healthcare in the 1970s defied basic laws of economics. The initial consumer, the patient, had little incentive to shop for better prices. Even the secondary consumer, the insurance companies, seemed unable or unwilling to constrain the upward trends. They appeased providers by paying what was demanded and passing costs on in the form of increased premiums to their corporate customers. The amounts that the insurers paid out increased exponentially. Blue Cross payments increased every year from 1966 to 1980 at twice the average rate of inflation, causing them to triple their average premiums (in constant dollars) over that time. In 1975, Blue Cross costs rose 24 percent.[65] The Blue Cross program of the National Capital Area (Washington, DC) raised payments between 1975 and 1978 from $2,000 to $3,500 for coronary bypass, from $1,650 to $2,500 for hip replacement, and from $750 to $1,000 for hysterectomy.[66]

Physicians had little incentive to constrain their charges; the general practice of the insurers was to simply take all charges for a particular procedure and reimburse at either the seventy-fifth or ninetieth percentile. For some procedures, one physician group could control so much of the market as to be able to unilaterally alter the usual fee.[67]

By 1977, with some Blue Cross programs raising premiums by an extraordinary 30 percent, corporate America began to respond. US manufacturing companies, faced with high benefits costs for their unionized employees and growing competition from abroad, realized that their healthcare costs were making their products uncompetitive. Chrysler Corporation hired Joseph Califano, President Jimmy Carter's first HEW secretary, to conduct broad cost-control measures throughout the company, and other companies followed suit.[68] Many of the measures were simply common sense: requiring second opinions for all procedures, carefully reviewing hospital bills, reimbursing for home services, and providing company-based wellness programs such as smoking cessation, alcohol treatment, and gym membership.[69] But many of the most promising cost savings solutions, such as steering employees to HMOs, reducing payments to hospitals and physicians, moving procedures out of hospitals to outpatient surgical centers, and limiting patients to certain in-network doctors who agreed to work for reduced fees, were beyond the abilities of corporate employers. They could exert some pressure on their employees' behavior, but they could not unilaterally change the nature of healthcare delivery.

❧

Lack of system in US medicine in the 1970s was not so much by design as by evolution. A creed of entrepreneurialism overlaid on a proud professional ethos had produced a fiercely independent physician cadre who opposed efforts at organization, planning, and coordination. The resulting cacophony had produced some superb medical care, but at the expense of efficiency and rationality. The nation was awash in urban specialists catering to the wealthier portions of the population who in turn consumed more medical services, tests, devices, and procedures than was optimal. Efforts to impose order on this antisystem produced vitriol and resentment. The *managed* in "managed care" was practically an epithet.

Proud independence was defiled (or at least adulterated) with greed. Both US medicine and US hospitals in the late 1970s could hardly claim to be above mammon. Increasing rates of surgical procedures and discretionary tests reflected more underlying greed than medical progress. The nascent for-profit hospital movement did not so much change the nature of hospital practice as abrogate the industry's long-running commitment to charity. Neither the American people nor medicine's professional guardians seemed willing to call attention to the behavior.

3

![black bar]

Reining in the Excess

Prepaid Practice Plans

As the 1970s drew to a close, the most promising route to reining in excessive billings and costs lay in HMO-like payment schemes and multi-specialty group practices. HMOs had spawned a variety of payment schemes—used prepayment, capitation, preventive care, and lower hospital admissions rates—to hold down costs. Together these approaches came to be known as "managed care" and offered new paths to parsimony. They tended to work in tandem with large prepaid practice groups to subtly shift pressures in healthcare markets.

Physicians, of course, had long come together in small partnerships to share overhead, share patient loads, and train new associates. The new model was directed at improving the quality of patient care while holding down costs. Growing out of recommendations first offered in the 1930s by the Committee on the Costs of Medical Care, prepaid group practices grew slowly through the 1950s and 1960s, reaching about 8,500 nationwide by 1975.[1] The practices offered patients the advantage of coordinated care between doctors who all worked in the same practice, and thus were more likely to confer with each other.[2] At the same time, neighborhood clinics and medical schools tried to replicate the model by creating multispecialty nonprofit clinics and faculty practice plans. By 1979, university-based faculty practice plans, in which salaried physicians affiliated with medical schools agreed to see private patients as part of a multispecialty practice group, were generating $700 million in fees annually.[3]

Prepaid group practices offered many advantages for physicians. As they grew, they allowed groups of doctors to hire professional practice managers who in turn hired and managed legions of schedulers, billing specialists, lab contractors, office managers, and payroll professionals. All of these support personnel eroded the physicians' income, but it allowed them to focus their efforts on practicing medicine rather than managing a practice and pursuing nonpaying patients. More broadly, the group practices offered the hope of a more holistic and patient-centered approach to medical practice, in which doctors would coordinate their efforts to optimize patient outcomes, rather than toward maximizing their individual revenue. Proponents of the model suggested that prepaid group practices, even in the absence of managed care contractors, could reduce hospital admissions, improve long-term outcomes, and generally enhance a patient's clinical experience.[4]

These conclusions proved to be inaccurate, however. Doctors benefited from working in a collegial atmosphere, and some certainly conferred with each other on difficult cases, but data generated in the late 1970s pointed to few cost savings generated by the practices. Doctors in group practices sought revenue no less aggressively than did their colleagues in solo practices or in specialty groups, and even the claims of lower hospital admission rates seemed to reflect the growing presence of HMOs rather than any strategic advantage of prepaid groups. Prepaid group practices might play an important role in future iterations of healthcare delivery, but alone, their ability to hold down costs was minimal.[5]

By contrast, HMOs did succeed in holding down costs, largely by keeping patients out of hospitals, but also by reducing the average length of stay of a patient once he or she was admitted to a hospital. Data on HMOs in the late 1970s largely confirmed the rosiest predictions of their champions. HMO members used less specialty care, stayed away from hospitals, consumed fewer drugs and procedures, used cheaper doctors (limited to doctors in the HMOs' rosters), and tended to take better care of themselves.[6] Moreover, HMO members expressed a high degree of satisfaction with their care and with their interactions with physicians. Although claims for the organizations could be exaggerated, on the whole their payment model curbed the worse physician behavior while steering patients away from specialty practices and hospitals.[7]

HMOs failed to grow rapidly, however, despite their accomplishments. Americans continued to resist them when they could; doctors generally avoided them; and investors viewed them skeptically. Patients correctly perceived that joining an HMO would limit their choice of doctor (and, in a worst-case scenario, deny them necessary treatment) and in the absence of strong financial incentives generally preferred more traditional insurance plans.[8] Doctors correctly predicted that joining an HMO would limit their incomes while costing them some level of professional autonomy. Investors frequently failed to understand the revenue model of the organizations.[9] Moreover, HMOs were simply difficult to establish. The hopeful investor needed to assemble a broad catalog of member physicians willing to work on established rates and under stringent practice limitations before he or she could sell the first policy. Barriers to entry were high.

More promising from an organizational standpoint were modified managed care organizations called independent practice associations (IPAs). IPAs grew naturally out of their more orthodox HMO cousins. As with HMOs, physicians who joined up with IPAs agreed to accept a reduced fee schedule and refer exclusively to other physicians within the association. Some primary care physicians in the IPA worked on capitation, but more frequently doctors charged their services back to the IPA, which paid them on the fee schedule until money ran out. Member physicians tended to regulate each other, as all had a vested interest in maintaining the solvency of the central pool lest they be forced to work for free late in the year when funds ran out. Patients or their employers paid a set monthly fee to the IPA (as was true with traditional insurance or HMOs) and agreed to use physicians within the network. Notably, a physician could sign on to an IPA network while maintaining non-IPA patients within their practice.

IPAs were much easier to set up, as they did not require physicians to surrender their existing private practices. They tended to avoid the most stringent restrictions of capitation payment and relied more heavily on third-party utilization review (often peer review) and annual oversight in which overly spendthrift physicians were admonished or even ejected from the network. Unfortunately, they largely did not work. Data available by 1978 showed that IPAs failed to hold costs down more than traditional indemnity plans. One study conducted in California, where the Kaiser HMO had achieved significant penetration, showed that IPA charges were 27 percent higher per patient than Kaiser charges over a year. Alain Enthoven, perhaps the preeminent health systems analyst of his generation, noted that ultimately the ability of an IPA to keep down costs relied on the "ethics of physicians."[10] Unfortunately, data suggested that in the absence of binding and enforced restrictions, ethics thinking tended to give way to profits.

The disappointing news from the vanguard of healthcare delivery by 1979 was partially good (HMOs worked) but largely bad (patients and doctors avoided HMOs when they could, and HMOs were hard to establish). More broadly, health planners and policy makers were beginning to learn that in the area of cost containment, there were no shortcuts. The strategies that worked best in bringing down costs tended to depress physicians' incomes, limit choice, leverage capitation, and keep patients away from specialists and hospitals. Although data suggested that none of these actions actually made people sicker, all were actions that patients did not like and would avoid as long as they could afford to. In healthcare, as in most economic activities, there was no free lunch.

Consumer Choice

Enthoven failed to be cowed by this depressing prognosis. He was convinced that the United States could be sold on HMOs provided certain market inefficiencies were corrected and a broad series of regulations were imposed on both corporations and individuals. In 1978, he published his Consumer-Choice Health Plan, in which he laid out his plan for widely distributing the fruits of HMOs to the nation using market forces, free choice, adjusted tax formulas, and gentle government oversight. The plan, whose influence extended for more than thirty years and undergirded such major government reforms as President Bill Clinton's Health Security Act of 1994 and President Barack Obama's Affordable Care Act of 2010, was simultaneously realistic and quixotic.

Enthoven believe that if most people were given a choice between competing health plans at work, including traditional indemnity plans and orthodox HMOs, and if they were forced to bear a substantial portion of the cost differential between the plans, many more would choose to enroll in managed care plans. Moreover, those who chose to retain their traditional indemnity plans could be forced to pay a larger share of the true cost of the plans. Thus, he proposed that the government require all employers to offer an array of choices, similar to how the federal government offered its employees a menu of choices. To push employees into making rational choices about their health plans, Enthoven would end the tax protection of health care benefits for employees (at the time, all health benefits were considered nontaxable compensation) and rely instead on a standard tax credit to be used toward the purchase of their first-choice plans. Not only would this force people to recognize the true cost of the plan they were purchasing, it would make the system of tax deductions and credits more equitable in that they would no longer be pegged to a specific employee's tax bracket but to an employee's actuarial cost of health consumption (dictated largely by age, but also in part by profession and health history). People who chose to enroll in more expensive plans would not get larger tax credits.

Enthoven wished to integrate Medicare and Medicaid into his scheme as well, with Medicare beneficiaries also receiving a tax credit to purchase a health plan on the open market, and Medicaid recipients receiving vouchers for 100 percent of the cost of certain plans, which they, too, could purchase on the open market. (Medicare, as a government insurance program, would be retained for the permanently disabled.) To a large degree, the plan would take tax deductions granted to high earners using expensive plans and transfer part of that wealth to the public to boost subsidies for the poor. At the same time, it would induce many people to join HMOs to save money and thus gradually reduce the entire national commitment to healthcare purchasing, while granting many more people the health advantages conferred by enrolling in an HMO.

Enthoven addressed one of the great challenges of his plan, the unwillingness of most health insurers to enroll individual subscribers who were sicker or older than average, by requiring that all insurers and managed care companies take on all potential subscribers at average community costs if they wished to qualify to receive federal tax credit payments. That is, an insurer that refused to play by the rules would risk marginalizing itself, as the vast majority of people would rely on the tax credits to pay for their insurance. Qualified insurers would not be allowed to discriminate based on sex, race, age, religion, or national origin. Most certainly they would not be allowed to discriminate based on prior health history. Moreover, every qualified plan must be open to new subscribers for one month every year (open enrollment) and provide detailed descriptions to all subscribers and potential subscribers of fees, payouts, premiums, co-payments, and deductibles. Enthoven's plan, in theory, would make purchasing health insurance a more open, transparent process.

Enthoven estimated the price of his plan for the federal government at $22.4 billion. The coming glut of doctors might pressure doctors into participating in HMOs, while the reformed tax laws and tax credits would force citizens to bear more of the true cost of their healthcare purchasing. Ideologically, the plan rested on the best aspects of market capitalism, entrepreneurialism, and American creativity. In a later guise, many of the most important aspects of the plan were incorporated into a philosophy of healthcare distribution which would be called managed competition. For now, the word *choice* was paramount.[11]

Enthoven's plan was not uncontentious. The medical community continued to resist many of the basic assumptions of managed care as an organizing scheme for medical practice, while most Americans in 1980 who had heard of managed care viewed it negatively. Few members of Congress were committed to broad-scale healthcare and tax reform in 1978 when Enthoven created his plan, and even the Carter administration, committed as it was to doing something about healthcare inflation, had not yet settled on managed care as an important vehicle to reining in costs. More telling, serious healthcare policy analysts questioned many of Enthoven's assumptions and attacked his plan as naive and unworkable.

Perhaps the most eloquent of Enthoven's critics, Eli Ginzberg of Columbia University, questioned the impetus behind the changes to the tax code that the plan required. Ginzberg wrote, "For market-competition advocates to support such a major intrusion of the federal government into collective bargaining is a reminder that reformers are no less likely than other groups to becoming enthralled with their own ideology."[12] Ginzberg also expressed deep skepticism that physicians could ever be induced to surrender their professional autonomy to managed care organizations, while outsourcing some of the decision making to third-party utilization review professionals. Also, he correctly discerned that most people very much wanted top-dollar coverage in their health insurance and would resist less expensive plans that saved money by imposing higher deductibles and co-payments on their members.

Most important for Ginzberg, Enthoven's plan rested on people consuming less healthcare by forcing them to realize the true costs of their own health consumption habits. But Ginzberg believed and advocated for increased healthcare consumption, whether measured by volume or quality. For him, the constant improvement of healthcare imaging, testing, knowledge, and intervention over the previous half century had been one of the signature achievements of modern society and to deny access to those discoveries was simply immoral. He wrote, "the public wants improved, not reduced, access to essential healthcare, and it wants to accelerate, not slow down, the progress of medical science."[13] This impulse to consume, in Ginzberg's estimation, doomed the Enthoven plan to failure.

In part, the disagreement lay in essential differences between the two scholars' approaches to life. Enthoven was a business school professor who had served earlier in his career as Assistant Secretary of Defense for Systems Analysis in the administration of President Lyndon Johnson. An economist by training, he had spent much of his career thinking about costs and benefits and optimal application of resources. Ginzberg, also an economist who had worked for the Department of Defense early in his career, had applied his expertise on manpower training and deployment issues rather than systems issues. Having served as the first director of the Conservation of Human Resources Project, Ginzberg tended to focus his work on how societies could optimally use their human capital. For him, education and healthcare were investments that a moral society made in its people, rather than goods to be distributed and consumed through the application of market forces.[14] The two men, both highly successful in academic economics, were strikingly different in their perceptions of a good society.

Lessons from Abroad

Could the United States turn to the health delivery models of other nations for guidance? Many other nations were claiming health outcomes equal to or better than the United States, while spending significantly less money purchasing care. While the United States spent 11 percent of its gross domestic product (GDP) on healthcare, France spent only 9.3 percent, Canada 8.5 percent, Germany 8.2 percent, and the United Kingdom only 6.2 percent. Life expectancy in these countries was longer than in the United States, maternal and infant mortality rates were lower, and prevalence of most infectious diseases were about the same. Indeed, many of these countries were rapidly improving their health outlooks, while the United States appeared to have hit a plateau. For example, Canada had lowered its infant mortality rate from 17.5 per

one thousand births in 1971 to 9.6 in 1981. During the same period the
United States lowered its infant mortality rate as well, but only from 20
to 12.6. The United States was falling behind.

Canada's system of ten provincial mandatory health insurance
programs, together called Medicare, evolved after World War II with
several of its Midwestern provinces creating mandatory hospital insurance plans. In 1966 the federal government mandated that each province
create a comprehensive health insurance program covering all of the
province's residents, which could work reciprocally with the plans of
other provinces. By 1970, all Canadian citizens carried comprehensive
health insurance covering most physician and hospital costs, paid for
through general income taxes, payroll taxes, and (in two provinces)
mandatory premium deductions.

Medicare was enormously popular among Canadians. The majority
of Canadians expressed high levels of satisfaction with the system, and
even wealthy Canadians (who were more likely to purchase additional
care out of pocket) generally liked it. Through central planning, fee
abatement for medical tuition, collective bargaining with provincial
medical groups, and restrictions on capital investment in hospitals and
infrastructure, the country had managed to avoid many of the worst
excesses of the US system. In Canada 40 percent of all physicians were
generalists (as opposed to 18 percent in the United States) and a higher
percentage of doctors practiced in rural areas (due to strong inducements from provincial governments). Canada managed to produce approximately as many physicians per capita as the United States (140
per 100,000, versus 132 per 100,000 in the United States) but had been
more successful in training the types of doctors most needed by the
public and in getting them to practice where they were needed most.[15]
Nonetheless, like the United States, Canada needed to fill almost one-
fourth of its residency slots each year with graduates of foreign medical
schools.

Could Canada be a model for the United States? Although many
politically progressive Americans looked longingly to their northern
neighbor, scholars who studied Canadian politics and society were
skeptical. Canada was historically a far more egalitarian society than
the United States was. A nation that had shunned immigration until the
twentieth century, its ethnically homogeneous population expressed
greater comfort than did Americans with higher taxation, more social
redistribution, and a larger role for government. Robert Evans, a prominent Canadian health economist, warned the United States away from

borrowing Canada's model. "I am not trying to sell it to you," he told a US researcher. "You cannot have it. It would not fit because you do not see the world, or the individual, or the state, as we do."[16] John Iglehart, a US health scholar who undertook an exhaustive year-long study of the Canadian system, came away with a similar view. He wrote, "There is a remarkable egalitarian quality about Canadian health care that reflects a society that attaches a higher value to social equity than does the United States."[17]

The Canadian system was attractive to US progressives not just because of its universality and its efficacy; it also managed to produce more with less. Scholars who studied the system postulated the roots of its fiscal efficiency and concluded that part of the savings was realized by simply paying doctors less, but part resulted from the streamlined administrative structure. In the United States, doctors and hospitals contended with multiple payers, each with multiple reimbursement rules, and thus had to hire substantial numbers of personnel simply to facilitate billing and reimbursement. Canadian doctors and hospitals, by contrast, had only one payer to contend with.[18]

It was true that each year Canada lost a certain portion of its best-trained physicians to the United States, where a surgical specialist could triple his or her income. Recognizing this, Canadian provinces debated whether to allow physicians to opt out of Medicare and see private-pay patients in an effort to induce them to stay and serve at least some Canadians, if primarily wealthy ones. The nation turned down the proposal, however. When Prime Minister Pierre Trudeau posed the Canada Health Act of 1983, which created financial incentives to discourage physicians across the provinces from billing above Medicare rates, the bill passed with unanimous support. Not a single conservative member of Parliament opposed the final legislation, largely in recognition of the extraordinary level of support Medicare drew across the political spectrum. It was no wonder that Iglehart, reflecting on the phenomenon, said that Medicare was regarded as "a social jewel" by the electorate.[19]

The UK National Health System (NHS) held costs down even further than Canada did but seemed even more ideologically alien to the United States. Tracing its genesis to the Beveridge Report of 1942, which laid out much of the UK social welfare state, the system had been implemented in 1948 by putting most physicians on salary and nationalizing almost all of the independent (private) hospitals. The system had brought modern healthcare to the masses (coverage was universal for both UK citizens and noncitizen residents) although quality was generally viewed as mediocre. Rudolf Klein, a social analyst in the United Kingdom, quipped that the goal of the NHS was not to universalize the best of British medical care but to "universalize the adequate."[20]

The NHS had different strengths and weakness than did Canadian Medicare. British doctors were insulated by distance from the lure of US physician incomes and emigrated at far lower numbers. But the system, chronically underfinanced, produced far worse queues than did Canada's, and British residents faced aggressive rationing for discretionary and "quality-of-life" procedures which Americans easily purchased. As a result, a far greater number of Britons (as much as 28 percent) purchased supplementary private health insurance plans in the mid-1980s, which they used to pay for physician services provided after hours in private clinics and offices. If Canadians focused on bringing middle-class medicine to the whole nation, Britons seemed more content with working-class medicine, while allowing more of the nation's wealthy to opt out.[21]

British life expectancy was roughly equal to US life expectancy, but Britons lived more uncomfortable lives. Dialysis treatments, organ transplants, hip replacements, herniotomies, and pelvic floor repairs were all in short supply. British emergency rooms and critical care wards regularly turned away patients deemed too old or too sick to benefit from expensive services. Health administrators in the British government emphasized to local district supervisors that cost-benefit analyses must be central to their decision making. When Neil Kinnock, leader of the Labour Party, accused Prime Minister Margaret Thatcher of gutting the NHS, Thatcher replied: "Let me tell you how really to terminate the health service. You do it by pretending there are no hard choices; you do it by behaving as though Britain has a bottomless purse; you do it by promising what you can't deliver; by assuring that all you need to do is snap your fingers, cry 'abracadabra' and lo and behold, the sky's the limit."[22]

In theory, the United States had much to learn from other nations' insurance and delivery systems. Even eschewing the UK's parsimonious example, US health planners could aspire to a less expensive, less administratively complex, fairer, and more effective program. Canada, Germany, France, and Japan all delivered care through private doctors and hospitals reimbursed by either private or provincial insurance programs, at substantially lower costs than did the United States. Residents of those countries lived longer, expressed higher levels of satisfaction with their care, and lived with less fear of insurance denials, job-lock, preexisting exclusion clauses, and (most important) loss of insurance. Their citizens were 100 percent covered from birth to death. Of note, however, these nations had begun constructing their patchwork of mandated private, public, and provincial insurance programs decades ago, before the combined lobbying power of private insurance, physician and hospital associations, and drug companies had made comprehensive health reform so difficult to legislate.

Rejection

US medical leaders in the late 1970s were hardly persuaded by the clear successes posted by Medicare and Medicaid and were unreceptive to government efforts to rein in excessive costs and billing. Leaders of the American Medical Association (AMA) and various state and specialty associations articulated highly conservative views endorsing the efficacy of markets and alluding to the threat of communist expansion. Thomas Ballantine, for example, the treasurer and secretary of the AMA, cited Friedrich Hayek's *The Road to Serfdom* in expressing concern about the federal government's impulse toward social control, and John Tupper, in his inaugural speech as incoming president of the California Medical Association, stated his bedrock principles: "Less government; less poverty through stimulation of industry and business; encouragement of the sprit of the independent pioneer; the spread of the voluntary effort throughout society."[23]

Many physicians eschewed embracing a consistent political stance, but tried to push the issue of cost and payment to the margins generally. For these doctors, the integrity of medicine lay in its professionalism and trust. Discussions of fees, payment schemes, deductibles, co-payments, and negotiated rates denigrated the ideals of the profession, enshrined as they were in the Hippocratic oath and centuries of selfless service to patients. These doctors were not so much ill-intentioned as naive, believing that somehow funds would make themselves available for the support of the medical enterprise independent of organizational schemes and legislative directives. Many of these doctors had come of age after the great expansion of private health insurance in the 1950s, and they failed to understand that this expansion had been paid for with increased consumer prices, reduced wages, and declining industrial competitiveness. One sanctimonious physician, commenting on an article on medical economics that had appeared in the *New England Journal of Medicine*, dismissed such exercises as "a study in cash flow and inappropriate to a medical journal."[24]

Other doctors, particularly well-reimbursed specialists, resorted to aggressively defending the unique success achieved by US medicine and suggested that only the free exchange of medical services in open markets could produce such high quality. Michael DeBakey, the celebrated Texas heart surgeon who invented the major component of the heart-lung machine and pioneered life-saving heart surgeries, was a prominent spokesman for this line of thought, denigrating the contributions of Medicaid, Medicare, federal (Hill-Burton) hospital construction funds, and health planning generally. DeBakey was more than simply arrogant; he was sloppy and self-serving with his use of facts. Claiming that the heavy hand of government regulation was destroying hospitals, he ignored the fact that the hospital industry was largely self-regulated through its national accreditation council. Moreover, in direct contradiction to the enormous expansion of access to hospitals brought about by Medicare, he tarred the government program as "metastatic" and "pernicious," imposing layers of requirements on hospitals to "keep bureaucracy's wheels turning." He concluded, "Clearly, government's oppressive grip on health care must be loosened."[25]

Organized medicine, particularly as embodied in the AMA, resisted managed care as well. Even though HMOs were private, voluntary enterprises conducting business with private employers (who often offered the HMO as one of a number of health insurance options for their employees), the AMA rejected their essential premise that a third-party payer had a reasonable interest in "managing" the physician–patient transaction. The management function, in the AMA's view, was intrusive and undermined the integrity of the doctor–patient relationship, while casting aspersions on the trustworthiness of physicians. HMOs, after all, were built on careful selection of doctors who agreed to abide by practice guidelines and allowed themselves to be audited and second-guessed by either their peers or by third-party utilization review professionals. The scenario was a "chilling nightmare of modernity" in the words of Eliot Marshall, a medical writer who followed the industry closely during these years. It was a first step toward the "corporate practice of medicine," in which nonphysicians overrode sound medical judgment in the interest of profits and cost control.[26]

Physician skeptics also denied the distortionary effect of insurers. The expansion of private health insurance had greatly increased the funds used to consume healthcare, but in doing so had introduced a highly interested third party. Insurers were inevitably getting more interested in precisely how their funds were being spent, and on what tests, procedures, and services they were purchasing on behalf of their beneficiaries. As US industry began to protest ever-rising premiums, health insurers were forced to question physicians' judgments, if not necessarily their motivations. For thirty years US doctors and hospitals had grown wealthier on a customer base purchasing services on expense accounts, but now the payers were beginning to audit those accounts. Doctors bristled at the scrutiny and rushed to accuse their interrogators of intrusiveness, commercial mindedness, and general ineptitude, but they could not escape the fact that their profession had benefited greatly from the rise and expansion of the third-party payers they were complaining about.

A different group of doctors, taking a more moderate stance, understood that inflation over the long term needed to be checked, but rejected the argument that the government was the appropriate agent of change. These advocates of the "voluntary effort" teamed up with the hospital industry to argue that doctors and hospital leaders were the individuals best placed to find inefficiencies in medical delivery, negotiate better contracts with equipment providers, seek more cost-effective ways of treating patients, and root out superfluous tests and procedures. The American Surgical Association (among others) advocated this approach, encouraging its members to work closely with hospitals, educate themselves on the true costs of the procedures they were performing, and join voluntary cost-containment oversight committees.[27] These advocates pointed to a few successful examples of voluntary cost cutting, such as those posted by Johns Hopkins Hospital in Baltimore, which managed to cut annual cost increases from 17 percent to 8 percent over three years and cut $5 million from overhead costs.[28]

A small minority of doctors resisted the obstructiveness of their profession's leadership and called for greater scrutiny, oversight, and government involvement. These doctors, disproportionately drawn from the primary care ranks and frequently working with a public health orientation, endorsed the efficacy and quality of medicine delivered through HMOs and generally supported efforts to expand the government's role in providing health insurance to more people. A report by the Institute of Medicine in the mid-1970s called for greater acceptance of HMOs and demanded more extensive research on comparative efficacy of different health services delivery schemes.[29] One Alabama physician admitted that the medical establishment had been charged "not unconvincingly, with special interests advocacy, with self-serving hubris, and with pursuing and preserving social power."[30] Many primary care doctors argued to have the fee scale rebalanced in favor of "consultative services, counseling, and simply listening to patients."[31] More than a few, represented by the small but influential Physicians for National Health Insurance group, insisted that only large-scale government participation in payment could rationalize a system whose many self-interested players were driving up costs for millions while enriching themselves.[32]

In addition to grappling with changes in payment, the medical profession was facing challenges to its authority. The benevolent paternalism that had marked the profession through the twentieth century was morphing to a spirit of egalitarianism. Younger patients demanded more active participation in their own medical decision making, and the impulse to cede to the physician's best judgment was giving way to a medical conversation between doctor and patient. Changes to the AMA's Code of Ethics in 1980 dictated that a physician should "deal honestly with patients"; a departure from its past language, which said that a physician could withhold information from a patient for his or her own good.[33] The willingness of younger physicians to embrace this changed medical culture boded well for acceptance of future organizational schemes.

Physicians who resisted government efforts at health reform, be they on cost containment, access, or reorganization, took comfort in their firm knowledge that US healthcare was the best in the world. In a certain sense, they were right. In 1979 the United States biomedical research effort, resting firmly on the billions of dollars distributed annually by the National Institutes of Health, was unparalleled. A disproportionate share of the world's biomedical breakthroughs emerged from US labs and medical schools. American patients had access to surgical procedures, scans, and diagnostic tests that residents of other wealthy nations could get only by traveling abroad. A US residency slot was considered by young doctors around the world as the gold standard in clinical training.

Nonetheless, physicians who celebrated these facts frequently ignored the millions of people who had no access to medical wonders due to lack of public or private insurance, as well as the increasing burden that inflated health insurance premiums were placing on US industry. The US manufacturing juggernaut, which had led the world for three decades after World War II, was finally being challenged by retooled factories in Japan, Germany, and southeast Asia, and the US economy was beginning to feel the drag of the overly generous employee benefits. Healthcare in the United States was still preeminent, but the status was likely unsustainable.

4

The Lure of Profits

For-Profit Hospitals

The US hospital could trace its roots back to medieval eleemosynary convalescent houses in which succor and prayer were plentiful and therapeutics were in short supply. Early colonists in New York, Philadelphia, and Boston started institutions in which local doctors could obtain visiting privileges to counsel and treat while patients waited to heal on their own or die. These hospitals were more sites of caretaking than healing, and the local minister was as important as the attending doctor. Not-yet-professionalized nurses attended the sick, who often resided in the hospitals precisely because they lacked the bonds of kin and community to allow them to recuperate at home. Virtually all of these hospitals had religious orientations.

Change came in the years after the Civil War, when anesthesia and analgesis made surgery more than simply blood sport. Carbolic acid in hospital operating rooms created theaters where sepsis could be held at bay and ether allowed surgeons the leisure of doing more than simply hacking off gangrenous limbs and removing obvious tumors. By 1880 Samuel Gross, a surgeon in Philadelphia, could proclaim: "Progress stares us everywhere in the face. The surgical profession was never so busy as it is at the present moment; never so fruitful in great and beneficial results, or in bold and daring exploits."[1] The US hospital was an institution being repurposed to a more therapeutic and medically intensive institution.[2]

In the late nineteenth and early twentieth centuries, new immigrant groups founded hospitals in rapidly growing industrial cities, reflecting their ethnic and religious orientations. Seattle, Denver, St. Louis, New York, Chicago, Boston, Newark, and New Orleans suddenly hosted hospitals whose names reflected their founder's roots. Lutheran, Swedish, Jewish, Presbyterian, Episcopalian, German, Scottish, and Methodist hospitals proliferated in cities that hosted large contingents of those populations, and Catholic hospitals everywhere flourished under the watchful eyes of their patron saints and beneficent orders. All of these hospitals were incorporated as private, nonprofit institutions, dedicated to serving their communities with succor and science and dispensing charity to those who were deserving of it. Many established bonds with local medical schools and teaching programs such that the most prominent hospitals, with the most generous boards, could host research enterprises, medical schools, medical students, interns, and a few specialized residents.

At the same time, many municipalities established public hospitals to serve those deemed less than deserving. Although a few public hospitals were substantially older (New York's Bellevue traced its roots to 1736), the preponderance were established in the early years of the twentieth century in response to large populations of migrant industrial workers who often lacked communal affiliations. These hospitals were funded by local tax revenues and gave away their services free or at heavily reduced rates. While they, too, might host teaching and research programs, their wards tended to be more crowded; their wait times were longer; their surroundings were less cheerful. Not all cities chose to establish public hospitals. Several, disproportionately in the South, subsidized hospital care for the needy through tax abatements and grants to private hospitals, which were expected to commit a portion of their resources and facilities to caring for the public.

Privately owned for-profit hospitals were nearly as old as private sectarian nonprofits, but through most of US history had tended to be small (with fewer than ten beds) and specialized. Many physicians in the nineteenth century had their own wards from which they gleaned patient fees, and while the growth of nonprofit hospitals had displaced many of these small clinics, they had never entirely disappeared. In the

1970s, a new type of for-profit hospital began to appear. Large, well equipped, and comprehensive, these new hospitals were designed to compete directly with established community nonprofit hospitals while eschewing many of the charitable and less profitable services to which their competitors devoted substantial resources. A number of for-profit hospital chains—Humana, Columbia, Hospital Corporation of America (HCA), National Medical Enterprises—grew rapidly. By 1984, for example, HCA owned or managed 260 hospitals in forty-one states and grossed $3.9 billion. By that year, for-profit (often called *proprietary*) hospitals accounted for 12 percent of all hospital billings in the United States, and 21 percent in the South.[3]

For-profit hospitals were not necessarily bad. For-profit enterprises tended to adopt new technologies more quickly, manage themselves more efficiently, and respond to market demands more adeptly. Nonprofit hospitals had long suffered a reputation of being run amateurishly, and for-profit corporations could promise to deliver hospital care with "traditional business approaches," better market analysis, more effective deployment of capital, and more rigorous approaches to labor.[4] For-profit institutions worked side by side with nonprofit institutions in other sectors—theater, education, and museums, for example—and differently structured institutions could parse the market to deliver specialized products. For-profit hospitals could complement the charitable mission of the nonprofits while creating a denser, more responsive hospital sector.

But several studies conducted in the 1980s suggested that none of this was happening. For-profit hospitals actually tended to have higher costs, due in part to the more expensive cost of capital (the for-profits could not float tax-exempt hospital construction bonds) but also due to the higher prices they charged for similar services. For-profit charges were nearly 25 percent higher per admission than nonprofit charges for similar diagnoses, even while they maintained lower nursing staff ratios and provided substantially less charitable care.[5] At the same time, the for-profit chains aggressively resisted caring for nonpaying patients, moving to "dump" charity cases at local public hospitals or quickly discharge them. One widely reported story in Memphis told how the local HCA hospital threatened to stop chemotherapy treatments for a patient who had run out of money. Only after the patient threatened to file suit for abandonment and extortion did the hospital relent and continue treatment.[6]

In the lingo of economists, for-profit hospitals exhibited rent-seeking behavior. They were hardly alone, as virtually every for-profit company and professional partnership in the country did the same. Hospital care, however, had long been viewed by the public as an enterprise that ought to shun rent-seeking behavior. Although it was reasonable for hospitals to charge for board and services to allow them to continue serving their communities, it was less reasonable to think that human illness and suffering might be fruitful ground for garnering profits. For-profit hospitals tended to develop specialized wards, services, and procedures not because of medical exigency but because these services were potentially profitable. They spawned spas, elective surgical suites, cosmetic surgical departments, and private rooms that competed with luxury hotels. The Humana hospital in Phoenix took out an advertisement in 1985 (one of many) stating: "Complete face lift . . . was $941, now $675; breast augmentation . . . was $504, now $315."[7]

Even while they sought revenues, for-profit hospitals aggressively cut costs. Some cost-cutting procedures made sound managerial sense. Humana centralized its purchasing and administrative functions in one office, reducing inventory costs and streamlining administration. Its procedures might well serve as a model for sclerotic nonprofits.[8] But for-profits also looked to cut costs by cutting nursing and auxiliary therapeutic staffs, hiring less experienced house staff, and cutting contracts with partner medical groups. Young doctors were cheaper to hire than were older ones, but almost all practicing physicians felt that their skills improved over time, with their growth curves not flattening out until their fifth or sixth decades.[9]

What of quality? The question was hard to answer because long-term outcomes of hospital stays and hospital-based procedures were difficult to establish. Certainly for-profit hospitals had their adherents. Well-insured private patients found the care and attention they received from for-profit hospitals very much to their liking. One patient at a for-profit Nashville hospital recalled, "The nurses have shown me kindness and love. It's not just that they take care of my needs. It's the way they come in and whisper 'Don't worry Bob. You're going to be all right.'"[10] But rigorous studies of hospital quality suggested that the opposite was true. A study conducted by Lewin and Associates, a healthcare consulting and analytics firm, found that for-profit hospitals employed substantially fewer staff members per patient than did nonprofits, and a study conducted by the Institute of Medicine found that at least a quarter of physicians with admitting privileges at for-profit hospitals felt that the quality of care was better at nonprofits.[11]

Measuring quality was one of the great challenges for healthcare scholars in the 1980s because outcomes were so heavily determined by patient condition on admission. Patients who were healthier, wealthier, lighter skinned, taller, better educated, and who claimed more friends, better diets, better insurance plans, and better daily habits inevitably healed faster, more completely, and more permanently. Whereas the quality of hospital medical and nursing staff could make a difference based on measures of sheer clinical competence, much of the outcome depended on inputs for which the hospital could not be held responsible. In the following decades, healthcare scholars refined their measurement techniques to control for many of these variables, but in 1985 outcome measurement was still primitive. Nursing staff levels were probably a good proxy for quality, as was the opinion of experienced attending and house staff, but many declarations of quality were based on little more than anecdotes and personal experiences.

The increasing importance of for-profit hospitals reflected a rise in rent-seeking behavior throughout the health system. For-profit hospitals sought rents most transparently, but nonprofit hospitals, physicians, drug manufacturers, and even academic medical centers began to lessen their commitment to charitable and non–revenue producing endeavors and turn toward increasing their revenues. Nonprofit hospitals, for example, which historically had relied on substantial amounts of community philanthropy, by 1985 were operating almost entirely on patient billings and expanding their facilities through bond-backed funds. In New York City, philanthropy as a share of nonprofit hospitals' budgets dropped from 25 percent in the 1940s to 1 percent by 1984. The lost funds were made up from exponential growth in billings. One physician noted that when he had joined New York's Presbyterian Hospital in the late 1930s, a patient with advanced pulmonary disease could run up a bill of $8 to $12. By 1984 a critical pulmonary patient might leave the hospital owing close to $100,000.[12]

Both for-profit and nonprofit hospitals tried new strategies in bringing in more patients who could pay full price for treatments. A number of large hospitals experimented with a modified managed care model called a physician hospital organization (PHO) in which the hospital created a network of affiliated physicians who would work on a modified salary basis in hospital-owned office space and admit to the host hospital. Doctors were attracted to the stable salaries and low overhead, and hospitals hoped that owning the physician practices would guarantee a steady stream of patients. Teaching hospitals were particularly successful at using this model, as they already had access to hundreds of affiliated clinical faculty who enjoyed dividing their time between research, teaching, and clinical work. The physician practice model became an extension of many academic medical centers' work in local communities, allowing them to extend their communal orientation in providing ambulatory care while again guaranteeing a steady flow of patients to the main teaching hospital.[13] The whole effort, dubbed "the patient capture initiative" by healthcare consultants, moved the system a step closer to corporatization and network integration.[14]

A number of hospitals went beyond PHOs to spin off ambulatory surgery centers, free-standing medical imaging clinics, day hospitals, and other sorts of outpatient venues for profitable procedures. All of these new institutions were designed, like the PHOs, to extend the hospitals' reach into the community, guarantee inpatient referrals, and increase the volume of profitable procedures. Hospitals experimented with birthing centers, hospices, physical therapy clinics, radiation oncology centers, rehabilitation centers, and (most profitable of all) imaging centers to see which services could stand alone and thus be delivered more efficiently than was possible in general community hospitals.[15] At the same time, following the model of the for-profit networks, nonprofits began to create alliances, mergers, and networks in an effort to replicate some of the cost-saving advantages of scale, such as unified administrative offices, used by the for-profits.

Rent-seeking behavior by for-profit hospitals and by some of the more profit-oriented nonprofit hospitals placed stress on the nation's public hospitals. Always the treatment of last resort for the poor and uninsured, public hospitals in the past had shared the public burden with nonprofit hospitals whose tax abatement and missions had compelled them to care for a reasonable share of the poor. But as for-profit hospitals aggressively skimmed off the most well-insured (and profitable) patients, a ripple effect through the industry forced nonprofit hospitals to become more miserly in doling out their own charity. The burden of the poor and uninsured rose for public hospitals in the 1980s while "dumping" proceeded apace. A study of hospitals in Texas found that of the $400 million profit garnered by all of the state's hospitals in 1984, 66 percent went to the for-profits, 31 percent to the nonprofits, and a shade over 1 percent to the publics. The seven largest public hospitals shouldered 64 percent of all of the state's charity care, and all of the state's nonprofit hospitals together took on only 6.5 percent of charity patients (and the for-profits took on 3.5 percent). Public hospitals had always taken on a disproportionate burden, and the burden was growing.[16]

Public hospitals made up one-third of the 5,500 general acute care hospitals in the United States in the mid-1980s but provided well over half of all uncompensated and Medicaid-funded care. Federal and state cuts to the Medicaid program heavily affected the budgets of these hospitals as they struggled to cut overhead and stretch their resources. Not surprisingly, hospitals that treated above-average numbers of Medicaid patients reported budget deficits at double the rate of hospitals that treated below-average numbers of Medicaid patients. The credit rating of various municipalities told the same story, with hospitals in those cities carrying triple-A rated bonds showing deficits half as often as hospitals in cities issuing subinvestment grade ("junk") bonds.[17] Moreover, in an ironic turnabout, generous Medicaid payments actually hurt public hospitals, for as these payments approached private insurance levels, Medicaid-insured patients become more attractive to private hospitals, which vigorously solicited them.[18]

The exploding AIDS epidemic of the mid-1980s exacerbated the problem. Most AIDS patients then—adult gay men—could not qualify for Medicaid, as the program's eligibility restrictions were built around impoverished women with children. Men with AIDS soon were unemployed, lost benefits, exhausted their savings, and wound up being treated as charity patients in public hospitals. Cities with large population of AIDS patients—New York, Newark, Los Angeles—struggled to fund care for the population. In New York, the city's Health and Hospitals Corporation treated two-thirds of all AIDS patients at enormous costs to the city. Congressman Ted Weiss (D-NY) stated, "We can see a situation when AIDS will overwhelm the local health departments."[19]

State and the federal governments reduced spending on Medicaid programs through the 1980s by lowering reimbursement, tightening eligibility, and restricting benefits. Some states limited hospital stays or coverage for certain procedures; others tightened their eligibility requirements in an effort to trim these patients' roles as beneficiaries. Twenty-seven states limited prescription coverage, which resulted almost immediately in Medicaid recipients using fewer drugs, frequently to the detriment of their health.[20] One internist practicing in rural Vermont wrote eloquently and bitterly about how his patients were cheated of health and vitality by a Medicaid system operating too miserly to achieve reasonable ends. "We have been doing the best we can against terrible odds. Here kids have been denied health and equal opportunity from conception, and I feel like a man defeated."[21]

The rush to profit raised broader ethical questions about the appropriate place of profit in healthcare. Doctors took an oath to serve the best interests of their patients, which meant that profits should cede to good clinical judgment. The question came up in cases of harmless but possibly redundant procedures, in which profitable medical decision making did not necessarily harm the patient, might help the patient, but was not necessarily indicated in a world of perfectly attuned benchmarks. Most doctors argued that their judgment was not undermined by the profit motives in medicine, but nearly every outcome study performed in the 1980s suggested that this was not the case. In fact, doctors appeared to be as susceptible to revenue-producing opportunities as were other professional and business people.

Hospitals were different. A hospital did not take an oath but committed itself to a mission. For-profit hospitals committed themselves to work on behalf of their shareholders, and nonprofit hospitals committed themselves to the health and welfare of the community. But commitment to shareholders did not bar for-profit hospitals from delivering high-quality care. The evidence that for-profit hospital care was inferior was weak. The moral dilemma came in the spillover effect of the for-profits in a community, as they skimmed off profitable patients whose payments would otherwise go to subsidize a nonprofit hospital's charity patients, or at least to reinvest in the hospital's infrastructure or outreach programs. Reverend Kevin O'Rourke of St. Louis University Medical Center pointed out the difference: "When interest is paid to improve facilities, the ultimate goal of health care is service. When dividends are paid to investors, the ultimate goal of health care is profit for those investors."[22] The question for healthcare watchers and policy makers in the mid-1980s was, could hospital care accommodate investor interest while remaining committed to its implied doctrine of service?[23]

For-Profit Drug Makers

The 1980s were a heady time for the large prescription drug manufacturing companies. Collectively known as "Big Pharm," the fifteen or so companies that dominated US and worldwide sales experienced extraordinary levels of profitability. In one year, from 1987 to 1988, total US sales increased by 15 percent and profits rose 10 percent. Merck, perhaps the most successful US pharmaceutical company of the era, posted 37 percent annual returns on equity between 1985 and 1990.[24] A variety of new enzymatic formulations—mostly used for prevention or long-term treatment of disease—led the way in profitability. Certain brand names of antihypertensives, prostate medication, anticholesterol treatments, and antibiotics all produced annual revenues of hundreds of millions or even billions of dollars.[25]

Such profits, however, invited criticism. For one, many of the drugs carried very high price tags, creating hardships for people responsible for paying for their own prescription drugs, including all Medicare patients and many privately insured patients. A month's supply of the AIDS drug pentamidine cost $125—five times the cost of the same drug abroad. Cyclosporine, used to suppress rejection of new organs, ran $10,000 a year. Erythropoietin (for kidneys) cost $6,200 a year, and AZT (to suppress HIV) was $6,400. Although there was no true "correct" price for a drug, the high profit margins of the drug companies suggested that many drugs were being priced exorbitantly. One telling statistic undermined corporate claims to penury: the price of all prescription drugs had risen nearly 20 percent a year, every year, since 1968.[26]

The large pharmaceutical companies drew increasing attention from regulators and physician leaders in the 1980s for their aggressive marketing work. The nature of the business required pharmaceutical manufacturers to earn the trust of doctors and educate them about their products, lest doctors fail to prescribe them. Drug companies used a variety of techniques to accomplish these goals, ranging from hosting medical conferences to hiring physicians to endorse their products in speeches and publications. But the most important tool they used was a roving team of pharmaceutical representatives ("pharm reps") who rode circuit in a particular area, meeting weekly with physicians at their offices to speak with them, hand out literature, discuss the potency and uses of new drugs, and sweeten the deal for physicians with gifts, dinners, theater and sports tickets, free samples, and merchandise emblazoned with corporate logos. Many doctors were surrounded in their offices by ad-bearing tote bags, pens, pads of paper, key fobs, mugs, umbrellas, and other corporate swag.

The sales representatives were the key to the sales strategy. By 1990, pharmaceutical firms were spending $5 billion a year employing 45,000 representatives to regularly call on the nation's 550,000 practicing physicians. That budget for direct marketing had increased by 40 percent over ten years, adding some 20 percent to the cost of each prescription.[27] While most doctors claimed that they relied on their own judgment to choose which drugs to prescribe, and were largely inured to the allure of dinners and gifts, the data indicated otherwise. Less than 5 percent of the drug representatives had formal pharmaceutical training, and only about a fourth of all the literature they dispensed contained data relevant to a physician's prescribing needs. Nevertheless, the industry's enthusiasm for funding the representatives suggested that that the efforts were working.[28] Studies through the 1980s demonstrated that the advertisements and sales pitches from the representatives were heavily influencing doctor's knowledge of and opinion of new drugs.[29] One English physician summed up the phenomenon: "few doctors accept that they themselves have been corrupted. . . . The degree to which the profession, mainly composed of honorable and decent people, can practice such self-deceit is quite extraordinary. No drug company gives away its shareholders' money in acts of disinterested generosity."[30]

Equally problematic were the encomiums physicians sold for specific drugs. Upon agreeing to endorse a formulation, doctors were sent on speaking circuits around the country for which they were paid up to $5,000 per speech. Although some spoke from successful experiences in using a specific drug to treat patients, many used remarks and slides prepared for them by the drug companies. Similarly, drug companies sponsored symposia and conferences in which invited speakers promised to present encouraging data about drugs manufactured by the sponsor. The frequency of the conferences rose rapidly in the 1980s. From 1974 to 1988, the number of sponsored speeches and symposia for all prescription drugs rose from 7,500 to 34,500.[31] David Kessler, the commissioner of the US Food and Drug Administration, expressed alarm at the phenomenon, which he felt corrupted the profession while spreading misinformation about new drugs. He implored his colleagues to resist the lure of money or at the very least be clear about whose money they were taking before they delivered speeches and educational talks. The law, however, did not require this, and few doctors heeded the call.[32]

The pharmaceutical industry defended itself against charges of bribery and profiteering. It was true that retail prices were high for new drugs, but so were the costs of development. A typical pharmaceutical research product consumed $360 million over a dozen years, and only one out of ten patented molecules was ultimately approved for sale. The industry doubled its investment in research and development from

1985 to 1992, yet kept the rate of inflation for new drug products to just a few points above the inflation rate of the consumer price index.[33] The percentage of all US health dollars spent on prescription drugs was actually shrinking at the time, from 12 percent in 1965 to 7 percent in 1991. The pharmaceutical industry spent a higher portion of its revenue on research and development (9 percent) than was true of any other industry (although computer software was close with 8 percent). Notably, US pharmaceutical firms provided half of the world's pharmaceutical research budget, with only the United Kingdom, Germany, and Switzerland contributing significantly after the United States.[34]

Each side had statistics, but a compelling argument in favor of the industry was the fact that even with inflated new drug prices, drug treatment still tended to be a bargain relative to other interventions. All drug sales combined totaled only 7 percent of the US healthcare market in 1991, despite the fact that well over two-thirds of all reported ailments were pharmaceutically treated. While a simple surgical procedure could produce billings of $40,000, the most expensive prescription drugs were generally only several hundred dollars a month. All in all, drug treatment was still the great bargain of the health care system.

What of accusations of corrupting physicians? This was harder to refute. All data pointed to the corrosive influence of drug marketing on physicians' decision making, yet even here the drug companies had a reasonable defense. It lay in the fact that while the information dispensed by their sales representatives might be tendentious and self-serving, it was better than no information. Studies of Soviet physicians in the 1970s, practicing in an environment where pharmaceutical marketing efforts did not exist, demonstrated that most doctors were unaware of new drugs and new drug regimens. Journal articles and official government announcements failed to reach large parts of the physician population, and the majority of doctors tended to stick with treatments and technologies they mastered in medical training. Doctors were busy, journal articles were boring, and information was best transmitted through old-fashioned retail sales. The solution seemed not so much to end drug marketing as to rein in the worst of its excesses by limiting the size of gifts, barring drug reps from young and impressionable residents, and carefully monitoring corporate literature for accuracy and reliability.[35]

As the 1990s began, prospects for the pharmaceutical industry were positive. Genetic engineering and recombinant DNA technology promised a flurry of new proteins in coming years that could be used to treat cancer, emphysema, Parkinson's disease, Alzheimer's disease, diabetes, and autoimmune disorders. Scientists at the four largest biotechnology firms—Genentech, Genzyme, Amgen, and Immunex—were working on miraculous formulations such as milk laced with genetically modified proteins useful for a variety of treatments, new antiviral drugs and vaccines grown right in the cells of host bacteria, and mice that could secrete sweat that was potentially useful in treating cystic fibrosis.[36] At the same time, traditional pharmaceutical research labs were finding it increasingly difficult to synthesize new molecules and fell back on making incremental advances in existing drugs (tweaks) rather than pushing for true innovation. Drug companies were being forced to sell harder rather than invent more brilliantly, leading Kessler to expand his criminal enforcement staff to crack down on marketing abuses. His first action, in May 1991, was to forbid Bristol-Myers Squibb from distributing corporate sales material masquerading as a peer-reviewed scientific journal.[37] The industry promised miraculous products, but at times produced very mundane ones.

❦

The appropriate role of profit in healthcare delivery was elusive. Free markets assumed that profits drove individuals and firms to innovate and compete with better products, higher quality services, and lower prices. At the same time, Americans had long cordoned off a sector of the economy to be protected from profits. Services in this sector— education, spiritual succor, religious communities, art and culture, and charitable works—needed to be protected from the harsh pressure of the markets lest their principals be eroded. Few felt that pastors and teachers should hawk their wares with the same promises of lower prices and greater consumer utility. Instead, services produced in these sectors should cleave to a more ethereal standard of community service, truth, and good.

Healthcare was odd. On one hand, Americans had repeatedly asserted their opinion that health services should not simply be sold in the marketplace to those consumers who could afford them. Centuries of charity care, public hospitals, and public dispensaries testified to this charitable impulse. On the other hand, the profit motive was probably more effective than the charitable motive to impel pharmaceutical companies to invent new drugs, device companies to create new technology, and hospitals to provide higher quality patient service. Unlike the world of faith, profit had a role to play in healthcare delivery.

But if profit became the overarching impulse in healthcare, the sector would surrender its professionalism. Doctors and hospitals had long been understood to hold themselves to objective standards beyond the simple need to please patients. Individuals and institutions used science as their guide and clinical benchmarks as their standard. A hospital that lost touch with this underlying guideline would quickly devolve from hospital to health spa. A drug company that pushed new products too aggressively, urging doctors to prescribe even when symptoms indicated otherwise, would lose the faith of the public. The government searched for the right balance in profit and mission to regulate the industry, but resisted using too heavy a hand.

5

Efforts to Rationalize

The Prospective Payment System

Of all the many sources of funds for purchasing medical care in the United States when Ronald Reagan became president, one stood out for size and influence: Medicare. The national program, implemented in 1966 to cover acute hospital and physician care for citizens over age 65, had evolved but had not changed dramatically. The program continued to be divided into Parts A and B paying for hospital and physician care, respectively, with enrollment in Part A being mandatory and enrollment in Part B being voluntary. Part A was funded through a mandatory 2.9 percent payroll tax on the first $51,300 of income (slated to rise to $130,000 in 1992); Part B was funded through general income tax revenue and a premium of $31.80 per month per enrollee. The premium was adjusted upward periodically to accommodate the rising price of physician care, but even so covered less than a quarter of the cost of Part B in the early 1980s. If the premiums were adjusted to cover the true cost of physician care, they would be $125.40 per month. It was one of the best bargains for consumers. In part, as a result of this gross underpayment, Medicare was slated to go bankrupt by 1990 if revenue sources were not significantly adjusted.[1] Notably, Medicare costs rose 14.5 percent from 1981 to 1982.

Medicare paid both physicians and hospitals in a complex system tied to "customary, prevailing, and reasonable" costs. The system impelled doctors and hospitals to endlessly raise their prices in an effort to reanchor the prevailing rate and force Medicare to raise its reimbursement. Although many physicians chose to "take assignment," that is, to bill Medicare directly and accept the Medicare reimbursement as payment in full, others billed their patient directly, who then applied for reimbursement from Medicare's parent agency, the Health Care Financing Administration (HCFA). HCFA reimbursed doctors at 80 percent of a set fee schedule (varying by state). Patients were responsible for the remaining 20 percent and substantial yearly deductibles for both Parts A and B.

As it stood in 1981, Medicare could not continue. The cost of the program had grown at an average annual rate of 6 percent since 1966, and the federal government, with a growing annual deficit, could hardly be expected to make up the loss. The Congressional Budget Office estimated that without structural changes in the tax code, the federal deficit would reach $250 billion a year by 1987, with Medicare making up nearly 10 percent of the entire federal budget.[2] Funds put into the system through the payroll tax and Part B premiums would account for a declining portion of the cost of the program, even as the ranks of the nation's elderly would swell. Phillip Keisling, a political columnist, pointed out that "the contract that society now has in force with the elderly for health care must be renegotiated. We have no other choice."[3]

In response, the Republican-led Congress proposed a series of reforms through the Omnibus Reconciliation Act (OBRA) of 1981 mandating a 25 percent increase on all cost-savings requirements by Medicare beneficiaries, and cuts of $5 billion, $7.5 billion, and $10 billion to the program over the succeeding three years.[4] The cuts would help, but hardly solve, the problem. Medicare would continue to outgrow its revenues, and rent-seeking hospitals and doctors were sure to find creative ways to increase their billings. Moreover, several major structural problems with the program, such as the customary and prevailing reimbursement policy, and the ability of nonprofit hospitals to roll their capital depreciation into the their operating costs (to be reimbursed by HCFA), remained intact. Hospitals would still have a perverse incentive to overexpand, and patients would continue to have little disincentive to overconsume.[5] The director of the Office of Management and Budget, David Stockman, ruefully reflected, "There's overuse of emergency rooms, there's overuse of hospitals, there's overuse of doctors."[6] Something more drastic would need to be done.

The answer came in the form of diagnostic related groups, or DRGs, as they quickly came to be known. Developed by two Yale University researchers in 1975, DRGs divided all hospital-based services into 468 diagnostic categories and assigned a set payment to each diagnosis regardless of the actual time a patient spent in the hospital, or the actual amount of resources allocated to him. The system was adopted by New Jersey in 1978 for its Blue Cross and Medicaid programs in an effort to restrain cost increases by hospitals.[7] Congress mandated the adoption of the system for Medicare payments in March 1983, and HCFA implemented it starting in October.

DRGs, which collectively made up the prospective payment system, adjusted the diagnostic categories for eighteen different regions which were the nine census tracts further subdivided into rural and urban payment areas. Adjustments were made for teaching hospitals and hospitals taking on a disproportionate share of charity patients.[8] By imposing set payment rates for specific diagnoses, Congress altered incentives for hospitals treating Medicare patients. Hospitals would no longer have an incentive to overtreat Medicare patients and extend treatment in an attempt to raise the bill. Rather, they would have an incentive to treat Medicare patients as quickly and efficiently as possible in an effort to squeeze profit from the DRG payment.

Critics of the plan pointed out a number of weaknesses. The different reimbursement rates failed to adequately account for differences in labor and real estate prices between urban and suburban hospitals in the same area and failed to adequately address the true range of labor costs between different DRGs, leading to a phenomenon known as "DRG compression." At the same time, hospitals might be tempted to alter the stated DRG for a given patient in an effort to wring greater reimbursement from the system (DRG creep) or might be tempted to undertreat Medicare patients so as to realize profits.[9] Hospitals complained that rates did not accurately reflect the cost of providing services for certain DRGs, and hospital administrators expressed concern that annual adjustments did not allow hospitals to invest in new technologies.[10] Last, the prospective payment system could not stop hospitals from providing superfluous care with procedures that were only marginal helpful, although the legislation did create a nationwide network of peer review organizations, which were intended to disallow the worst of these abusive practices.[11]

The prospective payment system was implemented in stages between 1983 and 1986, such that by 1988 the first retrospective studies on its efficacy were available. Initial reports were promising. Under the system, hospital days for Medicare patients nationwide fell by 28 percent (although concomitant increases in the intensity of treatment negated some of the savings associated with the decreased number of hospital days).[12] Each hospital stay fell by an average of nearly two days.[13] Efforts to measure changes in quality as determined by patient outcomes were indeterminate but seemed to show little decline with the advent of the prospective payment system.[14]

The prospective payment system was hardly perfect. It did not address overpayment in physician pay or gross disparities in income between different types of physicians, and it was not applied to mental health ailments of all kinds for the reason that government regulators did not feel comfortable estimating average costs for specific mental health hospitalizations.[15] Moreover, hospitals continued to maintain what many people felt were outsized profit margins, even after the DRG system was fully implemented, One government study estimated that under DRGs, nonprofit hospitals maintained annual operating gains (profits) of 14 percent—a healthy margin for most for-profit firms.[16]

A second tactic in bringing down the cost of Medicare was contracting with HMOs. A number of congressional leaders, in particular Robert Dole (R-KS), had resisted Medicare risk contracting for fear that HMOs enrolling Medicare patients would deliberately undertreat the most vulnerable patients, but by 1982 the opponents capitulated. In that year, the Tax Equity and Fiscal Responsibility Act established a program of Medicare risk contracting. Initially, HCFA established demonstration projects in various cities throughout the country, and in 1985 the program was expanded to all who were interested.

Medicare risk contracting paid HMOs (both staff and IPA models) 95 percent of the actuarial cost of a given patient as a capitated fee each month, under the assumption that HMOs could leverage various management devices to reduce the cost of providing care. Participating HMOs were required to provide the same menu of benefits offered by the traditional Parts A and B, but could provide more. A number of HMOs found that they could add preventive care and payment for prescription drugs, while holding co-payments to very low levels (a number charged only $1 per visit) and still make a profit on the patients. By 1987, 152 participating plans enrolled 903,000 patients, or about 5.5 percent of all eligible Medicare beneficiaries. Virtually all of the participating plans were able to reap profits from the program.[17]

Medicare risk contracting appeared to be an effective tool in holding down inflation in the program, but analysts were not confident that the program was working as intended. The HMOs contracting with Medicare had an enormous incentive to enroll only the healthiest (and therefore the cheapest) Medicare beneficiaries, while the youngest and healthiest beneficiaries tended to self-select their way into the program. Older, sicker enrollees tended to avoid the program for fear of jeopardizing their options to procure specialty care. Stories abounded of aggressive marketing toward retirees who were engaged in an active lifestyles (advertisements in golf and skiing magazines were designed to skim off this population), and office locations in areas where more vigorous elderly persons tended to live. One crafty Medicare contractor purposefully placed its enrollment office on the third floor of a walk-up building, offering a quick test as to the physical vitality of potential enrollees.

In looking for additional ways to cut the cost of Medicare, congressional leaders turned their attention to the subsidies paid to teaching hospitals. These subsidies, which had been preserved in the prospective payment system, were designed to compensate hospitals for the additional costs they incurred while training medical residents. The program recognized the public burden of training the next generation of physicians and the fact that teaching hospitals tended to treat a disproportionate share of the nation's sickest and poorest citizens.

The Graduate Medical Education subsidy (as it was known) had its share of detractors. Robert Rubin, the assistant secretary of Health and Human Services for Planning and Evaluation, notably observed that there was "no incremental cost involved in teaching in a hospital setting."[18] That is, although the medical residents required some degree of supervision and training, very early in their training they actually became a net asset for the hospital because they provided clinical and skilled nursing care for bargain rates. (At the time, a medical resident was typically paid about half the salary of a staff nurse.) They tended to work very long hours with no claim on extra benefits or overtime pay. Although teaching hospitals had long claimed that they incurred unusual costs in training residents, analysis did not support the claim.[19] Moreover, given that nearly a fifth of all residents in US programs were foreign nationals who in theory intended to return to their home countries on the completion of their residencies, Americans could rightly question whether or not US government funds should be going to train other nations' doctors.

HCFA leaders also looked to recover money lost on fraud. In such an immense program, fraudulent pricing was inevitable, and profiteering for devices and drugs was relatively common. One supplier marked up a $28 bed cushion and sold it to Medicare as a "dry flotation mattress" for $900. Another company sold a transcutaneous electronic nerve stimulator—a simple device creating modest electrical shocks to control pain from neuropathy—for $500, although Radio Shack carried a similar device for $50. A wheelchair parts supplier charged $250 for a replacement cushion in Pennsylvania, although a Tennessee-based company supplied comparable cushions for $42. The list went on. The inspector general for the Department of Health and Human Services noted ruefully, "A welfare queen would have to work mighty hard to steal $100,000. Somebody in the practitioner or provider community can wink and steal $100,000.[20]

Despite all efforts—risk contracting, DRGs, aggressive efforts to fight fraud—Medicare costs continued to rise. Medicare costs, along with medical costs generally, rose nearly 9 percent each year through the mid-1980s. Even as co-payments, deductibles, and Part B premiums increased, the government was forced to spend more each year covering a growing elderly population that managed to consume more medical care even as it spent fewer days in the hospital. Each cost-saving effort was countered by a parry from providers. As DRGs compressed payments, doctors and hospitals simply inflated DRGs. Doctors seemed adept at increasing the volume of tests and procedures for every diagnosis. Drug companies and device manufactures hired consulting firms that specialized in getting new drugs and devices approved for reimbursement, even as HCFA and Congress voiced opposition to the growing number of reimbursable products. The program was immense and unmanageable.[21]

Paradoxically, even as the total amount of money pumped into the health system increased, many participants found themselves strapped. The nation's health insurance companies suffered $10 billion in underwriting losses in 1988; most HMOs lost money; and the nursing home industry suffered its worst year in decades. Doctors generally maintained their incomes, but largely through increasing the volume and intensity of their services, meaning that they worked longer and more frantically to produce the same revenues.[22]

More significantly, hospitals lost money on their patient services. Increases in the costs of labor, equipment, drugs, and medical supplies consumed almost all of the increased revenue in patient billings, forcing hospital managers to become more entrepreneurial and profit-seeking. Over six years, occupancy rates nationally dropped from 60 to 48.5

percent even as more than five hundred hospitals closed their doors. Industry analysts estimated that nearly one third of the remaining five thousand hospitals in the country were vulnerable to closure. The financial hemorrhage could be attributed to the downward pricing pressure of the prospective payment system and managed care organizations, shorter hospital stays for most procedures and tests, and general managerial sloppiness. Arthur D. Little, a prominent healthcare consulting firm, estimated that less than half of all hospital supplies were purchased through purchasing consortia and cooperatives, even though hospitals bonding into purchasing groups achieved substantial discounts in supply costs.[23]

Hospitals turned to the federal government to make up the shortfalls, demanding increased payments within the PPS to offset their losses in private revenues. Congress responded with a series of increases for specific types of hospitals—rural referral hospitals, rural sole community hospitals, rural Medicare-dependent hospitals, urban disproportionate share hospitals, and teaching hospitals—in an effort to make these critical institutions whole. Through the Omnibus Budget Reconciliation Acts of 1989 and 1990, HCFA raised payments to these different hospitals based on a variety of factors, such as a high proportion of patients receiving Medicaid or Supplemental Security Income, high rates of referrals from rural hospitals, or high ratios of medical interns and residents to beds. Congress committed itself to generous payment premiums to the teaching hospitals in particular; even so, the teaching hospitals complained of inadequate revenues.[24] Clearly something was very wrong.

The prospective payment system produced strange results. The average length of a hospital stay for a Medicare patient fell 9 percent in the first year after the system was implemented, and for hospitals with a comparable case mix the length of stay fell 25 percent. At the same time, the costs per case rose 10 percent, suggesting that hospitals were gaming the new reimbursement rules by admitting sicker patients and caring for them more intensively. In-hospital tests were down, but ambulatory surgical billings had grown as a portion of reimbursable surgeries from 16 to 40 percent since 1980.[25] In another example of unexpected market responses to the system, nursing home admission rates in New Hampshire climbed by 100 percent after that state's Medicaid plan reduced payments for prescription drugs.[26]

The government could "declare victory" in response to the reduced lengths of stay, but the top-down price controls threatened the solvency of critical institutions in the health system.[27] The Gramm-Rudman-Hollings Balanced Budget Act of 1987 wiped away almost all reasonable fee increases built into the prospective payment system, meaning that many hospitals were starved for reimbursement, even as they did their best to cut costs, discharge patients more quickly, and move to an ambulatory model of care. Carol McCarthy of the American Hospital Association complained bitterly about the arbitrary quality of the reimbursement adjustments. She wrote, "Today, payment predictability is a sham.... Between October 1 1987, and November 21, 1987, for example, the previous year's Medicare rates were in effect; from November 21, 1987, to April 1, 1988, those rates were increased by .4 percent, or 2.7 percent, minus a 2.3 percent reduction mandated by the Gramm-Rudman Act; for the final six months of the fiscal year, one of four different updates apply, depending on a hospital's location."[28]

At the same time the prospective payment system was producing modest savings, other federal efforts at cost control were failing. The certificate of need (CON) program, mandated by the 1974 Health Planning Act, had largely failed, with research data collected through the 1980s showing few discernible reductions in hospital capital expansion wrought by the CON process. At the same time, Medicare's policy of reimbursing all hospitals for a large portion of their capital expansion dedicated to Medicare patients was negating any modest achievements the CONs could have. From 1986 to 1991, for example, Medicare funded $26 billion in hospital capital expansion and improvements, even as occupancy rates fell and hospitals closed their doors.[29] Gail Wilensky, HCFA's director, pointed out in exasperation that in the current system, "the more you spend, the more you get."[30] Although Wilensky was able to change HCFA rules to reimburse capital expenditures based on occupancy rates, the new rule fell far short of the systems in place in Canada, England, and West Germany, in which virtually all hospital expansions required approval from either a national or regional government. Each small step seemed only to distort provider behavior more, without achieving anything approaching effective cost control.

Induced Demand

Misallocation of healthcare capital was most visible in the increasingly bizarre economic world of healthcare technology. Noninvasive surgical suites, laser centers, MRI machines, and CAT scanners—all technology that in theory could *lower* the cost of providing excellent medical care—in every case seemed to increase the cost. The problem originated in ownership structure. In France, for example, where ophthalmologists used hospital-owned lasers for cataract surgery, the cost for a simple procedure in 1989 was $75. In the United States, where ophthalmologists used their own lasers, the cost for the same procedure was over $1,500.[31] The difference lay in the financial incentives of the physician. In many European countries, where the capital costs of medical care had been largely socialized, doctors viewed new technology as a tool to be used to either increase efficacy or reduce costs. In the United States, doctors (and hospitals) viewed an investment in technology as a potential revenue producer, to be exploited and leveraged insofar as the market would permit. The conflict of interest for the doctor was clear, yet long established tradition dictated that in the United States doctors equipped their own practices and then reaped whatever gains they could. Arnold Relman, editor of the *New England Journal of Medicine*, went as far as calling the arrangements "a form of kickback." "Oh yes," he told one interviewer. "I think it should be made illegal."[32] Defending the system, James Todd of the American Medical Association pointed out, "One thing about us Americans . . . we are crazy about technology. In the United States we expect miracles, and we often get them."[33]

Physicians were part of the problem. For a variety of reasons, they were sharply increasing the number of procedures and tests that they were performing through the 1980s. Whether a conscious effort to increase their incomes, a defensive posture to ward off malpractice suits, or an unconscious tic left over from training in procedure-rich academic medical centers, physicians were performing a great number of unnecessary procedures each year. The rate of cesarean delivery, for example, had exploded from 5 percent of all well-baby births in 1960 to 25 percent by 1988.[34] By one estimate, 32 percent of arterial plaque removal procedures were not necessary, as were 17 percent of coronary angiographies, 27 percent of hysterectomies, 17 percent of carpal tunnel surgeries, 16 percent of tonsillectomies, and 14 percent of laminectomies. Upper gastrointestinal scans and preoperative laboratory procedures were similarly overused.[35]

In virtually every case, overcapacity was closely aligned with overtreatment. Both doctors and hospitals found ways to fill their schedules and beds, and they tested, cut, scoped, and scanned until their practices were at capacity. In this medical world, Bostonians went to the hospital more frequently than did New Havenites simply because there were many more hospital beds per capita in Boston than in New Haven. One telling study conducted at Dartmouth Medical School found that two adjacent towns in Vermont, Stowe and Waterbury, differed sevenfold in their rates of tonsillectomies. Similarly, rates of prostate surgery of men in two Maine towns, Portland and Bangor, differed fivefold. The differences appeared attributable to the sheer number of physicians available to perform the procedure, but also in part to differences in prevailing practice styles. Doctors tended to adjust to local medical mores once they established practice in an area and paid little attention to "best practice" directives coming through peer-reviewed studies.[36]

Increases in numbers of procedures also reflected increases in the numbers of specialists, who tended to be more procedure-oriented. Between 1965 and 1990 the ranks of the nation's gastroenterologists grew by 1,000 percent, cardiologists by 900 percent, neurologists by 325 percent, and plastic surgeons by 300 percent. At the same time, the percentage of graduating MDs entering primary care residencies dropped by half, to just over 30 percent.[37] The ratios differed markedly from comparable Western medical systems where primary care physicians tended to make up 50–60 percent of all practicing physicians.

Young doctors chose specialty training for a variety of reasons, but certainly money was foremost. In 1990, median income for family practitioners was $93,000, whereas median income for cardiovascular surgeons was $400,000. The pay differential between primary and specialty care was substantial and growing. At some point the money overwhelmed most other considerations. Furthermore, specialty physicians actually worked fewer hours than their primary care colleagues, took fewer hours of call, and had more predictable schedules. One family physician in Ohio expressed his frustration: "Why bother with sixty- to seventy-hour work weeks, constant phone calls, all night emergency room visits, poor reimbursements, demanding patients, the need for instant exact decisions . . . concerning a million possible diseases, when you can 'specialize' in one organ, get paid $500 for a fifteen-minute procedure, only need to know a dozen drugs and side effects, and work part time?"[38]

Other pressures were skewing decisions. Recruitment efforts aimed at attracting the most scientifically accomplished undergraduates (rather than students with broader, more humanistic interests) tended to produce a class of engineers rather than healers: technically proficient but often lacking in compassion. At the same time, the generation after the Baby Boom (known as Generation X) eschewed some of the youthful idealism of their elders and admitted that earning a good income was more important to them than making a meaningful difference in the world. One study revealed that the percentage of college freshman who claimed that a meaningful philosophy of life was "very meaningful" dropped from 82 percent in 1966 to 40 percent in 1986.[39] One physician suggested that the lure of the specialties was enhanced in part by the extraordinary advances being made in those areas. Oncologists had gone from being largely ineffectual taxonomists a generation earlier to miracle workers, and heart surgeons were hailed as the medical rock stars of their time.[40] One pessimistic medical observer noted that generalists suffered from the "Rodney Dangerfield syndrome" in that they got "no respect."[41] A senior internist admitted that he could no longer encourage his students to seek careers in internal medicine given the long work weeks, intrusive payers and regulators, and shrinking resources, all to earn "markedly less than a subspecialist working fewer and less stressful hours."[42]

Some doctors pleaded with their colleagues to accept voluntary limits on their income for the good of the profession. High fees eroded public confidence in the intentions of doctors, and popular images of physicians jetting off to ski resorts, driving luxury cars, and living in large homes further convinced many people that doctors were largely practicing medicine for self-gain. Timothy Johnson, a physician-turned-television correspondent, suggested that a starting salary of $90,000, rising to $200,000 over a career, was more than adequate to achieve an upper middle-class lifestyle while allowing doctors to practice caring and responsible medicine. ("For those who believe that doctors should have the right to make much more, like some business executives they know," he wrote, "I would simply suggest that they go into business."[43]) A medical school professor at the University of Missouri proposed $100,000 to $150,000 as an "adequate income," given the median US household income of $30,000.[44] Virtually nobody took these suggestions seriously, but proponents of voluntary salary caps recognized that the drive toward money was eroding the integrity of the profession and the trust of the public.

Relative Value

Arguments over reasonable physician income came to an abrupt end in 1992 with the implementation of the resource-based relative value scale (RBRVS). The fee schedule of seven thousand different medical tests and procedures performed by every conceivable medical specialty had been devised by William Hsaio, a professor at the Harvard School of Public Health, for HCFA to use in adjusting Medicare payments. The RBRVS system was intended to be budget neutral; all increases in payments to primary care physicians were offset by decreases in payments to specialists. With the RBRVS, HCFA aimed to cut the total Medicare Part B budget by 6 percent by 1996. The fee scale attempted to bring specialty payments more in line with medical medians while adjusting for geography. Notably, the system did not reward physicians with records of better patient outcomes with higher fees. Moreover, the system did little to thwart the expected increase in volume that doctors would undoubtedly use to compensate for lower fees, although the HCFA did impose a 3 percent reduction in the fees to counter just this move.

The AMA responded vociferously to the proposed RBRVS, claiming that the system would erode physicians' fees from Medicare by 16 percent (not true) and that the government was imposing its plan with scant input from the profession (also not true). What was true was that certain specialty groups, notably anesthesiology, ophthalmology, radiology, thoracic surgery, and gastroenterology, faced substantial cuts in revenue, with further cuts possible as private sector payers mimicked HCFA's schedule. The physician's fee for a hysterectomy under the RBRVS, for example, would drop from $2,000 to $500, while a cardiac surgeon would see her pay for inserting a pacemaker decline from $1,900 to $320.[45] The Physician Payment Review Commission—a physician-dominated advisory board—also opposed the new system, claiming it would erode physician support for HCFA's cost-containment efforts in the future, but its only solution was that the government simply keep paying more.[46]

Many of the ninety-five thousand comments to the proposed regulations pointed out inconsistencies and inaccuracies in the coding methodology, and undoubtedly many of these comments were correct. HCFA was attempting to reform a vast and complex system that was devouring funds while producing suboptimal results. Imperfection was implicit in the effort, although HCFA would have future opportunities to refine and correct its mandate. Doctors still retained a certain respect both within government and without, but they had squandered their reputations and goodwill in pursuit of increasing incomes. The government was acting alone and was fairly confident of itself.[47]

Underlying the logistical challenge of implementing the RBRVS was the question of how powerfully money influenced doctors. Leaders of the profession claimed that while doctors expected to earn generous incomes, their minute-to-minute decision making was largely divorced from monetary concerns. A growing body of data collected in the 1980s belied the claim, however. HCFA documented substantial "code creep" even before implementation of the RBRVS and found that at least half of increased payments to physicians in the previous decade come from increases in volume and intensity rather than price hikes.[48] The case of Health Stop, a chain of for-profit ambulatory care centers that moved from paying its physicians on an hourly basis to giving them a percentage of total billings, was a sobering example. After the pay scheme was changed, doctors increased the average number of lab tests per patient by 23 percent, x-rays by 16 percent, total billings by 20 percent, and (amazingly) total monthly patient volume by 12 percent, despite the fact that the patient population remained unchanged.[49]

Compensation incentives could have obverse effects as well. Just as physicians could be induced to practice overly profligate medicine through pay structure, they could be induced to practice overly parsimonious medicine. HMOs, for example, which charged members a capitated fee for total care (the "per-member-per-month" system) created incentives for their staff physicians to do less, as each additional test and procedure needed to be charged against total revenues. While the various HMOs handled these pressures differently, a large number (67 percent by one measure) provided financial incentives for physicians to hold down costs by withholding part of the pay against potential deficits each month. If targets were not met, the physicians could be charged as a group for the monthly overage, or each one individually could be charged for his or her contribution to the deficit. (The latter system was relatively rare.[50]) Though these inducements did not erode physician pay substantially, regulators and patients rights groups were concerned that incentives to undertreat undermined the integrity of the doctor–patient relationship.

The ethical ramifications of payment debates were complex. On one hand, payment incentives could induce doctors to practice more financially conscientious medicine—HMOs that billed on capitation sent patients to the hospital substantially less often than did those that built fee-for-service into their payment mix.[51] On the other hand, payment incentives could discourage a physician from taking aggressive steps to diagnose and treat a patient presenting with ambiguous symptoms. Was it unethical for a doctor to "be paid more to do less for the patient?," asked one concerned doctor.[52] The ethical paradox of medicine—that doctors made money on treating the sick, rather than maintaining the well—was becoming harder to ignore, and the gatekeeping role physicians played in HMOs was only making matters worse.

Indeed, the profession was being pulled between poles along two axes: corporatization and scientificization. Medicine, always proudly a *profession*, was being forced into a more corporate model. Substantial numbers of physicians were moving away from solo practice or small partnerships to employment by large multispecialty groups, hospitals, PHOs, or HMOs. Some doctors began to envision themselves as part of *labor*, whose interests lay opposed to *management*—a new and alien definition for medical practice. Some doctors proposed creating physician unions to advocate for the profession as it negotiated contracts with the corporate entities that now owned hospitals, managed care companies, and large groups. Sanford Marcus, president of the Union of American Physicians and Dentists, wrote: "We become more convinced with each passing day that only by standing together as a determined and ethical trade union of doctors can we protect and preserve at least the best features of that legacy of 'professionalism' of which we are so properly proud."[53] Hospitals were becoming increasingly corporate, with multiple layers of management, a disempowered medical staff, corporate accountability mechanisms, and titles that evoked big business more than they did the historic roots of medicine. One medical school professor asked, "Why, for example, is the Chief of Psychiatry now a Vice-President? . . . And what, by the way, is a Nursing Project Coordinator?"[54]

At the same time, medicine had strayed from its historic roots in caretaking and progressed relentlessly toward complex therapeutics, which leveraged extraordinary new technologies. In just a quarter of a century the profession had mastered therapies involving genetic engineering, joint replacement, arterial bypass, lithotripsy, in vitro fertilization, laser surgery, transplantation, immunosuppression, histamine and beta blockers, micro-surgery, and even sex reassignment surgery. Imaging specialists had moved far beyond century-old x-ray technology to take advantage of computer-assisted tomography (CAT) scans, positron emission tomography (PET) scans, nuclear magnetic resonance (NMR, later MRI) scans, and digital subtraction angiography (DSA). The new PET scanners, for example, fired positron particles at various reactive dyes, which lit up screens and films as they responded by emitting bursts of energy, thus outlining various organs, tumors, vessels, and muscles.[55]

Technological advances accelerated medicine's evolution from empathy to action. At heart, the profession remained one of caring for the sick, yet increasingly the profession viewed itself as a branch of biomedical engineering, with the caretaking role being left to the nursing staff. When combined with corporatist pressure, which viewed doctors as employees rather than professionals, doctors behaved increasingly like organized employees whose main goal (as was true with all organized labor) was higher pay, better working conditions, more generous benefits, and shorter hours. It was no wonder that a distraught older physician, upon surveying his patients, heard frequent complaints of "My doctor's office is an assembly line . . . the personal touch is gone . . . I am treated not as a person, but as an appendix, a hernia, a heart attack a hemorrhoid."[56]

Waste

Waste was part of the problem. Some experts estimated that as much as a quarter of all tests, treatments, and drugs were medically unnecessary, which meant that they could not reliably be shown to have greater utility than doing nothing at all.[57] One well-publicized study found that 40 percent of all hospitalizations were either inappropriate or avoidable through aggressive use of ambulatory surgery.[58] Overlaying this profligate clinical system was a growing layer of administrators, billers, schedulers, compliance officers, and accountants who added more costs to the final bill while hardly improving care. Competition, the fallback solution for free-market thinkers, seemed powerless to reduce waste, as price-conscious consumers of insurance and health services were unable to discriminate between necessary and unnecessary services.[59] One corporate executive discussing the problem admitted, "We know more about what goes into the cost of the seventy-five-cent box of screws we use on the factory floor than we know about what goes into the cost of health care."[60]

Most unnecessary healthcare was consumed by well-insured individuals with corporate health insurance plans, meaning that consumers did not immediately bear the cost of their profligacy. Rather, employers bore the brunt of the imprudence, and large manufacturing corporations, with their carefully negotiated union health benefits, felt the waste most acutely. John Deere, for example, purchased fourteen days of hospitalizations annually for each worker, while General Motors, Chrysler, and Ford estimated that employee and retiree health costs made up nearly 20 percent of their manufacturing costs. Such waste may have been tolerable in decades past, when US manufacturing faced little competition from abroad, but newly retooled and invigorated Japanese and European manufacturing firms now threatened the solvency of US industry.

The response was to aggressively rein in employee health costs. Perhaps no US corporation did this as successfully as Chrysler Motors did in the 1980s under the leadership of Joseph Califano Jr., who had served as the secretary of the Department of Health and Human Services under President Jimmy Carter. In three years, Califano managed to cut health costs for Chrysler by $100 million while engaging the United Autoworkers in a productive and cooperative effort to cut even more. Under the program, annual premium inflation declined from 15 percent to 4 percent, while the increases in the cost of retiree Medigap policies were even lower. Califano forced employees to purchase generic drugs, seek second opinions for all referrals, move to ambulatory or outpatient surgery for many procedures, and consume health services through HMOs and prepaid group plans. The company began to aggressively audit medical bills and found that 72 percent, 66 percent, and 34 percent of all hospital admissions for its workers in St. Louis, Indiana, and Delaware were inappropriate. Primary care physicians were forced to justify tests and referrals, and employees received cash incentives to use less-expensive providers. The company also identified employees who overused or abused health benefits.[61] Within five years, many other large US companies adopted Chrysler's strategies and were able to replicate some of these cost-containment successes.

Some physicians and hospitals responded to calls for cost containment with a series of changes that could best be called a "voluntary effort." They hoped to assuage the public by assuring legislators that the industry could rein in costs by itself. Medical school deans claimed that by educating students in the art of cost-cutting, they could train a new generation of physicians to practice medicine guided by fiscal restraint. Physician groups claimed that they had no need for external review because they were best situated to judge the utility of their work and conduct cost-benefit analysis on their own decision making. Hospitals claimed to be able to manage more efficiently, bill less aggressively, and generally lower overhead and staff costs.

Some of these promises were made good. In Rochester, New York, for example, sixteen area hospitals cooperated in reducing inflation, occupancies, lengths of stays, and daily billings.[62] Medicare bills in

Rochester hospitals were 27 percent lower than the national average and the lowest of any metropolitan region measured. The hospitals voluntarily entered into a joint strategic planning venture to avoid investment in redundant facilities and technology in an effort to distribute hospital services efficiently across the region. Medicare, Medicaid, and Blue Cross paid funds into a regional hospital corporation, which distributed money to the constituent hospitals in a model parallel to that of an independent practice association. Despite dire warnings from skeptics, the autonomous belt tightening failed to create queuing for hospital services, nor did it undermine the quality of the outcomes.[63]

But Rochester's success in voluntarily holding down costs was aberrant. More typical were the half-hearted efforts by the nation's medical schools to teach fiscal responsibility to their medical students. Although three-fourths of the AAMC member schools expressed enthusiasm for the project, a GAO audit revealed that most schools used informal unstructured approaches to the subject, introducing the material in noncredit courses for which students were not held accountable. When surveyed, 65 percent of medical students who had been through some sort of financial awareness curriculum deemed the training inadequate.[64] Although the GAO determined that such training could potentially help hold down medical costs, the anemic quality of most of the training suggested otherwise.

Reforms at the State Level

The prospective payment system and the implementation of more scrupulous corporate oversight strictures were efforts by both the government and private payers to reduce healthcare costs. But alongside troublesome healthcare inflation, the problem of access continued unabated. Large numbers of citizens either were locked out of Medicaid, could not afford private insurance, or purchased inadequate insurance policies that excluded coverage for preexisting conditions. The number of uninsured people continued to rise, while the numbers of employers offering comprehensive policies to their employees shrank.

When the federal government failed to take substantial action on insurance reform, a number of states stepped in. States differed in the precise details of their plans, but all involved expanding existing employer-provided private insurance while broadening Medicaid and (usually) creating a public insurance program. In effect, states were falling back on insurance reform, rather than attempt health reform. States refused to tamper with training, ownership, and marketing. Instead, they reformed insurance regulations and Medicaid reimbursement: two activities in which the states had ample precedent. The results might be far from ideal, but they were politically tenable and administratively feasible.

All of the states that attempted reform in the late 1980s used some sort of mandate in which employers of more than a set number of full-time employees (the number varied from state to state) were required to provide basic health insurance to their employees (although not their employees' dependents). Most states required employers that refused to comply with the mandate to contribute to a fund that subsidized public insurance for the difficult-to-insure. States hoped that the mandates and public subsidies, coupled with more generous Medicaid programs, would insure more people. Some states created inducements to get more residents enrolled in managed care plans or required enrollment in such a plan in exchange for public subsidies. No state even considered nationalizing hospitals or physician practices or mandating practice hours or fees for private practitioners. This was health reform with a light government touch.

From 1985 to 1990, Hawaii, Massachusetts, Oregon, and Minnesota experimented with different variations on this same basic model. The states achieved varying levels of success, with Massachusetts's reform efforts thwarted by Governor William Weld. Minnesota took the most aggressive stance on insurance regulation, using its new MinnesotaCare to create a subsidized public plan for residents who earned up to 275 percent of the federal poverty limit, while prohibiting experienced-based pricing in its private markets. Hawaii implemented its own pay-or-play plan, using its state health insurance program to put uninsured Hawaiians into the local Blue Cross/Blue Shield plan. In two years, the state reduced the number of uninsured by more than 60 percent.[65]

Oregon's health reform differed sharply from that of other states and drew scrutiny and widespread opposition. As elsewhere, the legislature created a public insurance fund to catch state residents who fell between the cracks: too wealthy for Medicaid, yet unable to qualify for employer-based private insurance. In an effort to bring more Oregonians under the umbrella of its Medicaid program, the legislature imposed a cap on the per capita cost of the program by disallowing payments for a number of expensive but ineffective procedures. Under the leadership of John Kitzhaber, president of the state Senate and an emergency room physician, the legislature ranked 709 medical tests and procedures by cost efficacy. Procedures that were inexpensive yet highly effective were ranked high; procedures that were expensive and largely ineffective were ranked low.[66] Estimating the cost of funding each procedure across the newly expanded Medicaid population, the state's health department cut off reimbursement at procedure number 587.[67] When accused of medical malpractice by helping create a plan that would deny potentially life-saving procedures to beneficiaries, Kitzhaber responded that the "Hippocratic Oath needs to be adapted to the twentieth century."[68]

The Oregon plan allowed the state to provide at least partial coverage to every resident without exceeding the capacity to pay, but it invited accusations of racism, classism, and indifference to human suffering. Critics immediately found instances of residents whose ailments fell below the cutoff of covered procedures and were thus condemned to either prolonged suffering or penury. The starkest illustration were the five patients who died after having been denied transplants in the first months after the program was implemented.[69] Oddly, the program drew the harshest criticism from liberals, who feared that the model would usher in a new era of class-based medicine in which the wealthy received the full benefit of modern medicine and the poor would need to make do with less. The venerable liberal magazine, the *Nation*, editorialized about the "Oregon Disease," which entailed "health care rationing, class-biased welfare, and profit-driven medicine."[70] In its defense, two scholars studying the program pointed out that the legislature could either expand Medicaid to 1,500 Oregonians or could continue to fund bone marrow transplants for thirty-four patients.[71] Kitzhaber defended the program with the following compelling choice: "Is the human tragedy and the personal anguish of death from the lack of an organ transplant any greater than that of an infant dying in an intensive care unit from a preventable problem brought about by a lack of prenatal care?"[72]

The Oregon plan would newly insure nearly 300,000 residents, including 77,000 under Medicaid. But the stark judgments about suffering, utility, and cost efficacy implicit in the formula were intolerable for most people, who still were not willing to think rationally about medical costs. In July 1992, under pressure from the National Right to Life Committee, President George H. W. Bush challenged the Oregon plan for violating the recently passed Americans With Disabilities Act (ADA). The ADA, which had mandated that states grant equal or comparable access to all state services for disabled people, regardless of cost, held any program that disproportionately affected disabled people to a high level of scrutiny. To take one example, Oregon had refused to fund life-saving care for babies born weighing under eighteen ounces or born before twenty-three weeks of gestation. The plan's designers argued that the state only succeeded in saving one in ten such infants, at a cost of more than $250,000 per infant. Proponents of the ADA argued that the state had no right to deny the benefits to the babies, imperfect though they may be.[73] The legislature placed a moratorium on the plan, forcing Kitzhaber to rewrite the law in a way that would preserve civil rights.

Despite these setbacks, Hawaii, Massachusetts, Oregon, and Minnesota (and later Tennessee) demonstrated that states had a role to play in health reform. As the local arbiters of insurance law, state governments could tweak insurance regulations and Medicaid eligibility rules to insure more citizens. Hawaii, for example, managed to insure nearly 99 percent of its residents within a year of enacting its reform measures, while Oregon cut its uninsured population by three-fourths. Notably, no state made substantial efforts to reform the way medical care was produced or provided. No state worked to find easier or less costly ways to train physicians or worked to expand the ability of nonphysicians to provide primary care. No state legislated efforts to hold down the costs of hospitals rooms or prescription drugs. States dismantled their CON provisions, meaning that they now played no role in limiting capital expenditures for hospitals, labs, and clinics. No state created or expanded state-owned clinics, hospitals, community health centers, or traveling physician practices in an effort to leverage the power of the state to bring services to residents. States proved that they were willing to tamper with insurance, but not with healthcare.

❧

Changes in payment through the 1980s recalled the "Whack-a-Mole" game popular at amusement parks. Each effort to limit reimbursement and constrain costs resulted in unexpected modulation by providers, such that global costs never really declined. The prospective payment certainly seemed sound to health economists, impelling providers to work more efficiently, but providers responded by raising the volume of treatments they offered and inflating DRG codes. The RBRVS adjustments were born of multiple time-effort studies by physicians and other providers, but in the end failed to substantially reduce the dramatic disparities in incomes between primary care providers and specialists. Providers seemed able to raise demand for their services wherever they practiced, meaning that increased supply of doctors and hospitals failed to reduce prices, as classical economic theory dictated.

These changes were all made with reasonable intent and sound analysis, but none addressed the system as a whole. Foreign healthcare systems, which provided better outcomes at discounts of 20–40 percent, were not simply more efficient in individual cases; they were systemically more streamlined. That is, health planning, capitalization, training, and distribution comported with an overall rational plan, rather than following the whims of the market. The US healthcare system would require fundamental (often called "comprehensive") change to replicate these outcomes, but such change continued to be alien to provider organizations, political leaders, and the public at large.

6

━━━━━━━━━━━━

HillaryCare

Managed Competition

On April 4, 1991, US Senator John Heinz III (R-PA) died in a freak helicopter accident. In the race to claim his seat that fall, the state's Republican leaders nominated Dick Thornburgh, a former governor and sitting US attorney general. The state's Democratic leaders nominated Harris Wofford, a former Peace Corps volunteer and university president. Initially Thornburgh held a decisive advantage, and early polls suggested he would win the fall election easily. Wofford campaigned heavily on a platform that emphasized the need for comprehensive health reform to allow middle-class and blue-collar workers to retain health benefits after being laid off. With the help of political consultants Paul Begala and James Carville (who directed Bill Clinton's successful run for the presidency a year later), Wofford turned the election into an ultimatum on the future for middle-class workers in the United States. Reflecting on the race, Henry Aaron, an economist and political analyst at the Brookings Institution, noted that the odd election had tapped into a "large seam of inchoate discontent."[1]

Wofford's surprise victory persuaded many political observers that the nation demanded comprehensive health reform. Wofford had not based his call on the need to expand Medicaid, but had correctly perceived broad nervousness among workers that any layoff would effectively end their ability to purchase insurance. Health reform appeared to have become a populist issue, rather than simply another social welfare item to be augmented or cut. Moreover, Pennsylvania was one of several states, along with Ohio, Michigan, and New Jersey, that represented the US political center and thus drew the attention of politicians of both parties.

Not everyone agreed that the Wofford victory suggested a demand for health reform. Healthcare providers and payers across the country were hardly rushing to undo their bailiwicks, and physicians and hospital leaders continued to argue for maintaining the status quo. Survey data indicated that 73 percent of people favored a national health program, but that only 14 percent ranked it among their top two priorities for the federal government.[2] Democratic leaders in Congress had devoted little time or effort to discussing health reform, and no comprehensive plans were being debated at the time of Wofford's victory. Most scholars who examined the issue agreed that managed care would play a pivotal role in any future health reform, yet at the time relatively few people had even heard of managed care, much less understood precisely what it was.[3] Representative Willis "Bill" Gradison (R-OH), a congressional leader on health issues, admitted that Congress had no plans to tackle health reform in the near future.[4] A pair of political scientists, analyzing the special election, warned that "America has yet to be profoundly awakened to the social good inherent in universal health insurance."[5]

Congress was reluctant to engage in health reform in part due to the fiasco of the Catastrophic Care Act of 1988 (CCA). The CCA had attempted to address the growing burden of Medicare co-payments and deductibles on the elderly, which had grown from an average of $300 a year in 1966 to almost $2,400 a year by 1988. The law diminished the burden by expanding Medicare benefits to cover all inpatient costs above $560 a year, all physicians' services above $1,370 a year, and (for the first time) outpatient prescription drug costs above $600 a year. (Beneficiaries paid for half of their drug costs above that amount.) In addition the CCA covered almost all costs of skilled nursing care. Ronald Reagan considered it one of the great domestic successes of his presidency.[6]

Senior citizens responded to the program with vitriol. The expanded benefits were of little use to the 90 percent of seniors who had some sort of Medigap insurance, and the benefit which most wanted—long-term care insurance—had not been included.[7] The program was paid for by sharply increased income taxes and Medicare Part B premiums on the elderly, creating a 75 percent marginal tax rate for the elderly workers earning $10,000, and rising to a marginal rate of 102 percent (!) as non–Social Security income rose to $25,000.[8] Elderly citizens around the country organized write-in and call-in campaigns to their representatives, demanding the law's repeal. A group of senior citizens in Nevada circulated a recall petition that quickly garnered 150,000 signatures.[9] On October 4, the House of Representatives voted to repeal the law, and the Senate concurred two days later. The repeal measure passed the Senate by a vote of ninety-nine to zero (with one abstention).

The CCA debacle spooked Congress and the White House. President George H. W. Bush made only passing reference to health reform in his 1988 campaign, and he barely touched the issue during his four years in office.[10] But the Wofford victory, coupled with a nonbinding resolution in New Jersey calling on Congress to enact a national healthcare program, convinced Bush's budget director, Richard Darman, that the need for reform was pressing.[11] The Bush administration responded by developing its own plan, based largely on a plan produced by the Heritage Foundation, which used tax credits to allow uninsured people to purchase private health insurance and allowed self-employed people to deduct the cost of their premiums. The plan also capped the price at which premiums could be set.[12] The Bush plan differed from the Heritage Foundation plan in a number of ways, most importantly in that it did not require people to purchase health insurance (the "universal mandate"), nor did it end the tax deductibility of employer-provided health benefits. Writing in the *New Republic*, Michael Kinsley noted that the Bush plan was "pure Reaganism: all dessert, no spinach."[13]

The Bush plan defied the essential principle of insurance that risk had to be aggregated for the product to be worthwhile. In allowing high-risk individuals to buy in at capped premiums, without requiring that low-risk individuals buy in at the same time (often these were the same people at different points in their lives), the plan promised to create an insurance death spiral. Healthy people would wait until they were sick to buy in, at which point insurers would be legally compelled to sell them insurance products at rates below their actuarial risk. Insolvency would follow shortly.

Various groups around the country seized the moment to produce their own health reform plans, which generally fell into one of two types: employer-mandated health insurance in the mold of the Hawaii, Oregon, and Massachusetts efforts; or a single-payer model delivered at either the federal or state level as was done in Canada. The employer-mandated models, suggested by groups as disparate as the Health Insurance Association of America, the American Medical Association, and the National Leadership Coalition for Healthcare Reform, preserved the current system while mandating that employers above a certain size either provide health insurance for employees or pay a tax to create an expanded Medicaid program or a new public insurance program.[14] These plans sustained the private insurance industry and thus were politically more feasible. On the other hand, in sustaining the existing system, they all failed to address problems of administrative complexity and redundancy that came with the system. Moreover, because most did not mandate that individuals purchase insurance, they harbored the same problems of adverse selection as the Bush plan.[15]

By contrast, the plans calling for a single-payer reform, backed by the American College of Physicians and the Physicians for a National Health Program (PNHP), reflected declining faith that administrative inefficiencies in the present system could be corrected incrementally. The designers of the PNHP proposal estimated that the private insurance industry in the United States consumed an additional 5 percent of revenues in overhead costs above what the national Medicare program of Canada consumed and that the administrative burden of dealing with multiple payers (some 1,500 in 1990) doubled billing costs for private hospitals and physician practices in the United States.[16] To rectify these inefficiencies and create universal coverage, the PNHP proposal envisioned a shared national tax levied on individuals and businesses equal to present payments for private health insurance policies, which would flow to a central health insurance office, to be disbursed to state insurance plans. Hospitals would be placed on an annual budget from which all expenses would be deducted; private physicians would submit bills to a central reimbursement office. The private insurance industry would cease to exist, as would Medicare and Medicaid.[17]

Both approaches suffered from fatal flaws. The employer-mandate proposals could attract the backing of private insurance, hospitals, and physicians and would be far easier to implement given their light touch on administrative reform and Medicare. On the other hand, they would do little to hold down costs, reduce complexity, or prevent job-lock, and at least a few critics warned that they could bankrupt thousands of small businesses that could not afford to shoulder premiums for their employees while maintaining their slender profit margins.[18] Moreover, such proposals relied on the continued viability of state Medicaid programs to cover the poor, despite the fact that in many states Medicaid reimbursement rates were falling far below market rates. By contrast, the single-payer models, which offered reasonable hope of controlling costs, were politically untenable. The likelihood of simply superseding, and thus destroying, the nearly $1 trillion private health insurance sector was exceedingly small, and many individual physicians and hospitals would join the insurance sector in fiercely opposing such reforms. Single-payer models would likely limit people from purchasing care outside of the confines of the system—a limitation guaranteed to antagonize wealthier Americans—and would likely limit access to certain sorts of innovative, experimental, and highly refined procedures, drugs, and tests. One Canadian expatriate doctor feared the PNHP proposal for its likely effect on academic medicine. He wrote, "I would urge physicians and the public to consider very carefully some of the likely consequences of a national health program . . . Such a system tends to concentrate enormous power over health delivery in the hands of the government."[19] Other critics pointed out problems in the Veterans Administration health system as foreshadowing of problems to come. A group of concerned doctors wrote, "Schemes that depend on the ongoing wisdom and beneficence of the government may found on the rocks of bureaucratic and organizational imperfection."[20]

Plans in both categories focused on expanding access to health insurance, but neither group of reformers was willing to take on the paralyzing issue of cost containment. By 1990 it was becoming increasingly clear that the only promising path to long-term cost reduction was simply consuming less. Administrative reform might produce one-time cost savings, as might a move toward managed care, but Henry Aaron and William Schwartz, two prominent healthcare economists, demonstrated persuasively that savings wrought from bed closures and HMOs might be as little as $20 billion.[21] Other observers expressed doubt that greater physician awareness of costs, or more intensive physician education surrounding costs, would prove effective, given the incentives for doctors to always do and provide more and for patients to constantly consume more.[22] The knee-jerk antagonism toward the Oregon plan suggested nothing else.

The health reform bills proposed and debated between 1989 and 1993 reflected growing concerns of both legislative and medical leaders that the status quo was becoming increasingly unsustainable. The

Wofford victory, although not dispositive, was sobering; middle-class citizens were clearly worried about their continued ability to consume healthcare given the constant pattern of lay-offs, downsizing, and outsourcing within the US labor force. In the near future, the debates would galvanize the nation over the course of the 1992 presidential race and would come to dominate President Bill Clinton's first term in office. Even then few participants would confront rationing. Americans continued to deny reality, believing that endless, high-quality care for all could be achieved through the right mix of tax incentives, employer mandates, state and federal health plans, public gap plans, and personal fortitude. All were proven incorrect.

Bill Clinton entered office in January 1993 determined to make comprehensive healthcare reform the central domestic initiative of his first term. Although he had been conspicuously vague about plans for health reform throughout his campaign, he had promised to deliver "affordable, high-quality health care," through insurance reform, mandatory community rating, and a public health insurance plan, all coordinated by a new National Health Board, which would set rates and oversee insurance benefits.[23] He had further promised increased funds for education and prevention, stronger physician practice guidelines, expansion of electronic medical records, and more generous long-term care benefits within Medicare.[24] But the specific framework of his reform efforts remained a mystery through much of the fall.

Clinton's health reform could have taken one of several shapes. He could adopt a single-payer approach, as was used in Canada, but this model was fraught with political challenges and would face enormous industry opposition.[25] He could push for a pay-or-play approach as was backed by Senator Edward Kennedy (D-MA), but this approach would not appeal to his desire for truly innovative reform. Or he could look to Alain Enthoven's complex vision for comprehensive reform known as "managed competition."

Managed competition had grown out of a decade of work within the Jackson Hole Group to apply theories of management, competition, firm organization, and consumer behavior to the healthcare sphere. Enthoven, along with colleagues Paul Ellwood and Representative Jim Cooper (D-TN) envisioned a complex and highly coordinated system that would marry rational consumerism, market competition, regulated insurance, a universal insurance mandate, and a new type of group purchasing mechanism knows as a health insurance purchasing cooperative (HIPiC—pronounced "hipick"). Nearly all people would purchase private health insurance through the HIPiCs, and most of these insurance policies would contract with HMOs, which would, in turn, promote healthier habits and provide better preventive care. Doctors, bound by HMO incentives, would change their practices to favor more cost-effective therapeutics.

Managed competition preserved the existing private health insurance industry, but exposed it to competitive market forces in an effort to make it more responsive to consumer preferences. Employers would be required to offer multiple plans, but employees would only be allowed to deduct the premium of the cheapest plan offered, forcing them to confront the true cost of more profligate fee-for-service plans if they chose from those. Cheaper plans, presumably employing aggressive managed care strategies, would in turn negotiate discounted rates with physicians, who would be forced to aggregate into more cost-efficient prepaid practice groups. New government oversight agencies would rate the efficacy of various doctors and hospitals, allowing consumers to seek out those providers who achieved the best outcomes at the lowest costs, thus creating more transparent markets for choosing providers. Smaller employers and individuals, meanwhile, would be able to leverage the purchasing power of the HIPiCs to buy plans at competitive prices that would be otherwise unavailable to them given the small size of their risk groups. The elderly would continue in Medicare, and the poor would stay in Medicaid.[26]

Managed competition promised to restrain government action through the use of competitive markets, but even Enthoven was forced to impose government regulation in some areas. Ratings and outcomes assessment would need to be conducted by government agencies, as would tax reform. HIPiCs would need to be established and regulated by either state or local governments. Insurance companies would require continued regulation and oversight to force them to use community rating pricing on their premiums and to prevent them from excluding potential beneficiaries based on preexisting conditions. State insurance commissioners would need to adjust approved premiums based on the health status of pools of enrollees. Public subsidies would likely be necessary to help low-income individuals buy private insurance plans. Enthoven refused to prescribe a universal insurance mandate, however, relying on the appeal of community-rated premiums and tax advantages to induce consumers to purchase insurance, and he refused to offer a universal fee scale for doctors and hospitals, alluding vaguely to "performance-based systems of pay, somewhere between fee-for-service . . . and salaries, using peer judgment and various indicators of performance."[27]

Managed competition drew ire or outright condemnation from more progressive reform groups, which viewed the existing system of private insurance and private providers as profiteering, exploitative, and cumbersome. One muckraking journalist postulated that the plan was the intellectual brainchild of the Trilateral Commission, whose capitalist overlords—David Rockefeller, Allan Gotlieb, Mark LaLonde, and Adam Zimmermann—had captured Bill Clinton and his new secretary of Health and Human Services, Donna Shalala.[28] Theodore Marmor, a respected scholar of health policy, and one of the architects of the original Medicare program, tarred managed competition as a "wolf in sheep's clothing."[29] Health watchers of all stripes feared the impact of aggressive HMOs on quality, end-of-life care, and experimental procedures.[30]

But more important, managed competition preserved the Rube Goldberg quality of the US health system in which for-profit insurers with motivation to deny care, limit coverage, and extract profits would continue to have authority over clinical judgment and patient decisions. Doctors, hospitals, clinics, and imaging centers would continue to be uncoordinated and unregulated. The "system" would continue to lack systematization and would continue to harbor many thousands of independent agents and firms pursuing maximum profits as they negotiated a tortured landscape of private and government payers. Robert Dreyfuss, a progressive-minded writer in Washington, offered the following parable to capture the model: "A foundation offers an inventor a grant to build a better mousetrap. But in the fine print of the contract the inventor reads that the final mechanism must incorporate an old-fashioned player piano. So he designs a mousetrap that includes the piano. Of course, the result is bulky and expensive, and it catches few mice."[31]

HillaryCare

Early on Clinton opted for managed competition. The market-oriented philosophy of the program went along with his desire to direct the Democratic Party to a more business-friendly orientation. The idea of maintaining existing insurance firms and independent providers seemed far more politically realistic that remaking the health system anew. The party's enormous political debts to many components of the healthcare industry dictated that a workable plan would need to appease many stakeholders.

The stakeholders were legion and included pharmaceutical firms, hospitals, doctors, malpractice attorneys, organized labor, patient advocates, medical device firms, insurers, small businesses, nurses, and advocacy organizations for specific diseases. In 1992, pharmaceutical firms had donated $4 million to congressional candidates of both parties.[32] Over the first six months of 1993, the National Federation of Independent Business mailed out 600,000 postcards to voters around the country. At the same time, the AARP trained 1,400 members to speak about health reform at forums around the country, and the AFL-CIO readied 287,000 members to staff phone banks. The Hospital Corporation of America briefed 66,000 of its clinical employees and affiliates on lobbying points, and dozens of unions scheduled appointments with various representatives to voice their priorities in health reform.[33]

Health lobbyists aimed to preserve privilege and revenue streams for their clients and particularly targeted four powerful members of Congress who were best able to deliver this: Representative Peter Stark (D-CA), chair of the House Ways and Means Committee; Senator David Durenberger (R-MN), ranking Republican on the Senate Medicare subcommittee; Senator Lloyd Bentsen (D-TX), chair of the Senate Finance Committee; and Senator Max Baucus (D-MT), ranking member of the Finance Committee. These four together received nearly half of all healthcare lobbying funds directed at sitting members of Congress.[34] Tom Goodwin, director of public affairs for the Federation of American Health Systems, explained, "We spend our money on those members . . . most interested in maintaining the current system."[35] To this end, managed competition as a general approach allowed the Clinton administration to make substantial progress in expanding access to healthcare and possibly imposing some anti-inflationary measures on the system, without starkly limiting the ability of existing firms and players to make money. Bruce Vladeck, the director of the Health Care Financing Administration in the Clinton administration, noted, "The reason so many providers support managed competition is because they don't believe its cost-containment mechanisms will really work, and they're afraid the mechanisms in other proposals for health-care reform would."[36]

Healthcare lobbying funds and political action group funds bled into unexpected interstices. The US Catholic Conference and the Catholic Health Association vigorously advocated to bar funds for abortion from any proposed legislation.[37] Mental health counselors pushed hard for generous funding for psychotherapy and found a particularly receptive ear in Tipper Gore, wife of the vice president. Public hospital chiefs lobbied to strengthen Medicaid reimbursement, while nursing home owners lobbied to protect their Medicaid benefits. Even reformers, such as the Jackson Hole Group, drew money from the torrent sloshing through Washington. A *US News* investigative team found that the group had accepted hundreds of thousands of dollars in donations from Aetna Life and Casualty, Golden Rule, and the Mayo Clinic.[38] Doctors, individually and through lobbyists, funneled $16.4 million to members of Congress of both parties.

Clinton placed primary responsibility for developing health reform on his wife, Hillary Rodham Clinton, who in turn hired her husband's old friend and fellow Rhodes scholar Ira Magaziner to direct the effort. The choice of Magaziner was telling, as the man known best for his development of Brown University's "new curriculum" in 1969 had spent most of his career as a master of corporate and civic reorganization and bureaucratic streamlining. Through his early work in economic redevelopment for the city of Brockton, Massachusetts, and then through stints at the Boston Consulting Group and later his own Telesis consulting firm, Magaziner had shown himself to be a brilliant strategist of reorganization, but not necessarily a revolutionary thinker. Robert Reich, another Rhodes scholar classmate, who was appointed secretary of Labor in the Clinton administration, said of Magaziner, "It's funny. His insights are rarely startling. More often they are of the 'Why didn't I see that?' variety."[39]

As a master of complex processes, Magaziner assembled a team of more than five hundred healthcare experts, largely detailed from government agencies and Democratic congressional staffs, who met in secret over the early months of the Clinton administration. Notably, the Magaziner team failed to invite many powerful healthcare constituents to participate in the creative process and relied instead on management and reimbursement specialists, public health practitioners, healthcare economists, and performance and outcomes engineers. The Clinton health reform effort deliberately excluded representatives from physician and hospital groups, and in the process failed to acknowledge the tremendous influence that many of these interest groups retained with legislators and with the general public. (Years later, when President Barack Obama assembled his own health reform team, he sought to learn lessons from the Magaziner effort not so much from specific flaws in the final proposal but from political flaws in the development process.)

The plan that emerged, the Health Security Act of 1993, drew heavily on Enthoven's managed competition approach, albeit with some notable changes. The plan used an employer mandate to require all employers to purchase comprehensive health insurance for their employees through newly created regional health alliances. (Large employers could choose to create their own "corporate" alliances through which they could offer competing health insurance products.) The regional alliances, a manifestation of Enthoven's HIPiCs, would offer various health insurance policies, ranging from fee-for-service plans to HMOs to prepaid group practice plans. All employers would be required to pay 80 percent of the average cost of the plans, with the remaining costs coming from the employees. The plans, notably, would be offered by existing private insurance firms.

If the employer mandate was the first foundation post of the plan, broad new insurance regulation was the second. All insurance plans offered in the alliances would be required to offer comprehensive benefits, and all premiums would be community-rated. That is, all policies offered by any one insurance company would need to cost the same, regardless of the age, risk profile, or preexisting health status of the beneficiary (although insurance companies could price products for singles, couples, and families differently). In outlawing insurance adjustment for preexisting conditions, Magaziner hoped to assuage the general fear that so many peopled harbored of losing their jobs and being unable to purchase an individual insurance premium. Under the Clinton plan, all insurance premiums would cost the same for all comers, regardless of health status.

Health alliances, an employer mandate, and mandated community rating formed the tripod on which the plan rested, and it promised to greatly expand the number of people who would be able to purchase insurance. The plan did more, however. It restructured Medicaid by putting Medicaid-eligible beneficiaries into the regional alliances to purchase private insurance. It granted subsidies on a sliding scale to the poor so that they could purchase insurance in the alliances. It mandated minimal levels of mental health and substance abuse benefits that eligible plans would need to offer, and forced Medicare to offer a prescription drug plan for the first time. Notably, it left a number of separate sectors of the US health system untouched, such as Medicare, the Indian Health Service, the Veterans Administration, the health insurance plans used by the US Postal Service and the armed forces.

The use of alliances and an employer mandate were consistent with the theory of managed competition. The Magaziner plan, however, layered a number of mandates onto the basic managed competition structure in an effort to rein in costs and curb excesses. It mandated that 60 percent of all residency slots in the nation's teaching hospitals be in primary care. It imposed financial burdens on all employees to make middle-class citizens more aware of the true costs of their healthcare purchasing decisions. Most important, it placed nationwide caps on the growth of health insurance premiums, limiting premium inflation to the consumer price index by 2000. The importance of a premium cap suggested that the administration did not really trust the market forces at the heart of managed competition to hold down health costs.[40]

The plan required substantial subsidies to allow lower-income beneficiaries to buy insurance through the alliances. These subsidies would be financed through a variety of new taxes (on cigarettes, for example) and through substantial savings in the Medicare program, which would cut reimbursement to physicians in coming years while charging wealthier Americans higher Part B premiums. Nobody knew if the plan would actually pay for itself. Given the modest anti-inflationary measures built into it, the Congressional Budget Office estimated that the plan would save citizens $150 billion a year by 2009. Other, more conservative forecasters suggested that the plan might cost $250 billion more by the same time. One analyst said that President Clinton's challenge in health reform was the same as his challenge in balancing the budget: "to persuade the middle class that they will have to make real sacrifices."[41] Given that the plan did not touch the personal tax deduction for employer-provided health insurance contributions, the administration appeared to be reluctant to ask the middle class to make a real sacrifice.

More broadly, analysts questioned the ways the plan would distort labor markets. Employers might choose to hire fewer workers but work them longer hours, favoring greater overtime pay in lieu of more required contributions to insurance premiums. Workers might choose to leave unfulfilling jobs, knowing that they could now purchase reasonably priced health insurance through the regional alliances. Elderly workers might choose to retire earlier, while some newly insured people might choose to consume more healthcare. Certainly young self-employed or unemployed workers would now be paying more for insurance, just as their elders would now be paying less; the premium regulations in the plan amounted to a massive intergenerational shift in costs. Nobody knew how many physicians might choose to no longer accept Medicare assignment once reimbursement rates were adjusted sharply lower.

Attacks

The right attacked quickly. The first target was the sheer size of the proposal. The 1,300-page bill introducing the plan to Congress consti- tuted a massive overlay on the existing system of new agencies, regula- tions, subsidies, and tax changes. David Frum, a conservative columnist, called it "the most ambitious peacetime assertion of state power over civil society since the National Recovery Act of 1935."[42] William Niska- nen, the chairman of the libertarian Cato Institute, described the plan as "the most radical, arrogant, unreal, and unwise policy proposal by any administration in my lifetime."[43] James Todd, the executive vice presi- dent of the American Medical Association, noted that by the time he had reached page seventy of the bill, he had "counted five new agen- cies, and . . . learned about a whole now bureaucracy that the President wants to impose over health care in this country."[44]

Big did not necessarily mean bad, and an effort to reform structural problems in a complex system arguably required a big, complex piece of legislation. Most efforts at creating social safety net enterprises in the past had required creating new agencies and regulations, reformed tax codes, and appointing administrators to new positions. That said, large new agencies tended to take time to become functional, and accu- sations of potential bureaucratic sclerosis were hardly paranoia. Jack Welch, the celebrated CEO of General Electric, questioned the function- ality of the purchasing alliances, which he compared to large, quasi- governmental monopsonies that would likely by mediocre and ineffi- cient. "If you believe regional purchasing alliances in fifty states can weed out $200 billion in waste, go visit your local motor vehicle depart- ment," he suggested.[45] Other conservative critics questioned the large onus placed on small businesses, which would now be required to fund 80 percent of the cost of their employees' health insurance, and of the potential deadening effects on insurance markets that might come about due to the new stringent regulations on minimum benefit levels.

Many critiques from the right, however, were simply scare- mongering. Critics derided the plan as Marxist, socialist, totalitarian, and statist, although it was none of those things. Malcolm Forbes, the publisher of *Forbes* magazine, warned that the plan would bankrupt "hundreds of thousands of enterprises."[46] Betsy McCaughey parlayed her sensationalistic attack on the plan into a spot with George Pataki on the New York Republican gubernatorial ticket. John Goodman, the president of the National Center for Policy Analysis, offered the bizarre (and wholly incorrect) insight that individuals purchasing services from hospitals would be far more effective in negotiating lower prices than would large insurance companies or regional purchasing alliances. He told a group in Jacksonville, Florida, "People paying their own money at the hospital get the lowest price around."[47] In fact, the truth was precisely the opposite.

A different line of attack was more legitimate but raised troubling questions about the nature of civil society in the United States. One of the central aspirations of the Clinton plan was to distribute risk more broadly in an effort to distribute the cost of healthcare over a lifetime and over an entire society. Underlying this goal was the idea that most people were simply not responsible for the vagaries of their own health, and thus should not be hurt financially for the misfortunes that might befall them. Certainly some people were more conscientious at staying fit and refraining from drinking and smoking, but few could claim credit for remaining free from cancer, heart disease, stroke, mental illness, and the general dissipations of age.

Yet conservatives attacked the Clinton plan for the community rating mandate it put on insurance pricing, pointing out that no auto or fire insurance company would ever price policies independent of risk exposure. Peter Samuel of Greentrack International derided community rating as "forced income redistribution," which, in a sense, it was.[48] But it was no more income redistribution than was using progressive taxation to provide schooling, transportation, defense, police protection, and sewage treatment to all citizens, regardless of their ability to pay. The issue was philosophical: was health insurance so fundamental to civic participation as to demand broad subsidy? Many conservative thinkers thought not.

Another philosophically legitimate but politically tendentious attack on the plan centered on price controls. The Magaziner team had rightly discerned that most people were concerned about healthcare inflation and had worked to build at least modest price controls into the program through caps on insurance premiums and a long-term reduction in Medicare reimbursement. Conservative critics viewed such limits as incursions into the free market (which they were) and thus ideologically unacceptable. Marcia Berss wrote in *Forbes*, "Stripped of its verbiage and convolutions, the Clinton health plan is little more than a form of price control."[49] Kenneth Abramowitz, a healthcare analyst at Sanford Bernstein and a reliably conservative critic, noted, "Price controls have never worked in any society. The last one they destroyed was called the Soviet Union."[50] Other critics feared the government placing price controls over specific procedures and salaries, or limiting capital investment in the health sector's infrastructure. These fears and accusations were not so much wrong as they were out of touch with the concerns of most citizens. Wealthy people enjoyed being able to purchase some of the most innovative and advanced healthcare procedures in the world and had little need for government price controls. But most middle-class people feared the inexorable rise in healthcare prices and sought government intervention.

Not all attacks came from the right. Centrists and liberals expressed disappointment with the plan. It did little to simplify the Byzantine system of payment which larded the system with such a heavy administrative burden—a burden so heavy that the GAO had estimated that its cost alone could cover all uninsured people should the United States ever move to a single-payer system. If anything, this burden promised to grow heavier under managed competition, as more people moved to HMOs, which more carefully monitored billings. By some estimates, major hospitals spent an average of $100 simply to create a patient's bill, and the Mayo Clinic reported that in recent years it had hired more than seventy employees just to take calls from insurance companies.[51]

A number of politicians and health reform advocates were skeptical of the great promises made for HMOs in rationalizing healthcare consumption and reducing costs. HMOs spent less on specialists and hospitals than did traditional plans, but this was due in part to the generally healthier populations they had historically enrolled. Moreover, HMOs maintained large administrative burdens, spending up to 9.4 percent of their budgets on administration, rather than the 2.5 percent claimed by their more optimistic champions. David Himmelstein and Steffie Woolhandler, two liberal critics of the Clinton plan, pointed out that Prudential's managed care plan in New Jersey employed "eighteen nurse reviewers, five physician reviewers, eight provider recruiters, fifteen sales and twenty-seven service representatives, and about one hundred clerks," to administer a plan covering 110,000 members.[52] In Canada, by contrast, the administrative workforce for a comparable group of enrollees would have been a tenth the size.

The plan did little to end the profligate use of gratuitous care people consumed in the last six months of their lives.[53] It did little to rein in excessive malpractice litigation to cap malpractice awards or to thwart doctors from ordering redundant tests. It failed to cap the rising cost of medical school or limit the amount of new investment hospitals could make in infrastructure. It placed great hope on the role of competition between plans to force prices down, and it made promises for managed care that managed care had not yet proven that it could deliver. One White House staff member noted of the projected cost savings from HMOs, "these numbers are as squishy as any numbers on Earth."[54]

Perhaps most important, the plan promised to expand access to private health insurance without changing the way medical care was actually produced, packaged, distributed, and sold. Other nations bundled patients and medical groups, or placed global caps on hospital and physician budgets, but this plan used the crude cudgel of price caps on insurance premiums. Other nations vigorously applied outcomes research to create benchmarks for effective but parsimonious care, but this plan did little to offer guidance and oversight to physicians and hospitals. It did promise to limit the number of specialty training slots over the long term, but it could do little regarding the surplus of specialists already trained who sold their services and wares around the country. It did nothing to rein in price growth for pharmaceuticals, medical devices, and complex new procedures. In short, the plan asked little sacrifice of the middle class, even as it imposed broad new mandates for spending on employers.

"It's hardly begun, but we're already feeling overwhelmed by the healthcare debate," wrote Robert Samuelson that October.[55] The magnitude of the transformation, the complexity of the plan, and the viciousness of the surrounding rhetoric all served to frighten people from seriously engaging the debate. New terms such as *alliances, mandates, gatekeepers,* and *capitation* all pulled at citizens' comfortable view of their family doctor. The debate had hardly begun, but people were already alienated from their choices.

Many Americans were daunted by the sheer length of the bill and the number of changes it would bring to the US health system. Senate Majority Leader Robert Dole (R-KS) gained traction with skeptical constituents by showing a Byzantine diagram of agency relationships in televised hearings, while asking, "How do you spell 'manic depressive'?"[56] One language scholar remarked on the "Orwellian" tone of the term *health alliance*. ("Good morning, Mr. Jones, we're from the Alliance and we'd like to talk to you about how your therapy is going."[57]) The Health Insurance Association of America funded one of the most successful political ad campaigns in history by using a fictional husband and wife named Harry and Louise—a concerned professional-looking couple who sat at their kitchen table puzzling over the details of the plan.[58] The couple's fascination with policy minutiae was hardly credible, but the ad had "recall," in the judgment of Barbara Lippert of *Adweek*. The concerns raised by the couple resonated with many others, even if they reflected the tendentiousness of the HIAA.

Making the politics of the plan more complicated was the competing plan offered that year by Representative Jim Cooper, which was also built on the managed competition approach. Cooper positioned his plan as a less onerous alternative to the administration's plan when he deliberately omitted the employer mandate but encouraged individuals to purchase private health insurance from the alliances with more generous federal subsidies. Describing his plan as one based on universal access (rather than the universal *coverage* described under the Clinton plan), Cooper won the support of a number of conservative Democrats and liberal Republicans, including John Breaux (D-LA), Sam Nunn (D-GA), David Boren (D-OK), Bob Kerrey (D-NE), and Dave Durenberger (R-MN) in the Senate and Dave McCurdy (D-OK), Charles Stenholm (D-TX), and Fred Gandy (R-IA) in the House.[59]

In omitting the mandate, Cooper and his co-sponsors demonstrated their lack of understanding of health insurance. Community rating required a mandate to buy in, lest individual buyers wait until they were sick or old to purchase a policy, thus driving up premiums and forcing the insurance company into a death spiral. Most people consumed more healthcare as they got older and sicker, meaning that a sound insurance system forced people to overpay for insurance when young so that they could underpay when old. The employer mandate of the Clinton plan acknowledged this reality, albeit without creating an even more fiscally sound universal mandate. Most Americans, however, did not understand this basic law of health insurance and thus found the Cooper plan preferable. In effect, Cooper was promising a free lunch, and few people were sophisticated enough to understand that it was an empty promise.

Further exacerbating the politics of the Clinton plan was the general unattractiveness of Magaziner himself. A physically awkward man with the air of a policy wonk, Magaziner seemed to antagonize both legislators and voters each time he tried to explain the plan. One member of the White House staff remarked, "He costs us two or three votes every time he goes up to Capitol Hill."[60] The secrecy of the design process had drawn widespread suspicion from citizens, and Hillary Clinton's imperiousness had alienated many centrist Americans during the campaign. In short, even those who might have supported the plan if they had understood its provisions viscerally opposed it by the time it was introduced in Congress. Fearful legislators were sensitive to the disapproval in their districts.

Many groups lobbied against the plan, but none more stridently than the National Federation of Independent Business (NFIB). The NFIB marshaled 600,000 small business owners to lobby members of Congress against the bill, citing a federation study predicting that the plan would cost 1.5 million jobs. Small business and family farm owners from across the United States urged their representatives to vote against the plan, claiming that the employer mandate would potentially bankrupt them. Ronald Williams, owner of Anywhere Travel in Salina, Kansas, wrote, "If this health plan is mandated by the federal government, you will have twelve new people on the unemployment rolls in Salina because I will be forced to shut my business down."[61] While hard-left Democrats representing the coastal cities were largely immune to such pressure, the more conservative Democrats representing Midwest and Southern constituents were not.

Managed care companies, which might have been expected to support the plan given the mandate for an HMO option in the alliances, also allied themselves against the plan. Skeptical of the goodwill of the administration (they were particularly distrustful of Donna Shalala, secretary of Health and Human Services, who had pushed for a single-payer solution throughout the previous year), the managed care companies feared the cap on premiums, the single-payer option for states setting up exchanges, and the potential for long-term global budgeting within the alliances. Aetna, CIGNA, MetLife, Prudential, and Travelers banded together to create the Alliance for Managed Competition, whose purpose was to oppose managed competition by denigrating the administration's plan as not "true" managed competition. In short, neither Wall Street nor Main Street trusted the administration's commitment to a free and unfettered marketplace.

Organizations that might not normally be expected to express opinions on health policy weighed in. The United Methodist Church expressed distaste for a system that was not single-payer. The Knights of Columbus vociferously rejected abortion funding in the alliances. The nation's Roman Catholic bishops called for a system providing "universal access to comprehensive quality care subject to cost containment and controls, characterized by equitable financing and genuine respect for human life and dignity," in a veiled reference to omitting abortion funding and socializing the payment system.[62] Not to be outdone, David Zwiebel, the general counsel to Agudath Israel of America, an orthodox Jewish organization, pushed for better prenatal and pediatric benefits in the alliances and warned of expanding coverage at the expense of comprehensiveness of benefits.[63]

Administration backers tried hard to defend the plan, pointing to its projected low costs, its market orientation, and its ability to expand access to health insurance for virtually all people. Paul Starr, one of the administration's most consistent defenders, wrote that the plan "presumes neither a free lunch nor any fiscal fantasies," and pleaded for the universal mandate in an effort to ensure the solvency of the alliances.[64] Walter Zelman, who had chaired a task force on universal coverage in California, argued ardently for recognizing the impending crisis in US healthcare, which demanded an immediate and comprehensive response, which the administration's plan provided. The Clinton plan preserved competition, choice, and capitalism, Zelman wrote, while eschewing one-price universalism and single-payer consolidation. It was a "unique blend of health reforms" which could move the country to the consensus it needed to overcome the great political barriers of health reform.[65]

But the administration's defenders offered too tepid a defense of a plan that many feared more for its philosophy than its stipulations. The plan felt like big government, even if it really was not. People broadly accepted the government's role in regulating insurance products but could not quite accept that the new plan was largely federal reregulation of health insurance. Millions of Americans had long wished for employer-provided health insurance, yet feared the sound of the word *mandate*. Americans, it seemed, did not quite sense the crisis described by Zelman, nor had they come to the consensus necessary to force through a major piece of domestic legislation. The middle class was suffering in 1993, but hardly at the level they had suffered in the 1930s when Franklin Roosevelt had successfully expanded the nation's social safety net.

The Clinton plan failed to address many challenges to the US health system. True, if implemented, its employer mandate and regional alliances could bring many uninsured people under the umbrella of insurance, and its caps on insurance premium hikes could lower the total cost of US healthcare. However, it relied inordinately on unproven mechanisms of managed care to reduce costs, while doing little to rectify many inefficiencies in the way healthcare was actually produced and distributed.

Above all, the Clinton plan was built on a highly optimistic prognosis for managed care. The basic building blocks of managed care, such as capitation and utilization review, had drawn the support of health planners for two decades, yet much about managed care was unknown. It was unclear, for example, whether managed care could hold down costs as its covered population grew. Historically, managed care plans had only enrolled a small percentage of all insured people, and these beneficiaries had tended to be significantly younger and healthier than average. Under the Clinton plan, managed care plans would no longer be able to count on this unusually healthy beneficiary group. Moreover, managed care plans actually spent a higher percentage of their budget on administration, suggesting that the administration was understating the long-term administrative burden of the program. One study of Medicare managed care plans, for example, found that they spent 10–13 percent of their budgets on marketing, utilization review, and other administrative tasks, versus the 2 percent spent on these functions by fee-for-service Medicare.[66]

Managed care plans might not prove workable in large parts of the country. Because managed care was based on a capitated prepaid group practice model, building viable managed care plans required that there be enough local physician practices to create groups that were large enough to distribute the risk of high-cost patients. No individual doctor could afford to bear the risk associated with capitated payment for a patient with a serious chronic disease. Yet large parts of the country were not well served by doctors, and rural areas could hardly support the density of physician networks necessary to make managed care work. Managed competition might work well in areas where there was enough competition to create a vibrant market, but it could not work well in the many rural counties with few practitioners and only one hospital.

The Clinton plan did little to impel physicians to practice less profligately and intensively. True, large numbers of young doctors would be denied admission to specialty residencies, but they might choose to increase the technological intensity of their primary care practices. Both physicians and patients in the United States had insatiable appetites to purchase and use medical technology and expensive new drugs, and little in the plan promised to change this behavior. People would be required to pay 20 percent of the cost of their health insurance but would experience relatively little cost at the time they purchased services. Little in the plan suggested that doctors would enthusiastically take on roles of health educator or preventive health counselor. One medical school professor described a malaise he called "medical student myopia syndrome," characterized by "boredom, inattention, and hostility towards preventive medicine courses."[67]

The Clinton plan did little to halt unfettered hospital expansion, which had resulted in a hospital occupancy rate of under 70 percent.[68] The bloated hospitals had already been built (largely with borrowed funds) and would require years to pay off. Even as hospitals rushed to merge in the aftermath of prospective payment, newly merged institutions continued to confront historically high debt burdens. Nothing in the Clinton plan would force hospital management to become more efficient. Two scholars at Georgetown University, Jack Hadley and Stephen Zuckerman, found little evidence that larger hospitals were run more efficiently than were smaller ones.[69] The nation had built far too many hospital beds, and the bill would come due regardless of price caps imposed on the insurance industry.

Doctors complained bitterly of the aggressive lawsuits they faced and the outrageous punitive awards given to litigants, driving up the cost of malpractice insurance while inducing doctors to practice defensively. Little in the Clinton plan addressed this problem, which doctors viewed as a major barrier to practicing more parsimonious medicine. James Todd, vice president of the AMA, argued forcefully that "something must be done about the current malpractice mess" in critiquing the Clinton plan, pointing out the numerous ways the antagonistic environment was toxic to good medical care.[70] While certain states, notably Texas, had begun to cap malpractice awards by 1993, many states with Democrat-controlled legislatures would likely refuse to address the issue. A defensive medical labor force was inimical to cost-conscious medical practice.

Medicare would stay largely intact; Medicaid would continue to underpay physicians and thus prevent them from taking on large numbers of poor patients; and premium-capped insurance companies would squeeze providers, thus forcing many into a growing pool of doctors who would accept only cash. The Clinton plan did little to change the way doctors trained, hospitals administrators managed, patients behaved, and pharmaceutical companies marketed. While it would enlarge the pool of insured people, its cost-control mechanisms were ham-fisted. Americans might hope to each receive one of the new health security cards which the president showed on television the night of his State of the Union speech in 1994, but they might find that the card had few takers when they went out to the medical market to use it. One sober physician, explaining his decision to no longer accept Medicaid patients, admitted, "I finally couldn't keep myself from seeing them as a financial loss."[71] Declining insurance reimbursement might push doctors to view non-Medicaid patients in the same light.

There was no single flaw in the Clinton plan that guaranteed its failure, but the growing weight of its many weaknesses, coupled with strains of irrational and partisan opposition, brought it down. Bob Dole, the Senate minority leader, argued vociferously against its passage on the Senate floor in the spring of 1994, forcing Senate Majority Leader George Mitchell (D-ME) to offer a compromise bill that August. Even the compromise bill found few backers. By the end of the summer, the effort was effectively dead, and Mitchell halted the legislative process. The perceived crisis in US healthcare, which has appeared to demand a forceful and comprehensive response from the energetic new administration, had proven less compelling than many observers had supposed. There had been no crisis: simply growing discontent with the growing limitations and burdens of an increasingly complex and frustrating payment bureaucracy. The Wofford election had been misread, and few Americans in 1993 were upset enough with their care, or frightened enough about the future, to pressure their legislators into passing comprehensive reform. Analyzing the demise of the bill a few years later, Jacob Hacker, a political scientist, wrote, "If the received wisdom in the wake of Clinton's victory was that *reform* was inevitable, today's commentators are equally certain that *defeat* was inevitable."[72]

7

Managing Care

Movement to Managed Care

The Clinton health plan had failed largely because it compelled people to move from their traditional fee-for-service insurance plans to a managed care plan. Americans resisted the move, correctly realizing that moving from indemnity insurance to managed care would restrict their choices and limit their ability to see specialists. Betsy McCaughey, in her widely read critique of the plan titled "No Exit" had frightened many people with her scenarios of second-rate care delivered by cost-conscious managed companies which all would be required to join.[1] At the time of the Clinton health proposal, fewer than one-third of citizens who had private health insurance were enrolled in a managed care plan, and scarcely any Medicare beneficiaries were so enrolled. But in an ironic turn, in the years immediately after the proposal's failure, the United States moved rapidly into managed care. By 1998, 85 percent of those who received their health insurance through their employer were enrolled in some sort of managed care, as were most who purchased individual policies. Eighty thousand Medicare beneficiaries and many Medicaid recipients were moving to managed care plans each month.[2] The Clinton plan had prematurely envisioned a managed US healthcare landscape, but it had been only slightly ahead of its time.

People enrolled in managed care plans almost exclusively to save money. Individuals and employers who purchased the plans realized savings of 40 percent or more on premiums, while the federal government induced elderly beneficiaries to join Medicare managed care plans by allowing them free or subsidized prescription drug plans, lower co-payments, and reduced annual deductibles. Managed care plans, in turn, used their contracts, utilization review policies, and market leverage to reduce hospitalizations and specialist consultations while lowering payments to physicians. In two years, for example, Blue Shield of Washington, DC, reduced the fee it paid to obstetricians for standard prenatal care and delivery from $3,500 to $1,125.[3] One study found that HMOs reduced hospital admissions for Medicare beneficiaries by 40 percent, and another found that HMOs that implemented a $25 co-payment fee were able to reduce emergency room visits by nearly 15 percent.[4] Even indemnity plans that used aggressive utilization review were able to reduce hospital expenditures by 12 percent.[5]

The payment reductions were hardly unencumbered, however. Almost immediately following the bulge of managed care enrollments, patients and providers began to complain of heavy-handed abuses by the managed care companies. In Connecticut, for example, a physician hospital organization (PHO) run jointly by Danbury Hospital and Heartland Health System imposed monopsonistic pricing on the many physician practices, forcing the doctors to deliver at least 30 percent of their outpatient services at the hospital.[6] In New Jersey, the Merit Behavioral Care Corporation, an organization that specialized in reducing costs for psychiatric care, became infamous for denying treatment requests by psychiatrists treating severely ill patients, including those suffering from suicidal thoughts or withdrawal symptoms from alcohol and other substances. The firm's general rule was to limit most patients to eight therapy sessions, regardless of diagnosis.[7] The mantra of Oxford Health Plans, a New York–area HMO, was (in the words of one utilization review nurse), "When in doubt, carve it out." That is, deny coverage and wait for the patient to appeal.[8]

Doctors were frustrated by the cumbersome new system of checks, oversight, and denials. Whether looking out for the best interest of their patients or trying to get paid for services they had delivered, doctors hired new reimbursement specialists to negotiate by phone and mail with the managed care organizations and cajole and threaten them into approving reasonable coverage and fair fees. A six-person ophthalmology practice in Providence, Rhode Island, for example, enlarged its staff to include four full-time billing specialists, five transcribers, and a business manager. One of the physicians spoke nostalgically of the "clean claim"—the claim for insurance reimbursement that was approved without delay, negotiation, or obstruction. "It's like pornography," explained one of the doctors. "I don't know what it is, but I know it when I see it."[9] Other physicians gave up in disgust and limited their practices only to patients willing to pay cash for services.

Not all accusations of abuse were sound. One myth that circulated in the late 1990s was the presence of the "gag clause"—the stipulation that a physician being reimbursed by a managed care company could not speak frankly with a patient about treatment options that were unlikely to be reimbursed. Such accusations threatened to erode any remaining trust between patients and doctors, and even prompted members of Congress to investigate. The US General Accounting Office conducted an in-depth investigation into such practices and found the accusations baseless. Of the 529 HMOs it investigated, none included clauses in their contracts with physicians that restricted discussion of any treatment options with their patients.[10]

Managed care techniques in their many guises had been evolving for decades, but the 1990s were marked by the broad movement of patients into capitation arrangements. In the first four years of the decade, the number of HMO enrollees whose physicians were paid through capitation nearly doubled.[11] By 1996, 60 percent of all managed care plans (and nearly 70 percent of HMOs) used capitation for some portion of physician reimbursement, shifting the cost of imaging procedures, tests, and referrals to specialists (in whole or in part) to primary care physicians.

Capitation could work in a number of ways. Total capitation paid primary care physicians a set sum from which all cost of care must be deducted, usually up to a certain maximum amount per year at which point the managed care company indemnified the group using a reinsurance mechanism. More common was modified capitation, in which a portion of the monthly fee was withheld from the physician group to be awarded contingent on the group hitting certain targets for testing, specialist, and hospitalization costs. In this latter system, in which the physicians practiced austerity in an effort to earn a monthly bonus, the doctors had substantial financial incentive to defer tests or even withhold treatment. In one notorious incident, a California physician refused to order a sigmoidoscopy on a patient complaining of abdominal and rectal pain in an effort to capture part of the $450 cost of the test for his practice. The patient, later found to be suffering from colon cancer, died twenty months later.[12]

Capitation changed incentives for physicians. By shifting financial risk to doctors, for the first time doctors had strong financial incentives to keep their patients healthy, or at least not order tests and referrals they suspected would add little value. While historically patients had relied on physicians' commitment to professional standards, the underlying economics of the profession had worked constantly to undermine physicians' own best intentions. Third-party utilization review had created an antagonistic relationship between physician and payer without fundamentally altering a physician's incentives. But capitation changed the fundamental dynamics. One physician admitted that with capitation, "real managed care has finally arrived."[13]

Physicians struggled to adapt their practices to capitation terms, and many complained about falling incomes or new restrictions on their treatment options. Many complained that profiteering behavior by managed care companies was robbing them of their ability to provide high-quality care to patients, but others admitted that the real problem was that an era of wealth and professional freedom was coming to an end. One physician excoriated his colleagues for resisting accountability to parties "other than oneself and one's patients," while another wrote of doctors "whose incomes and professional power were nurtured by the open-checkbook fee-for-service system."[14]

Tales of extreme austerity in payment practices by managed care companies prompted President Bill Clinton and multiple members of Congress to propose various pieces of legislation all under the general rubric of a "patient's bill of rights." Though none passed, all of the bills proposed minimal required standards of care that managed care organizations must pay for, as well as various forms of transparency and disclosure to expose the conflicts of interest that capitation and bonuses imposed on physicians. Some of the proposals allowed patients to sue their managed care providers for denial of coverage that led to negative medical outcomes, and others mandated specific lengths of stay for obstetrical delivery, emergency visits, and access to specialists.[15] When Congress failed in these efforts, various state legislatures rushed in to reassure a concerned public that they would end the practice of "drive-by deliveries" and patient dumping.[16]

Doctors found practicing in a managed care environment frustrating and injurious to their income and suspected that it undermined their ability to deliver high-quality clinical care. Many illnesses and injuries were best treated as quickly as possible, and delay in some cases could mean permanent loss of function or even death. Marcia Angell, a long-time editor of the *New England Journal of Medicine* and a highly respected voice in the medical community, could hardly conceal her contempt for the managed care model when she wrote of the companies, "their financial success depends on doing as little for [the patients] as possible."[17] High-quality managed care companies, which might be genuinely committed to providing excellent medical care, were forced into price wars against companies that marketed low-priced premiums and were thus forced to deny care more aggressively.[18] In addition, the price pressures of managed care tended to dissuade physicians from providing charity care in ways they might have done in the past, disproportionately denying care to low-income communities. One survey of medical school deans showed that more than half believed that managed care pressures were heavily affecting traditionally underserved patient populations.[19]

Horrific anecdotes abounded: limbs lost to late diagnosis, joints set incorrectly because scans were not done in a timely fashion, cancer claiming a life because chemotherapy had not been started early enough. One nurse in California wrote of her odyssey through the managed care system after falling and injuring her wrist. After six months of delays and denials, during which she was diagnosed with a simple sprain and told to rest the joint, she paid cash to consult with a hand specialist who agreed to perform joint surgery in an effort to preserve the utility of the hand. Notably, her managed care company refused to reimburse her for the procedure. The worst part of the ordeal, admitted the woman, was the hand surgeon's regretful musing, "If you had seen me sooner, I could have ..."[20]

Managed care's effect on quality was hardly linear, however. For every horror story of botched diagnosis and needlessly delayed therapy, there were many other stories of unnecessary tests and procedures avoided, many of which carried their own risk. In California, for example, United Healthcare managed to sharply reduce the rate of cesarean sections by demanding that physicians delay epidurals until the laboring woman was dilated to five centimeters. The time delay increased discomfort, but allowed many women to avoid unnecessary abdominal surgery (the US cesarean rate was twice that of most European countries).

United Healthcare saved $4,000 on each cesarean section avoided, plus an additional two days of hospitalization, and the dangers of botched surgery were avoided as well.[21] Other managed care companies achieved lower rates of hysterectomies, CAT scans, and lower spine surgery, thereby allowing patients to avoid surgical risk and procedure-related injuries.

One question was whether nonprofit HMOs behaved any less rapaciously or provided care at higher quality than did for-profit HMOs. The question became moot in 1994, however, when the Blue Cross and Blue Shield Association, the national umbrella group for the nation's sixty-member organization, ruled that Blue Cross and Blue Shield plans need no longer register as nonprofits. Many of the plans, which were rapidly losing membership to profit-seeking HMOs, converted to for-profit status and shed state requirements that they price all premiums on a community-rated scheme. The largest of the plans, Empire Blue Cross and Blue Shield of New York, began converting in 1995, having lost over a third of its membership during the preceding three years. The initial public offering of the new for-profit company's stock in 2002 raised $417 million—one of the largest such offerings in the history of the health insurance industry. The new company, dubbed WellChoice, seemed to have lost any connection to the public ethos of its predecessor. It aggressively managed care, sought low-risk enrollment groups, and generally behaved as a profit-oriented managed care company would be expected to.[22]

By 1998, the climate had shifted. Many consumers demanded looser restrictions on their health plans, and lobbied employers to offer plans that allowed them to seek care out of network, or at the very least to consult with a specialist without first seeking permission from a gate-keeping primary care physician. Blue Shield of California, for example, created a new "open model" HMO in which all 290,000 of its members could consult with a specialist without receiving approval from a primary care provider first.[23] The looser preferred provider organization (PPO) and point of service (POS) plans that employers began to offer demanded a greater monthly premium payments than the more restrictive HMOs and often demanded higher annual deductibles and co-payments from their members, but people flocked to them. Wall Street, however, did not. The very tenets of cost control that had made HMOs so attractive to investors were being lost in the less restrictive arrangements, and traders lowered their estimates of the firms' future profitability. Aetna lost a third of its market value in the latter half of 1997, and Oxford lost even more. Managed care companies had been forced to enroll more physicians to give their customers greater choice in the medical marketplace, but with each new doctor they lost pricing leverage over other physicians in the plan. Between 1990 and 1997, the portion of managed care plans that allowed patients to seek care from out-of-network physicians rose from 36 percent to 80 percent.[24]

The movement of people to managed care had been so rapid through the 1990s that the industry lagged in understanding customer preferences. True, few were willing to pay the extraordinarily high premiums to purchase traditional indemnity polices after 1995, but it was true as well that many were willing to pay a modestly higher premium to gain the right to seek care out of network and bypass the primary physician gatekeeper. By 1998 the managed care industry was still adjusting to rapidly changing consumer preferences and still creating new products with the right mix of price, freedom, cost controls, and utilization review. The PPOs of 1998 fit more comfortably with the type of products most people demanded, but lacked much of the ability to control costs that had made HMOs so attractive to investors and employers a mere half-decade before. The world had changed rapidly in just a few years, and bizarrely the changes had been almost wholly unanticipated by the team that created the Clinton health plan.

Physicians Push Back

The rush to managed care depressed physician income from the mid-1990s. General practitioners lost 10 percent of their income during the period, and some specialists lost significantly more. Physicians turned to their professional associations and nascent physician unions to counter downward pressure from managed care organizations, but initially their efforts achieved little. Doctors still largely practiced in small partnerships, and they had few tools with which to respond. Moreover, aggressive recruiting of graduates of foreign medical schools into US residency programs, coupled with a substantially larger pool of US medical school graduates, undermined any efforts physicians made at negotiating with managed care companies. By the end of the decade, the nation had 261 doctors per 100,000 in population, when most experts recommended 145 to 185 as adequate.[25]

Doctors responded in different ways, ranging from simply producing inflated bills for managed care companies to unbundling services to hiring efficiency experts to manage their practices. Fifty-eight percent of physicians admitted that they would be willing to offer an insurance company "deliberate deceptive documentation," and many hired professional management companies to trim costs and grapple with insurers for higher reimbursement.[26] Some doctors took to capturing what had traditionally been revenue to hospitals by opening their own outpatient surgical suites, and others switched their practices to a "concierge" model in which patients paid between $5,000 and $20,000 annually for membership. The concierge model was morally odious; it cemented the distinction between first- and second-tier medicine that previously had been ill-defined and guaranteed that patients with disposable income could receive more attentive and personalized care than those without. Doctors who turned to the concierge model defended their decision by noting that the intention was not increasing their incomes but limiting their patient base to a volume small enough to allow them to practice higher quality medicine. In a sense, they were exchanging their mass-production model for an artisan one—guaranteed to be more professionally satisfying if not necessarily more lucrative.[27]

The most effective strategy with which physicians countered managed care was banding into large groups. In previous decades doctors had migrated from sole proprietorships to small partnerships, but now they began to aggregate into very large practices with dozens of physicians. Using a strategy one analyst described as "teaming up to keep the bullies from picking on us," doctors formed groups large enough to dominate local markets for medical services, and thus become "price makers" rather than "price takers."[28] Managed care companies, which previously had been able to play many small practice groups against each other, now had to negotiate with a handful of practice groups who could use their market share to force rates higher. The groups could use excess revenues to hire new physicians or purchase existing practices and thus solidify their hold on a local market. Large groups in urban areas proliferated in the 1990s; by the end of the decade nearly half of all physicians graduating from residency programs went to permanent salaried positions in either physician groups or managed care organizations.[29]

Large physician groups streamlined administrative and billing costs, purchased in bulk, distributed the costs of large pieces of medical equipment more broadly, and negotiated better malpractice rates. Physicians working for the groups took fewer (though more intensive) days of call, spent little time on practice administration, worried less about the ebb and flow of patient volume, and risked no capital in buying into a partnership. Physicians in the large groups could also extend their clinical knowledge by consulting with the many colleagues with whom they shared a work site and could refer their patients to specialists who were already part of the group.

The price physicians paid for joining the groups was substantial, however. Joining the group meant surrendering the hope of being one's own boss or owning one's own business. Even equity partners (in those groups organized as partnerships) found that their day-to-day work experience was more akin to that of a salaried employee. The professional managers of the large groups, in conjunction with a management committee of senior physicians, created volume and revenue targets for staff physicians. Staff physicians risked losing their annual bonuses should they fail to meet the targets.[30]

On the other hand, a certain portion of physicians preferred the regularity of salaried practice. Many appreciated the greater ease of balancing family obligations with a more dependable work schedule, and older physicians tended to appreciate the reduced call and the option to work part-time and pass part of their patient load to colleagues. Many primary care physicians found that their incomes actually rose with salaried practice, although the highest-paid specialists inevitably experienced substantial pay reductions with their forfeited partner draws. The model seemed stable, however, and its rapid growth through the 1990s suggested that the old sole proprietorships and even the small concierge models would be only a marginal part of medical care delivery in the future.

Closely related to the salaried physician at a large physician group was the hospitalist—an evolving job in which a primary care physician or internist, working on salary at a hospital, took charge of admitted patients, oversaw care, maintained close contact with the patients' primary care physicians, and discharged patients back to their primary care physicians. Hospitalists were hardly new—in England they had been the dominant provider of hospital-based care for a generation. But the model was relatively new to the United States, where physicians in private practice had long used local hospitals as their personal workshops.[31] Hospitalists developed closer relationships with nurses and other hospital-based clinicians, worked more closely with hospital administrators, and moved patients through the hospital more rapidly. In Denver, the local Kaiser affiliate began hiring many hospitalists in 1995 and was able to cut the average length of stay by a half day.[32]

Hospitalists tended to cooperate closely with emergency room triage teams and postoperative staff, and thus worked with more accurate information on specific patients. They combined the holistic orientation of primary care providers with the institutional familiarity of senior residents. Although the US medical community did not eagerly embrace the model, hospitalists promised to pay dividends in lower costs and better coordinated care.

Physicians responded successfully to the pressures that managed care imposed on their incomes and freedom, but many remained leery of the new landscape. Managed care radically transformed the incentives in medical practice and forced doctors to reconsider their priorities and commitments. Was the goal of medical practice to optimize patient outcomes within a constrained budget, or was it to simply do everything? Some physicians admitted that underlying their commitments to patient care was a commitment to self-preservation, purchased through a successful practice, community standing, and money. Others wrestled with the newly apparent tensions in medical practice and struggled to create balance.

Physicians expressed ambivalence about the new reality. While one study noted that 82 percent of doctors in 1999 were either "very satisfied" or "somewhat satisfied" being a doctor, most were quick to point out the ways managed care was degrading medical practice. That is, they were "satisfied" with their professional lot despite the pressures of managed care rather than because of it. One glum physician admitted that the word *frustrated* might be better replaced with *angry, dispirited,* and *hostile.* He wrote, "Would you expect good medical care from someone trained as an accountant? Have we sold our souls to this business devil, never having read the contract? Is this just? Can we continue seeing more and more patents to satisfy our fiscal managers, knowing that the quality of our work must suffer and that the sanctity of our oath to our patients is being violated?"[33]

When pressed, physicians admitted that they were being induced to ration care through financial incentives and threats of professional punishment. By 1998, nearly a fifth of all doctors faced some sort of financial incentive by a managed care company to undertreat, underrefer, underprescribe, or underhospitalize. Physicians were paid to boost "productivity" and ensure patient satisfaction, and were cautioned against bad-mouthing the managed care company.[34] Yet when asked candidly whether they were being paid to ration care, few could bring themselves to admit to it. "The word is so loaded that some cannot use

or hear it without thinking of policies that discriminate against vulnerable population groups," wrote two physicians at the University of
Pennsylvania. Rather, doctors tended to substitute euphemisms such as
"emphasizing truly beneficial services."[35]

Some physicians lashed out at the Kafkaesque tangle in which they
found themselves and condemned the perfidy of profit-seeking insurers.
"For-profit health care is essentially an oxymoron," wrote Bernard
Lown, a professor of cardiology at Harvard Medical School. "The moral
contradiction is beyond repair."[36] Others admitted that the dilemmas
were more subtle. Indemnity insurance had induced doctors to overtreat
in the interest of increasing their incomes, and many procedures had
generated extraordinary bills the patients were often unaware of. For
example, in vitro fertilization, which rapidly became popular through
the 1990s as women with fertility problems turned to the technique to
get pregnant, generated enormous bills for the budding IVF industry.
One study estimated that the average cost to produce a successful pregnancy using IVF was $67,000 per couple in the first round, rising to
$114,000 per couple in later rounds.[37] Thoughtful physicians admitted
their own fallibility and uncertainty, and questioned their ability to
discern how much value they were adding. It was difficult to appropriately value many medical procedures, and uncertainty in outcomes
only exacerbated the challenge. In a thoughtful essay in 1995, Jerome
Kassirer admitted, "The problem is that the marginal decisions—those
difficult choices about what is beneficial—often have little scientific
basis and are extremely difficult to make."[38]

Other physicians seemed more certain. Perhaps the most strident
critics of managed care were the married physician team of David
Himmelstein and Steffie Woolhandler. Himmelstein and Woolhandler
were appalled at the essential immorality of managed care incentives,
which in their words were "the inverse of fee-splitting." Whereas in the
past, money-grubbing doctors had created unsavory (and illegal) kickback arrangements with other providers in an effort to raise their incomes, under managed care agreements physicians signed a contract
wherein they agreed to not refer to other providers in the community in
an effort to raise their incomes. The arrangements, in Himmelstein and
Woolhandler's judgment, were equally unethical, as both put money
before a patient's interest. Managed care was actually worse, as it dissuaded doctors from treating certain patients at all, lest they be forced
into a capitated arrangement with a patient suffering from a chronic
disease. The two reported an incident in which the chief of a university

hospital warned his team that they could "no longer tolerate patients with complex and expensive-to-treat conditions being encouraged to transfer to our group."[39] That these inducements were often invisible to the patients only confused the matter more, as the patients were unaware of the incentives under which the physicians operated. The same had been true of fee splitting, of course. "In both instances," wrote Himmelstein and Woolhandler, "secrecy increases the ethical taint."[40]

Managed care impelled doctors to increase the volume of patients they saw and decrease the time they spent with each one: a pressure that exacerbated the trend toward dehumanizing patients. The heavy emphasis on basic sciences in medical training already seemed designed to strip young physicians of their intrinsic empathy and push them toward a more cerebral approach to patient care, but new financial pressures accelerated the transformation. One concerned medical observer suggested that molecular biology was actually driving a "wedge between the physician-to-be and his or her future patients," and Eric Cassell, a physician and highly respected public health scholar, suggested that young doctors worked under the erroneous assumption that medicine involved the "application of impersonal facts to an objective problem."[41]

Physicians rightfully valued their time, but as the 1990s wore on they seemed unwilling to take the time to dispense even rudimentary information to their patients. Various surveys conducted in the mid-1990s showed, for example, that physicians failed to ask patients about their symptoms, failed to solicit thoughts and opinions from patients, and failed to counsel patients on more holistic approaches to disease prevention, such as increasing sleep and exercise and eating better. In one fourth of instances in which doctors prescribed medicine, they failed to discuss potential side effects with patients. One survey found that physicians described the "best" patient as compliant, respectful, and reticent. Resigned patients admitted general levels of satisfaction with their physicians, but upon closer questioning admitted that "satisfaction" indicated that the care had been "functional." One psychologist who interviewed patients during this time concluded, "Patients may say they're satisfied because they walk into the doctor's office with low expectations about how personal the care will be—like an airline passenger who expects cramped seats and mediocre food but is satisfied if the plane arrives on time."[42]

Notably, the most dissatisfied patients were those suffering from difficult-to-treat chronic conditions. Patients with chronic headaches, lower back pain, torn ligaments, anxiety, depression, arthritis, and bowel ailments all reported levels of dissatisfaction with the medical system of 15 percent or more. Not coincidentally, it was precisely these types of ailments in which the scientific grounding of many doctors fell short and in which their time constraints became more pronounced. Patients suffering from chronic conditions required palliative care and reassurance, yet these services and sentiments were devalued under managed care payment schemes. Angry and dissatisfied patients responded in kind with demands for physician–patient relationships built on a quasi-colleague model of cooperative care rather than on "paternalistic benevolence," in the words of a sociologist studying the phenomenon.[43] Many physicians, who had spent years mastering the arcane intricacies of genetics, biochemical sequences, and molecular interactions, were bewildered by the demands and resisted them when they could.

Women doctors tended to come out on top in this time-pressed landscape. Though underrepresented in the surgical fields, women had entered primary care and internal medicine in large numbers starting in the early 1980s and tended to place more emphasis on communication and empathy. They were more willing to take extra time with patients, dispel misconceptions, and defuse stress. They tended to place more weight on a patient's social context and tended to dig deeper into a patient's reported health history and living situation. Even their body language spoke of validation and outreach when interacting with patients, with female physicians smiling more and using nonverbal cues to validate concerned patients.[44]

Hospitals Respond

The rush to managed care affected hospitals even more deeply than it did doctors. As managed care companies worked to squeeze costs from the system, they sharply reduced payments to hospitals, which in turn worked to discharge patients more quickly. Cities with too many hospitals found themselves with thousands of empty beds, superfluous nurses, and excess emergency rooms. Hospitals scrambled to adapt to the new fiscal environment, with more aggressive and creative institutions reinventing themselves as parts of integrated care networks with ancillary ambulatory clinics, surgical centers, and day hospitals.

Perhaps no city reeled from managed care as violently as Philadelphia. With six medical schools, eighty hospitals, and fourteen thousand doctors, the city was possibly the most medically oversupplied in the United States, and its old and independent hospitals had been slow to adopt to new pressures in the medical payment system. As managed care enrollment in Philadelphia swelled from 530,000 to 2.4 million between 1986 and 1995, the city's hospitals suffered declines. Inpatient hospital days during this period dropped from 5.2 million to 4.6 million per year, while operating margins for all hospitals dropped from 1.3 percent to 0.3 percent. By 1993, over a fourth of the city's hospitals were operating at a loss, and matters stood to get worse. Industry analysts predicted that managed care enrollment would rise to 3.3 million by 2000: nearly two-thirds of all area residents.[45]

Hospitals in other cities fared little better. The vaunted Beth Israel hospital in Boston, part of the Harvard Medical School teaching network, lost $100 million over two years.[46] In Los Angeles, the UCLA medical center cut its full-time staff by 25 percent to accommodate the drop in specialty reimbursement, which at times approached 60 percent, and in Rochester, Minnesota, the Mayo Clinic responded by developing a network of feeder clinics and smaller hospitals throughout Minnesota and Wisconsin and opening satellite facilities in Arizona and Florida. UCLA also sharply reduced the number of incoming residents in its specialty training programs, and many hospitals looked to slash purchasing and labor costs or reduce nursing ratios on their wards. One scholar of the US health system noted that many of the nation's most famous and prestigious tertiary care hospitals had fat "marbled through the system like a prime steak."[47]

Overall, in the latter half of the 1990s the nation lost 370 emergency rooms (out of 4,600), although the closures were not evenly spread. Rural areas lost 11 percent of all of their emergency rooms, and heavily oversupplied coastal cities lost even more. Massachusetts, for example, lost a fourth of all of its hospitals in less than a decade, and nearly a third of its hospital beds. In some cities, hospital occupancy rates went from 68 percent (where it had stood for decades) to nearly 95 percent, causing queues and complicated patient transfers. At many hospitals around the country, six-hour wait times at emergency rooms were not uncommon.[48]

Hospitals responded with a variety of cost-cutting techniques, the most prominent of which was sharply reduced lengths of stay (LOSs).

Throughout the country, in the late 1990s, hospitals reduced the standard LOS for an uncomplicated vaginal birth to twenty-four hours, earning it the sobriquet of "drive-by delivery."[49] Patients recovering from procedures and conditions of all types found themselves discharged on aggressive schedules, with firm dictates to call if conditions changed. One veteran nurse admitted that patient care had become "an exercise in frustration."[50] Rather than ascertain that a helpful family member be present for aftercare, hospitals now recommended home visits from nurses and paramedics to help with remaining complications. Martha Griffin, a nurse at Brigham and Women's Hospital in Boston, described the situation: "Patients used to leave the hospital because they were ready to leave. Now the goal is to get them out, to move patients along the continuum, whether they are ready to go or not. . . . Today we are sending people home who need complicated wound care. They have stitches in their chest and leg where they were cut open or drains were put in. They have staples in their chest. They have wounds with a high risk of infection. . . . What we are doing is turning the home into a hospital."[51]

Hospitals cut cost by downgrading the quality of caretaking personnel they hired. Registered nurses, whose median salaries had doubled over the previous decade, were a particularly attractive target for cost-cutting, and around the country hospitals worked to either reduce the number of bedside nurses or replace RNs with LPNs or patient care "technicians" who might only have a few weeks of training before being placed on the wards. Hospitals ceased these "deskilling" efforts (as they became known) only after multiple complaints from patients and physicians or, in the case of several hospitals, threats of nursing walkouts. At both Presbyterian Hospital in New York and Brigham and Women's in Boston, negotiations for new nursing contracts broke down over provisions to replace hundreds of nurses with technicians.[52]

Equally odious was the growing practice of "dumping," wherein private hospitals rapidly transferred uninsured (and potentially nonpaying) patients from their emergency rooms to local public hospitals. The practice was illegal yet rarely punished. Data from the US Department of Health and Human Services found that of ninety-one hospitals found to be dumping in 1994, only five were fined. Probably many more hospitals engaged in the practice but went undetected.[53]

More systemically, hospitals began to bind themselves together into partnerships, networks, and PHOs. Across the nation, stand-alone hospitals, often pillars of nonprofit and public service within their communities, sought out partners with which to merge to create integrated care networks. Some seemed obvious—a number of small, financially tottering hospitals and medical schools in Philadelphia merged to create Allegheny Health—whereas others seemed shocking, irrational, or both. In Boston, in the merger of the century, Massachusetts General and Brigham and Women's merged to create Partners; in New York, Mount Sinai and New York University attempted to create a system to dominate the East Side of Manhattan. In Boston (again), Beth Israel merged with New England Deaconess to create Beth Israel Deaconess (an ecumenical marriage of the city's Jewish and Methodist hospitals), and in the San Francisco Bay area Stanford began negotiations with the hospital of the University of California at San Francisco. Still other hospitals began to purchase physician practices in an effort to guarantee a steady supply of patients.

The mergers were driven more by panic than by rational business modeling. Many hospitals looked to create nothing more than a bigger system, assuming that after the merger economies of scale would naturally present themselves. Others thought more carefully, as they sought to make in-roads into satellite communities in an effort to ally themselves with feeder hospitals, which would refer more complicated cases to the tertiary care academic hospital which usually lay at the heart of the new system. Some mergers foundered on poor planning, inconsistent fit, or culture clashes, while other newly merged institutions found that they could advantageously combine some of their functions while maintaining independence along other lines.[54] In general, the hospitals that successfully dominated a market after merging fared better, as did those that aggressively cut beds and nurses and combined administrative units. Academic hospitals tended to have the hardest time, given their decentralized decision-making systems and their many grant-funded fiefdoms. One savvy observer noted that the problem of PHOs was that the patients (in the purchased practice) who were most familiar with the hospital services were, of course, "exactly the people you don't want to sign up in a health plan."[55]

Managed care drove some nonprofits into the arms of large, for-profit hospital companies, which eagerly bought up the financially healthiest nonprofit hospitals during these years. Between 1980 and 1995, 270 nonprofit hospitals converted to for-profit status either on their own or following purchase by a for-profit chain. This frenzy of conversion raised the percentage of all US hospitals that ran on a for-profit basis from 13 percent (where it had lain in the forty years following World War II) to 18 percent in 1995.[56]

Conversion to for-profit status worried many industry observers for fear that the new hospitals would ignore their historical commitments to their host communities. Nonprofit hospitals tended to use their profitable services to subsidize uncompensated care, education, outreach, prevention, and certain services for the chronically ill. But data that emerged from the conversions in the late 1990s suggested that the communal losses were not as great as expected. Several researchers found that uncompensated care did not decline sharply after hospitals converted to for-profit status, suggesting that the hospitals that had been targeted by the for-profit chains were frequently those providing the least amount of charity care to begin with.[57] Rather, what the newly converted for-profit hospitals showed themselves adept at was aggressively cutting costs and raising billings in an effort to force their new properties to produce greater profits. Columbia/HCA, for example, the largest and most profitable of the chains, cut or reduced hours at nearly a quarter of all positions in a four-hospital chain within four months of purchasing it, while forcing up charges and pressuring Medicare for better reimbursement. A research team at Dartmouth Medical School estimated that in regions dominated by for-profit hospitals, Medicare spending was nearly 15 percent higher, whereas in the thirty-three areas in which the dominant hospital converted from nonprofit to for-profit status between 1989 and 1995, Medicare spending rose nearly 50 percent faster than in other regions.[58] At a time when many nonprofit hospitals were losing money or barely breaking even, Columbia/HCA posted profits of 20 percent.[59]

Perhaps the greatest losers in the shuffle were public hospitals, which tended to be funded by a combination of local and state funds drawn off of general tax revenues. These workhorses of the charity world suffered substantially as managed care pressure on hospitals made Medicaid reimbursement more attractive to private hospitals. With declining revenues from Medicaid, the percentage of patients treated by public hospitals who had no coverage (and virtually no private funds) rose to 33 percent. Moreover, many of these patients suffered from chronic, difficult-to-treat ailments, such as AIDS, substance abuse, tuberculosis, and mental disorders. Cash-strapped cities cut subsidies to public hospitals in response to the exodus of Medicaid patients to private hospitals, and many of the hospitals consolidated or closed down completely. From 1980 to 1995, the number of public hospitals in the United States declined from 1,800 to 1,390, and the number of beds shrank by 20 percent. Though part of the shrinkage was an appropriate response to the movement of Medicaid patients to private hospitals, the public hospitals emerged from this period generally weaker and less appealing to talented nurses and physicians.[60]

Teaching hospitals, which hosted the nation's residency programs and most of its clinical research, faced special challenges. Long the recipient of Medicare subsidies to offset their expenditures on graduate medical education, these unique institutions were larded with specialists and expensive patients. A study done by the healthcare consulting firm Lewin/VHI, showed that costs per patient were 30–40 percent higher in teaching hospitals than in nonteaching hospitals.[61] Teaching hospitals had come to expect the subsidies to cover their unique costs and were accustomed to receiving generous treatment from private health insurers as well, but managed care and reductions to Medicare under the 1997 Balanced Budget Act were putting an end to the largesse. The combined pressure threatened the solvency of academic hospitals. The accounting and consulting firm Price Waterhouse estimated that a fourth of the nation's teaching hospitals would be bankrupt by 2005.[62]

The answer for the teaching hospitals, as was true for nonteaching hospitals, was to merge and cut. The new Partners system created by the merger of Massachusetts General and Brigham and Women's reduced the number of its beds from 1,700 to 1,514. In Washington, both Georgetown and George Washington University Medical Schools sold their hospitals. Many academic health centers around the country created physician practices wherein they paid their clinical faculty fixed salaries not to teach and do research but to treat patients who would subsequently be admitted to the teaching hospital.

Teaching hospitals were particularly vulnerable to the pressures of managed care because of their heavy use of specialty physicians and services. Congress grappled with its role in preserving the unique institutions and generally allowed market forces to have their way with the system. Some members of Congress representing rural areas moved to create target numbers of primary and specialty training slots in an effort to ensure that rural areas had access to adequate numbers of primary care physicians. Representatives of urban areas, with their many specialist practices and multiple medical schools and teaching hospitals, pushed back. Senator Daniel Patrick Moynihan (D-NY) was particularly eloquent in defending specialty residency slots from congressionally

mandated cuts. "This invites the wrath of gods," he lectured his colleagues. "This invites the death, the closing of a great moment of medical
discovery, unprecedented on Earth. . . . This is, if I may say . . . a sin
against the Holy Ghost."[63]

Underlying the issue of subsidies to teaching hospitals was a general
debate over quality. Were all hospitals equally capable? If not, should
reimbursement be adjusted so that higher quality hospitals received
more generous reimbursements? As far back as 1979, Harold Luft led
an investigation showing that hospitals differed substantially in the
mortality rates of their patients, even controlling for the health of the
patient population. The best hospitals tended to be those with the highest
volume for a given procedure—direct evidence that practice made
perfect.[64] In the years since, multiple studies had shown substantial
differences in mortality rates, recidivism rates, and success following
discharge between different hospitals, with the best hospitals posting
morbidity rates 15 percent lower than the worst hospitals for the same
surgical procedures.[65] A study done in the late 1990s showed that the
hospitals ranked as among the "best" by the newsmagazine *US News and
World Report* had significantly lower mortality for heart attack patients.[66]

In fact, the relationship of cost to quality was unclear. Through the
late 1990s, as hospitals sought to cut costs in response to the pressures
of managed care reimbursement, some actions seemed to affect quality
while others did not. Cutting nurse-to-patient ratios or deskilling ward
staff brought patient complaints, overly long wait times, and general
frustration from attending physicians. Hospitals retreated quickly from
these efforts, despite lacking outcome data indicating that patients
were suffering. But in response to managed care, hospitals also cut
whole units that had been unprofitable, resulting in institutions less
adept at serving the needs of a whole community but not necessarily
less capable of serving the needs of an individual patient. The word
quality itself came under attack, as industry analysts questioned whether
reputations for particularly good service, food, or decor were reasonable
indicators for evaluating hospital care. The only truly relevant metric
was recovery and morbidity rates, and no data in the late 1990s showed
a rise in these rates concomitant with cuts in reimbursement. Managed
care made hospitals meaner, less pleasant, and less charitable, but not
necessarily less salubrious.

Large-scale movement to managed care initially restrained healthcare costs. Healthcare inflation dropped to just above the inflation rate of the consumer price index, and insurance premiums stayed nearly flat through the mid-1990s. By 1998, however, cracks were becoming apparent. As consumers pressured their employers to place them into less restrictive managed care systems (such as PPOs and POS plans), managed care organizations found that they were less able to hold down costs. Inflation began to creep back into the system, and premiums rose by 7 percent that year. The following year, some HMOs raised their premiums by 15 percent, and employers who moved their employees to PPO plans saw premium hikes of 40 percent. The magical cost reductions that managed care had worked on healthcare delivery appeared to have been transitory.[67]

At the same time, the number of people who lacked health insurance rose rapidly. The portion of those under age 65 who held private health insurance coverage dropped from 75 percent in 1989 to 71 percent in 1995, and the percentage of children (under age 18) covered by private insurance dropped from 73 percent to 66 percent over the same period.[68] Altogether, nearly 15 percent of all citizens lacked insurance by the end of the decade. Individuals who were self-employed or contracted independently with large companies were particularly prone to losing insurance coverage.

The US public did not make rectifying the problem a high priority. Some political analysts suggested that uninsurance rates would need to hit 30 percent before the public demanded broad reform. In Texas and California, for example, official uninsured rates were 20 percent, and total uninsured rates (if one counted undocumented aliens) probably broached 30 percent, yet neither state seemed inclined to reform its insurance system.[69] The fact that the uninsured were disproportionately the unemployed and the working poor, who tended to be unheard in electoral politics, compounded the problem.

At the same time, states were moving greater numbers of their Medicaid enrollees into managed care plans, either through choice or by fiat. Various changes to Medicaid enacted under the 1997 Balanced Budget Act allowed states to experiment with managed care contracting for their Medicaid enrollees in an effort to either save money, better coordinate care, or both.[70] As in the general population, the percentage of beneficiaries enrolled in managed care rose sharply, reaching 40 percent of the entire Medicaid population (12.6 million) by 1998. Costs came down and quality appeared to improve. States found that Medicaid enrollees whose care was managed were less likely to resort to the local emergency room for nonurgent visits and were more likely to have a primary care physician to coordinate their care.

By 1998, nearly thirty million Americans lacked health insurance of any sort. Although unemployment had declined substantially under President Clinton, the economy seemed incapable of providing the sorts of full-time jobs with benefits that had been the backbone of private insurance coverage for a generation. The situation seemed to invite federal intervention, yet the Clinton administration was reluctant to make a second effort at comprehensive health legislation. Rather, it turned to incremental reform.

8

Quantity and Quality

More Is Not Necessarily Better

Years of rising healthcare costs raised the question as to why the sector seemed so inclined to excessive inflation. A number of economists and planners suspected that a major factor in healthcare inflation was the endless stream of new pharmaceuticals, procedures, and medical devices that flooded the market and demanded reimbursement from all payers. Whereas in most industries technological innovation tended to reduce prices through competition and manufacturing efficiency (demonstrated notably in the computing and telecommunications sectors), in healthcare innovations tended to produce more expensive products and procedures, which drove out cheaper established therapies.

The conundrum proved more complex under close examination. Many innovations, particularly new drugs, created tremendous savings in society, although these savings were sometime obscured. The oral polio vaccines developed in the 1950s, for example, saved an estimated $30 billion annually in polio treatment and incalculable savings in regained labor, despite incurring the cost of universal inoculation. Lithium treatment reduced hospitalization costs for bipolar disorders by $145 billion between 1970 and 1995. A vaccine to prevent bacterial meningitis probably saved between $350 and $450 million annually. Even greater savings were produced by fluoridating water ($10 billion annually) and treating stomach ulcers with antibiotics ($600 to $800 million annually).[1]

For all of the savings wrought by new treatments, many drugs and medical devices proved inflationary. Newly patented drugs drove older generic drugs out of the market despite frequently being little better. New devices allowed for complex procedures that could not have been attempted previously, thus increasing the overall healthcare bill. New procedures necessitated hospitalization, postoperative care, skilled nursing, and (often) follow-up drug regimens, which all added to the cost of the procedure.

A good example of the phenomenon was endoscopic surgery—a new technique that used cameras and remote-controlled tools to allow for very small incisions in surgery. On its face, the new technique would seem to reduce costs. Patients recovered quicker than before, with fewer postoperative complications and less pain. But the tools required to perform endoscopic surgery cost between $35,000 and $50,000 (in contrast to standard surgical tools, which might cost a tenth as much) and required precise sterilization techniques between procedures. Whereas standard surgical tools could be quickly sterilized in an inexpensive autoclave, endoscopic tools (which could not tolerate the heat of the autoclave) required immersion in a precisely controlled chemical bath housed in a "smart" chemical sterilizer which cost $16,000.[2] In the end, endoscopic procedures cost substantially more than did traditional procedures, even after factoring in the reduced recovery times.

Researchers working in both university and industrial labs produced innovations largely separate from cost considerations. Their training oriented them toward molecular discoveries and procedural breakthroughs. They were rewarded for producing innovative results (in the case of academic researchers) or marketable products (in the case of industrial scientists). In no case were scientists encouraged to consider the potential cost of their innovations to the ultimate consumers. Donna Shalala, secretary of the Department of Health and Human Services, bewailed the problem, postulating, "What we need to do is to get scientists to think about the more appropriate use of that technology." Kenneth Shine, president of the Institute of Medicine, agreed: "As scientists we have never taken more than a casual interest in how these pricing and application decisions happen. I don't think that the average scientist is going to spend a lot of time on health care costs."[3] Although it was nearly impossible to estimate the true cost of new technologies to the nation's healthcare payers, Joseph Newhouse, an economist at

Harvard's Kennedy School, estimated the annual bill at $30 billion in the mid-1990s.[4]

Pharmaceutical companies exacerbated the problem of inflationary innovations by drawing closer to academic medicine in the 1990s. Whereas previously there had been a fairly clean divide between academic and applied biomedical researchers, corporate subsidies to scholarly researchers and institutions undermined the boundary and spurred university scientists to work more closely with potential end users of their data. A study in the late 1990s revealed that 90 percent of all authors who had published research in peer-reviewed journals about prescription drugs in the previous year had received corporate funds to aid their research. The American Heart Association, the umbrella group supporting research in cardiac disease, received $11 million in donations from the biotechnology company Genentech and subsequently recommended a product produced by Genentech, while an editor at the *British Journal of Psychiatry* was paid $4,000 annually by a company that produced a drug the editor endorsed in a research paper.[5]

Practicing physicians had been compromising their professional autonomy with pharmaceutical sales representatives for decades, but now physician-scientists began to similarly give way. Pharmaceutical companies went beyond the traditional free sandwiches and pizza for medical students and residents, and free dinners, trips, and giveaways to practicing physicians, and worked to influence academic medicine. The watchdog agency Public Citizen estimated that the "medical education services suppliers industry" in one year funneled $115 million to grand rounds, $114 million to symposia, $64 million to advisory boards, and $60 million to publications.[6] Concerned physicians described the phenomenon of faculty at university medical centers "selling their patients to industry," and one rueful academic psychiatrist admitted, after taking corporate stipends, "I deluded myself into thinking I was educating physicians and not being swayed by sponsors."[7] One cynical physician answered the rhetorical question, "Is academic medicine for sale?" with a simple answer: "No. The current owner is very happy with it."[8]

Ties between industry and academic medicine induced clinical researchers to alter data, make clinical recommendations in favor of certain products, and even avoid certain types of research programs altogether if they might potentially endorse products or procedures at odds with a sponsor's interest. Tom Bodenheimer, a researcher at UCSF, reported that clinical researchers who received corporate funds were more likely to report results favoring a product produced by the sponsor, while other researchers pointed out the general bias in clinical research away from holistic and low-impact formulations and toward pharmacologically intensive regimens.[9] Marcia Angell editorialized, "House officers should buy their own pizza, and hospitals should pay them enough to do so. . . . Academic medical centers should be wary of partnerships in which they make available their precious resources of talent and prestige to carry out research that serves primarily the interests of the companies. That is ultimately a Faustian bargain."[10]

Pharmaceutical firms proved to be masterful at increasing sales volume and profits. In the latter half of the 1990s, the ten largest drug manufacturers produced annual profits of roughly 20 percent of revenues, making the industry the most profitable in the nation.[11] Companies jealously guarded their monopolies and worked hard to prolong the period under which new molecules were protected by patents. They were creative in developing molecules with very minor deviations from existing ones, which could be patented anew and pushed out to replace older molecules reaching the end of their patented lives. Their marketing efforts continued to expand, absorbing 40 percent of all industry expenditures by 2000, compared with the 20 percent spent on basic research.

Drug companies posted a major regulatory victory in 1997 when the Food and Drug Administration allowed them to advertise prescription drugs on television for the first time, provided they share information about risks associated with the drugs.[12] The regulatory change paved the way for a tremendous upsurge in direct-to-consumer advertising. Between 1991 and 2000, pharmaceutical companies increased their spending on advertising from $51 million to $2.3 billion.[13] At the same time, sales reps increased the intensity of their efforts with physicians, distributing sample packages of medications in addition to the usual pens, notepads, tote bags, and golf balls. The free samples, packaged with corporate icons and drug names prominently displayed, were particularly alluring to patients (and therefore physicians) although one doctor admitted, "I feel like I am handing my patients a billboard."[14]

TV ads subtly changed the doctor–patient relationship. Under their influence, increasing numbers of people went to their doctors already knowing which drugs they wanted to try. Physicians faced the difficult dilemma of prescribing what they thought most appropriate and cost-effective, versus pleasing insistent patients. Larry Sasich, a researcher with Public Citizen, reflected that the ads created an adversarial relationship between doctor and patient, with the doctor now serving as a barrier between the patient and her desired product. Sasich noted, "What you're basically asking the doctor to do is unsell the drug that sounds so good to the patient. That's difficult."[15]

Drug ads worked, particularly for lifestyle drugs—those designed to alleviate nonserious symptoms. Claritin, for example, the most heavily advertised drug in the country, posted a 21 percent increase in sales the year after its manufacturer, Schering-Plough, began advertising the drug on television. Certain branded drugs, notably Vioxx and Celebrex, increased market share rapidly despite offering scant better treatment than generic pain relievers during the same period. Overall, branded drug sales increased by 12 percent annually in the years following the legalization of TV ads for prescription medications.

Industry advocates defended the ads by claiming that sales increases were due partly to previously undiagnosed patients seeking help. The claim was impossible to prove. More patients sought treatment for depression, anxiety, incontinence, acid reflux, overactive bladder, seasonal allergies, and joint pain, and the increase in sales probably followed from increased awareness of potential treatments for these ailments. But doctors expressed concern that patients were now seeking relatively expensive care for minor ailments which may have been treated in the past with over-the-counter medicine or lifestyle changes. People were susceptible to drug advertising, just as they were susceptible to most types of advertising, and physicians were loathe to resist their entreaties.[16]

The net effect of changes in the drug industry in the late 1990s was probably nil. Generally drugs were very cost effective. At the same time, new brand-name drugs were often no more effective than existing generics and were always far more expensive. Under the relentless onslaught of drug advertising (in 1999 Schering-Plough spent more money advertising Claritin than Coca-Cola spent advertising Coke), patients sought treatment for ailments that might have previously gone untreated. The effect on health, functioning, and the nation's health bill was difficult to determine.

Evidence-Based Medicine

Although US physicians trained using similar curricula and protocols, they differed in their success rates. Studies showed that doctors in some parts of the country achieved successful outcomes at many times the rate of physicians in other parts of the country, and even within the same region the rate of negative outcomes for a given procedure could differ 10-fold between different institutions. The leader on these studies was John Wennberg, the director of the Center for Evaluative Clinical Sciences at Dartmouth Medical School, who (with colleagues) published the *Dartmouth Atlas of Health Care*, which detailed the high degree of variation in diagnosis and treatment across different parts of the country. Dartmouth researchers estimated that over 40 percent of variance in treatment disparities between regions was caused by the number of doctors and hospitals in an area rather than the frequency of a particular disease or diagnosis.[17] In one study, for example, researchers asked 135 practicing physicians to describe their approach to treating a urinary tract infection; the physicians responded with eighty-two different treatments.[18] A huge number of treatments—perhaps as many as 85 percent— had never been validated with clinical trials, and a growing body of evidence suggested that a significant percentage of all treatments caused more harm than good.[19]

These variations in treatment raised troubling questions of quality. Physicians and patients had a hard time actually defining quality, but the Institute of Medicine produced a reasonable response to the dilemma in 1990, defining *quality* as the "degree to which health services for individuals and populations increase the likelihood of desired health outcomes and are consistent with current professional knowledge."[20] In theory all physicians aspired to this standard, yet through the 1990s government agencies became increasingly concerned that the public had no way of measuring the quality of physicians' output. The Health Care Financing Administration, working with the National Committee for Quality Assurance, responded by creating the Health Plan Employer Data and Information Set (HEDIS) from which independent researchers and state-level agencies could create various physician "report cards" by which the public and payers could judge the efficacy of various clinicians. From 1989, states issued report cards on doctors' success rates in treating different ailments, although different states and medical watchers used different criteria for their grades. The report cards goaded physicians to practice medicine more consistently and carefully, or at least update their skills and knowledge by attending continuing education courses.[21]

Differing health status for different patients, as well as differing disease intensities, had always made defining healthcare quality difficult.

How did an assessor rate two different doctors who treated different patient groups, with different levels of pathologies, compliance behaviors, home lives, support systems, and access to nutrition? Private hospitals provided routine surgical procedures to wealthy, well-insured, and generally healthy patients and posted vastly superior results to public hospitals, which attempted risky procedures on poorly insured and sicker patients. One could hardly judge the quality of either the doctors or the institutions based on outcomes alone. But in the early years of the twenty-first century, a number of health scholars began to urge the industry to adopt standard practices based on clinical research generally known as evidence-based medicine (EBM). If widely adopted, EBM promised to impel doctors to do for patients not what they thought was best but what data indicated was best.[22]

EBM faced huge obstacles. Collecting data was expensive and difficult as patients had to voluntarily agree to having data collected and processed by researchers, who would then make complex models of the outcomes of millions of medical cases. Research teams needed to be paid over years as they collected and analyzed data, and the funds could hardly be drawn from manufactures of products that were under review. Once data indicated clear treatment protocols, convincing doctors to abandon standard treatment practices and adopt new evidence-based procedures was difficult. In one well-known case, many cardiologists refused to prescribe beta-blockers for survivors of heart attacks for 25 years after an initial study revealed that the drugs could substantially reduce the chance of a second heart attack. The change was simply too much for confident and established cardiologists.[23]

Not only did doctors resist altering their practices to comply with new outcomes research, they were vulnerable to suasion by pharmaceutical representatives and paid speakers at medical conferences. Required attendance at continuing medical education may have actually exacerbated the problem, as many of the speakers at these seminars were sponsored by pharmaceutical and device firms and were thus pressured to endorse certain medical interventions. Decentralized as US medicine was, no umbrella body existed to issue practice guidelines and benchmarks for clinical work. In 2004, no private insurance company offered to pay bonuses for superior outcomes.[24]

The most promising work in the field came from the United Kingdom, whose National Health Service (NHS) had mandated the creation of the National Institute for Health and Clinical Excellence (NICE) in 1999. NICE collected and analyzed research on clinical outcomes to issue guidelines and directives for the NHS to follow. Procedures and drugs approved by NICE were required to be offered by the NHS (although nonrecommended procedures could be funded at the discretion of regional directors). In the first decade of its existence, NICE issued ratings for hundreds of different technologies, tests, procedures, and drugs and issued nonrecommendations for many newer, more expensive formulations and procedures. The result was cheaper, more efficacious medicine delivered consistently throughout the country.

Other nations followed suit, with Germany establishing the Institute for Quality and Efficiency, and France and Australia starting similar agencies. All worked to collect existing data and perform meta-analyses producing clinical "benchmarks," which physicians were strongly encouraged to follow. The United States established a similar agency, the Agency for Healthcare Research and Quality (AHRQ), in 1989, but it could only produce guidelines and informational press releases and lacked enforcement powers, even for doctors taking Medicare patients.[25]

If quality was elusive, one thing that almost everyone could agree on was the need to avoid outright errors. An *error* was defined as a medical diagnosis or therapeutic intervention that clearly ran counter to agreed-on medical norms and procedures. Errors had historically been ignored in medicine; few researchers studied the problem before the end of the twentieth century. In 1999, the Institute of Medicine shocked many people when it published *To Err Is Human*, which offered detailed descriptions of errors made in the US healthcare system.[26] The report claimed that forty-four thousand Americans died annually from medical errors, which made errors more deadly than AIDS, car crashes, or breast cancer. Other investigators estimated that medical errors cost the country $500 billion each year: the equivalent (in the words of one researcher) of "three jumbo jet crashes every two days."[27]

Erroneous healthcare was clearly poor-quality healthcare, yet exposing errors was difficult. In 2004, few doctors used electronic records, and those who did use them did not centralize records on any one system or server. While the nation had records of Medicare payments and hospital admissions, it had no comprehensive records of ambulatory care, nor a code for a specific error. Doctors and hospitals had every incentive to hide errors rather than publicize them, and many errors were ultimately inconsequential.

Moreover, simply using errors as a proxy for quality was unwise. Although erroneous medicine was bad medicine, good medicine was more than simply the absence of errors. Good medicine was correct medicine, but it also optimized potential outcomes while minimizing costs and risks. Good medicine used the least intrusive, most established, least costly intervention to produce an expected outcome. The United States had produced a medical system that was capable of inordinate responses to unusual and extreme challenges but by other measures tended to use cumbersome, intrusive, and expensive therapeutics and procedures when simpler ones could be expected to work as well. Establishing benchmarks, as was being done by the AHRQ, was a helpful start, but mandated compliance with the benchmarks would take longer.

9

Ethical Wrangling

Extreme Medicine

For a very long time, the primary barrier to physicians achieving optimal results was capacity; doctors were constrained by their own inability to control bleeding, halt infection, excise a tumor, constrain a cancer, or repair broken tissue. Physicians and biomedical scientists tirelessly expanded their own capacities to heal, leveraging research, technology, drugs, tests, and surgical techniques. Always the limiting factor had not been the desire to heal but the limits of the doctor's ability.

In the late 1960s, physicians and others began to question the ethical propriety of healing, even when the capacity to do so existed. New technologies and techniques, many aimed at providing treatment at the beginning and end of life, raised questions about the appropriate role of medicine in ending or prolonging life. Infants who in the past would likely have died were frequently able to survive through the use of highly efficient incubators and neonatal intensive care. At the elderly end of the spectrum, equipment such as respirators and feeding tubes could sustain a human life into perpetuity, even in the absence of cognitive function.

The new state of the living dead ("brain dead" or "permanent vegetative state") became horrifyingly clear to the many people observing the case of Karen Ann Quinlan, a young woman from New Jersey who descended into a narcotics-induced coma in early 1975 but was sustained for years afterward on a ventilator and feeding tube. Ethical and religious thinkers debated her case at length. Were doctors compelled to continue to care for a body that showed no hope of recovery and appeared to be essentially dead? Was there an ethical distinction between "pulling the plug"—that is, actively taking her off life support—and refusing to put her on life support in the first place? At an even more basic level, did medicine or society even have an accepted definition of death?[1] Amitai Etzioni, a sociologist at Columbia University and one of the first academics to seriously engage these ideas, wrote in 1974, "How long should we keep the body of our father, mother, or perhaps our daughter or son, functioning once the brain is defunct? Should 'heroic' measures be taken on behalf of a child born to us, unequipped to live without such interventions, and—at best—condemned to a life of *severe* impairments?"[2]

At the same time, late-term abortion techniques such as hysterotomy raised troubling questions as to when a fetus became a baby. Was it at a certain weight? A moment of viability? The dawn of cognition? The question was troubling for all, regardless of one's personal views on abortion, and seemed to render physicians incapable of practicing their craft. As survival age for premature infants declined from thirty-five to twenty-eight weeks, and babies weighing as little as 1.7 pounds could be maintained in an incubator and nurtured to health, the field of obstetrics found itself in a quandary. One New York physician said, "We have the capacity to treat fetuses that are sick. But we also have the capacity to abort those mothers who elect to abort. Here, two separate stages of obstetrics meet."[3]

Even more alarming were new techniques of testing the health of an infant in utero, using the new procedure amniocentesis and the growing potential of genetic screening. Ethicists worried about the future potential for genetic engineering, cloning, selective abortion, and sex selection. Though these were not realistic in 1975, none seemed far off. Was it ethical for doctors to help women abort fetuses simply because they were the wrong sex or might prove to be mentally disabled? Was it permissible to grow fetuses outside of the womb and implant them in an unrelated mother, as had been successfully accomplished in 1974 in a laboratory in England? Already a scientist at Oxford, John Gurdon, had replaced the nucleus of a frog cell with a nucleus from another frog cell.

One observer wrote caustically about the ability to "skim the trash out of the gene pool by determining who shall be permitted to breed."[4]

Such concerns drew governmental and professional responses. Senator Walter Mondale (D-MN) pushed through legislation in 1972 to create a National Advisory Commission on Health, Science, and Society to address ethical and policy questions raised by new technologies and capacities. Mondale had attempted to create the body since 1967, and his initial efforts had met with derision from the physician community. But by 1972 enough progress had been made in beginning- and end-of-life techniques to force the issue. At nearly the same time, the National Academy of Sciences created the Committee on the Life Sciences and Social Policy directed by a well-regarded biochemist from the University of Chicago, Leon Kass. Daniel Calahan, a theologian interested in medical issues, created the Institute of Society, Ethics and the Life Sciences in Hastings-on-Hudson, New York. These organizations all focused their work on questions of sex selection, in vitro fertilization, life-sustaining treatments, genetic engineering, cloning, and abortion.[5]

Even more troubling for the budding field of bioethics were reports emerging in the 1970s of abuses in the US human research program. Such reports were hardly new—the horrors of Joseph Mengele's research on concentration camp inmates during World War II had spurred the world to create ethical research protocols at several conferences in the 1950s and 1960s, all of which placed the integrity and autonomy of the research subject first. Yet such guidelines had failed to wholly oust unethical practices. The US Public Health Service was humiliated by revelations in 1972 of research in Tuskegee, Alabama, on the effects of untreated tertiary syphilis in four hundred black men, despite the fact that the disease has been easily curable since 1950 with an ordinary course of penicillin.[6] Similarly, in 1973, a proposal to implant electrodes in the brain stems of violent criminals at the Lafayette Clinic in Detroit in an effort to neurologically castrate them provoked a lawsuit and widespread outrage, despite the fact that the prisoners had consented to the surgery in exchange for the possibility of parole. Mentally disabled children in the Willowbrook State Hospital in Staten Island, New York, were deliberately exposed to hepatitis to test the efficacy of a new vaccine developed by Saul Krugman, a researcher at New York University.[7]

Prisoners and mentally disabled children soon became viewed as a class of persons considered "vulnerable" and therefore largely shielded from the efforts of human subjects researchers.[8] If the essence of ethical research was informed consent, such vulnerable populations could neither be meaningfully informed nor truly give their uncoerced consent. So deprived were prisoners in their general circumstances that some researchers questioned the validity of a financial contract with the population. One group of prisoners, for example, was paid $30 a month to participate in a series of experiments that created nausea, caustic burns, and confusion. One prisoner explained the allure: "Hey, man, I'm making $30 a month on the DMSO thing [dimethylsulfoxide]. I know a couple of guys had to go to the hospital who were on it—and the burns were so bad they had to take *everyone* off it for a while. But who gives a shit about that man? Thirty is a full canteen draw and I wish the thing would go on for years."[9]

Such research pointed to the relatively low regard which many biomedical researchers held for their patients and research subjects and spoke to a broader malaise in the profession.[10] In the general balance of the healing arts, medicine seemed to be favoring its scientific side over its humanism, sacrificing the dignity of the patient on the altar of research. George Silver, a public health scholar, noted, "In their zeal to extend the frontiers of medical knowledge, many clinicians appear temporarily to have lost sight of the fact that the subjects of their experiments are in all cases, individuals with common rights and in most cases sick people hoping to be cured."[11]

Biomedical ethical challenges were still nascent in 1975. Extreme treatments to extend life at both ends had only just begun, and the AIDS epidemic had yet to make its mark on the ethics of human research. Nonetheless, doctors were facing the ethical limits of their craft and being forced to admit that the rectitude and utility of their training was not without moral ambiguity. Edmund Pellegrino, one of the early giants of biomedical ethics, noted as early as 1975 that the path to healing was a "joint process" in which "two human beings decide whether those measures are worth continuing," an effort to find the "moral thing to do."[12]

Although medicine had always taken as its charge to do no harm and to heal where possible, a growing corpus of disturbing cases through the 1970s illustrated the potential pitfalls of too much medicine. In the aftermath of the Karen Quinlan court decision, in which Quinlan's parents successfully sued to remove her ventilator, new cases surrounding beginning and end-of-life issues forced the courts and society as a whole to wrestle with broader questions of the utility of medical care. The case of Joseph Saikewicz, for example, ruled on by the Massachusetts Supreme Judicial Court in 1976, involved a 67-year-old man with an IQ of 10 suffering from acute myeloblastic monocytic leukemia with only months to live. Treatment might prolong his life for a few years only. A state-appointed legal guardian chose to withhold treatment from Saikewicz, claiming that the treatment would be only marginally helpful and would cause the patient pain and distress. The court sided with the guardian, and Saikewicz died on September 4.

Bioethicists and concerned observers debated the rectitude of the decision with some arguing that physicians and medical establishments ought to be free to make medical judgments, and others arguing that the state had a special obligation to intervene on behalf of its most vulnerable citizens. Doctors feared that the mere act of bringing the case to court had set a precedent compelling them to seek judicial permission any time they withheld treatment, leading to the bizarre case of a physicians implanting a heart pacemaker in a brain-dead patient.[13]

Similar issues were raised in the case of Shirley Dinnerstein, a 67-year old woman with advanced Alzheimer's disease, unable to speak, swallow, or cough. Doctor's sought permission to place a "do not resuscitate" order on her. The case was brought before the Massachusetts high court, which refused to judge on its merits, claiming that there was no available life-altering treatment to be ruled on. Again, the greater question seemed to be not so much what the correct course of action was but whether physicians had the authority to use their own best judgment. Most doctors and hospital administrators sided with granting the benefit of the doubt to the healing professions, but aggressive patient advocates questioned the judgment of doctors, claiming that nonmedical factors (such as the wealth or physical attributes of the patient) could sway them. Charles Baron, a law professor at Boston College, pointed out: "If you can't put someone in jail or take them off welfare or attach their wages without a court hearing, it seems all the more important that you have a hearing before you take someone's life away."[14]

On the whole, though, bioethical concerns were marginal for most physicians. True, gynecologists needed to decide whether to perform abortions, but most end-of-life decisions hinged more on the limits of life-sustaining technology than on judgments regarding the quality of life that such technology could provide. The Quinlan and Dinnerstein cases were slightly ominous. Medical technology and clinical ability were advancing rapidly. The age of viability for a fetus declined almost every year. Respirators and feeding tubes advanced concomitantly. It seemed only a matter of time before large numbers of patients at the extremes of life's beginning and end would demand a complex and unified ethical response from the medical community.

Ominous, too, were the potential costs of all of this technology. Extending life was enormously expensive. Premature infants could accrue hundreds of thousands of dollars in hospital bills in their first two months of life. Patients in near-vegetative states in nursing homes and hospitals required almost constant care as well as access to expensive machines, drugs, and nutritional formulations. Even as bioethicists wrestled with abstract notions of rights and utility, healthcare managers and policy makers questioned whether the nation could afford these services, regardless of the moral considerations. Keeping people alive was expensive, and advances in science, technology, and clinical techniques seemed only to inflate the costs more.

Withholding Treatment

In April 1982, a baby who came to be known as "Infant Doe" was born in Bloomington, Indiana, with Down's syndrome. The baby had an easily repairable esophageal atresia and tracheoesophageal fistula (a condition wherein the esophagus, rather than connecting to the stomach, feeds into the infant's windpipe). The baby's parents chose to withhold treatment and allow the child to die, rather than be faced with the challenges of raising a Down's child.

This case raised difficult ethical questions regarding parents' authority to withhold medical treatment from a child, the medical profession's obligation to aggressively treat all patients, and the state's right to intervene in medical decision making for patients who could not decide on their own behalf. In this particular case, President Ronald Reagan responded with a memo to his Secretary of Health and Human Services, Richard Schweiker, instructing him to notify healthcare providers that all who received federal funds (including Medicaid and Medicare) were forbidden from withholding care from handicapped citizens under terms of the 1973 Rehabilitation Act.

The Baby Doe case starkly highlighted questions coming to the fore in 1982: What was the ethical obligation of medicine to treat in the face of issues surrounding cost and quality of life? Were doctors and hospitals obliged to perform extraordinary procedures and dispense experimental drugs when such actions were highly costly and had little chance of success? Were providers allowed to consider the potential quality of life of the patient after treatment as part of their decision making? In response to the Baby Doe memorandum, Richard Given, the chief justice of the Indiana Supreme Court, reminded the public, "We can't legislate miracles. We can't pass a law saying doctors have to save every child that's born."[15] The American Academy of Pediatrics responded with a position statement challenging the actions of the Reagan White House. It said, "Handicapped persons . . . need health care providers who will carefully examine the appropriateness of specific medical intervention . . . Withholding a medical treatment will frequently be both legally and ethically justified."[16] Marcia Angell, the highly respected editor of the *New England Journal of Medicine*, wrote more frankly that the government's directive was predicated on the notion that "all life, no matter how miserable, should be maintained if technically possible," and that "the quality of life had no bearing on medical decisions."[17]

Severely impaired infants were hardly the only patients who raised troubling issues regarding obligations to treat. Was a hospital obligated to attempt an organ transplant in the face of high odds of failure and higher costs? In fact, Massachusetts General Hospital in Boston had explicitly decided in 1967 not to perform heart transplants, as such procedures ran counter to its ethos of providing the "greatest good for the greatest number," and reaffirmed its decision in 1980. Construction costs to build a new transplant center could run into the tens of millions of dollars, and costs of personnel and materials for each procedure could exceed $100,000. One analyst estimated the cost per additional year of life provided by a heart transplant was nearly $34,000, compared with $10,000 per added year for coronary artery bypass surgery.[18] Typical costs for a stay of a newborn in a neonatal intensive care unit (NICU) approached $100,000, and "million-dollar babies" were not unknown. "What are we *not* doing with that money?," asked Dena Seiden, a bioethicist from Union Theological Seminary. Even as expenditures on extraordinary procedures rose, federal support for the Women and Infant Children program declined. "Once a hospital has decided to build a NICU, it has already so skewed its resources that a large commitment to prenatal nutrition and screening may not be possible," argued Seiden. "It is not hard to predict what kinds of health care patterns we will be seeing."[19]

Ethicists divided themselves into two camps: absolutists and distributionists. Absolutists took the sanctity of an individual life as a starting point and generally refused to place that life within a broader social context. People in this camp did not consider the quality of life of a patient and did not consider the social costs of treatment—in Seiden's words, "What are we *not* doing with the money?" Surgeon General C. Everett Koop, an observant Christian, stood in the absolutist camp. Ardently antiabortion, he refused to consider the potential quality of life of an infant who might be a candidate for life-saving surgery. In one interview, Koop labeled 1973 a watershed year in people's perception of the value of human life as the point in time that "we began to kill 1.5 million babies a year."[20]

Distributionists grounded their ethics in distributive justice, derived from the Kantian imperative. Distributionists, or "relativists" as they were sometimes derisively called, took life to be a qualified good: simultaneously potentially wonderful and hellish. In their view, an ethical approach to medical care required that (1) the quality of life of a patient after treatment ought to be considered in the treatment directive, and (2) the cost to society of dispensing a treatment ought to be considered as well. Treatments that were expensive, experimental, and added little hope of improvement or survival ought to be weighed carefully against alternative uses of societal resources. Lester Thurow, an economist who wrestled with the societal parameters of public choices, wrote, "the health care problem is not a federal or state budget problem. It is a social problem. The expenditures are the same regardless of whether the money is spent through the federal budget or private insurance. Somehow, we have to learn to say 'no.'" Thurow called for a shift in medical decision making and demanded that doctors stop treatment when "marginal benefits are equal to marginal costs," and not when "all benefits cease."[21]

States responded sluggishly to the tangled issues confronting them, with some requiring patient advocates for all decisions for minors or disabled persons, and others passing "right to die" laws to ensure that patients could halt treatment in the face of futile life-saving efforts. Doctors found themselves caught in theological, philosophical, and political shoals and looked to ethics committees for guidance and legal protection. Although some celebrated the extraordinary (and remunerative) options that they could exercise in service to their patients, others admitted that new treatments had created more problems than they had solved. "The new technology has created a terrible monster," said Roger Johnson, a physician in Denver.[22]

Some health scholars vigorously opposed the moral inconsistency of the absolutists, noting that healthcare was regularly rationed in the United States, if invisibly. The fact that specialist physicians and tertiary care hospitals were not well distributed effectively rationed care to poor, rural, and disenfranchised Americans. Victor Fuchs, a health economist at Stanford University, made the compelling case that in the past (before the implementation of Medicare), wealthy elderly persons had eighty-six operations per one thousand people each year, while nonwealthy elderly persons had sixty-six. It could hardly have been the case that the less wealthy simply needed fewer operations. Fuchs wrote, "The system was rationing care even though individual physicians may not have been."[23] Americans, in particular, seemed uniquely incapable of recognizing the moral inconsistencies of not taking costs and benefits into account when making treatment decisions; the English, for example, were more accepting of the societal limitations on medical resources and the consequences of misusing them.

Who, then, should decide? If the state was overreaching, and churches were treading into areas of civic governance, should decision making devolve to the patient alone? Doctors were uncomfortable leaving complex treatment decisions to nontrained people, particularly people enduring serious illness. One physician-philosopher wrote, "A physician who merely spreads an array of vendibles in front of the patient and then says, 'Go ahead and choose, it's your life,' is guilty of shirking his duty, if not malpractice."[24] But others questioned the objectivity of physicians who, after all, stood to gain financially by making greater efforts to treat against all odds. Ironically, opponents of capitated managed care made the same argument in reverse, expressing concern about physicians' judgment in the face of financial incentives to undertreat. Neither the US legal system, nor the evolving code of treatment ethics, gave weight to considerations of distributional justice. Norman Daniels, an ethicist at Tufts University, wrote of the uniquely US ethical conundrum: "Saying no to beneficial treatments or procedures in the United States is morally hard, because providers cannot appeal to the justice of their denial. In ideally just arrangements, and even in the British system, rationing beneficial care is nevertheless fair to all patients in general. Cost-containment measures in our system carry with them no such justifications."[25]

Physicians and hospital administrators were in a bind. New technologies and advances in treatment raised questions that they were ill-equipped to answer. Faced with political turmoil, potential malpractice litigation, and demanding patients, providers generally opted to overtreat rather than undertreat. In coming decades, providers revisited these questions repeatedly and slowly devised more subtle and distributive approaches to these ethically difficult situations.

Do Not Resuscitate

A number of end-of-life issues resurfaced in 1990 with the US Supreme Court decision concerning Nancy Cruzan. Cruzan had entered a permanent vegetative state after an auto accident in 1983; her condition differed from Quinlan's in that she required only a feeding tube (Quinlan required a feeding tube and a ventilator). Her parents, wishing to terminate feeding, gained approval of a trial judge, whose decision was overturned by the Missouri Supreme Court. The family appealed the case to the US Supreme Court, which denied them the right to terminate feeding. Writing for the majority, Chief Justice William Rehnquist decided the case on the narrow grounds that the US Supreme Court lacked the authority to deny a state's authority to require a person to give explicit permission to have life-sustaining treatment withdrawn.

Critics of the decision complained that Rehnquist's opinion was "out of touch with reality" given the rapidly expanding capabilities of medicine to sustain life. George Annas, a bioethicist, wrote, "People do not write elaborate documents about all the possible ways they might die and the various interventions doctors might have available to prolong their lives."[26] Rather, most people made their wishes known to family and friends in more general and oblique terms, stating that they did not want "heroic measures" taken, or would "never want to live as a vegetable." A group of ethically minded physicians and lawyers noted that the court's decision was "at best sterile, applying a formula without regard for circumstances and seemingly without cognizance of the complexities of life and death in a modern hospital."[27] More bluntly, the granddaughter of one terminally ill man stated, "He said if he needed a machine to stay alive, we should take him behind the barn and shoot him."[28]

Other cases recapitulated the Cruzan dilemma. Jean Elbaum, a 60-year-old woman, entered a permanent vegetative state in 1986. Her husband, who claimed to have been given explicit direction from his wife to eschew heroic life-sustaining care, attempted to have her feeding tube withdrawn but was rebuffed by the nursing facility where she was residing. When the husband stopped making payments to the home, the home sued him for $18,500 in overdue bills. In the Elbaum case, a New York court ruled for the husband, who successfully had the feeding tube removed, although the debt to the nursing home was not excused.

Notably absent from debate surrounding the Cruzan case were discussions of cost. By 1990, Cruzan was consuming $130,000 in care annually, paid for entirely by the state of Missouri, and her case was hardly unique. One patient at Hermann Hospital in Houston, lying in total paralysis from a bullet wound to the neck, consumed nearly $10,000 in care each week in the three weeks after the incident, covered entirely through the state and the hospital's charity care fund. By the time he finally asked to be allowed to die five years later, he had incurred a bill of $727,000.[29] In one extreme case, a mother of conjoined twins insisted on their undergoing a separation procedure despite estimates that the chance of a successful outcome was less than 1 percent, at a cost of hundreds of thousands of dollars. One critical bioethicist wrote that the procedure was "not therapy in the usual sense: it was an experiment," and that it was "grimly ironic that we live in a society that permits [such a] procedure . . . but at the same time permits its infant mortality rate to be one of the highest in the industrialized world."[30]

The lack of discussion surrounding cost was bizarre but in some ways mirrored broader societal reluctance to truly confront limits on the costs of medical care. Like doctors, most ethicists had been trained to ignore money in their decision making, elevating concerns of autonomy, dignity, pleasure, and cognition over costs. Cost-benefit algorithms that were standard in other industries were essentially *verboten* in healthcare. Ethicists tended to word their ideas in the language of absolutes: a patient's *inalienable* right to self determination, or the state's *absolute* concern in promoting life. Ethicists, lawyers, judges, and doctors were extremely uncomfortable placing a value on a patient's pain, pleasure, or future life. At Montefiore hospital in the Bronx, for example, resident ethicists admitted that the patient's wishes were "paramount" and that the only relevant concern was in deciphering precisely what those wishes were. A colleague concurred: "We don't want to see any patient denied possibly helpful treatment because someone *else* may consider it too much of a burden or not worth the bother."[31]

The Ethics of Spending

Physicians could not perform miracles. Aging bodies and decaying neurological systems could not be repaired, only supported. Despite tremendous pressure on physicians and other providers to make extraordinary efforts to rectify, repair, and replace body parts, doctors and hospitals questioned the ethical propriety of investing time, effort, and most of all money in patients who had little chance of improving. Some began to offer palliative care rather than treatment.

Doctors who resisted treating patients faced professional opprobrium. The ethos of the profession had long been oriented toward treatment at all costs, and many physicians took pride in exploring every treatment option for every patient, regardless of how scant the chances of success were. In 1995, the Council on Ethical and Judicial Affairs of the American Medical Association reiterated the principle of unfettered commitment to patient care regardless of ulterior considerations.[32] But in a marked difference to previous such mandates, a number of physicians and ethicists responded with their own directives, arguing that in a world of limited funds, doctors needed to think more broadly about societal, rather than merely individual, health. Doctors, they argued, could choose to withhold care or offer palliative care, rather than attempt aggressive treatment.[33]

Debates over palliative care extended the discussion of rationing which had begun a decade previous, and which had become more compelling in an era of managed care. With transplant organs in limited supply, years-long queues for transplant procedures common, and managed care companies exercising increasingly tighter financial oversight, physicians questioned the prevailing mandate of providing endless care. The denial in 1995 of a new heart to a 34-year-old patient with Down's syndrome raised the specter of ugly arguments over the moral worth of organ recipients, in addition to the likelihood of their successful recovery from the procedure. In contrast, Mickey Mantle had jumped to the front of the queue for a new liver the previous year despite years of excessive drinking. One observer feared for the "Solomonic decisions" hospitals would face in the new environment.[34]

Even for the nonelderly, old arguments regarding experimental procedures garnered new weight. In vitro fertilization (IFV), for example, which offered the potential of pregnancy and parenthood to previously infertile couples, was hardly the panacea its advocates suggested. The procedure cost between $7,000 and $11,000 per cycle in the early 1990s, and carried with it substantial risk of embolisms, internal bleeding, stroke, and infarction. The procedure increased the chance of multiple births (and their attendant complications) at least 30-fold, and the chance of maternal complications 10-fold. The procedure led to a successful live birth in less than 15 percent of cases. Including lost wages, multiple efforts, and weighted costs of complications, the true cost of a successful birth using IVF was substantially more than $100,000.[35] No wonder, then, that IVF had been deliberately excluded from funding under the Clinton health plan.

More problematic were the extraordinary surgical efforts made to free conjoined twins, repair neonatal hearts and lungs, and transplant limbs and faces. The procedures cost hundreds of thousands of dollars and rarely produced successful outcomes. In one horrific case, Ken and Reitha Lakeberg, parents of conjoined twins in Chicago, pushed for surgery to separate the twins despite the promise of certain death for one of the children and almost certain death for the other, a potential medical bill of over $1 million, and no health insurance with which to indemnify the family. One medical ethicist termed the procedure a "research experiment" rather than a "treatment," and urged the parents to withdraw life support and allow the twins to die. Ethicists urged physicians to counsel the parents to cease their efforts.[36]

As chief payer for heroic end-of-life procedures, Medicare was particularly affected. Program administrators questioned the disproportionate share of public resources going to provide heroic, and frequently futile, procedures for beneficiaries whose natural life was ending. Between 27 and 30 percent of all Medicare payments each year paid for care for patients who would die that year, meaning that mean spending on a Medicare beneficiary in her last year of life was $13,316, versus a mean of $1,924 a year for all other Medicare beneficiaries. More troublesome was that payments in the last month of life totaled over 40 percent of funds spent in that year, meaning that 10 to 15 percent of all Medicare funds were spent on patients in their final month.[37]

One response was "living wills" or clinical directives—written orders made by the patient to withhold treatment, not resuscitate, and refrain from heroic efforts in the event of a stroke, coma, or infarction. The Patient Self-Determination Act of 1990 required providers treating Medicare or Medicaid patient to ask them if they had living wills and, if the answer was no, offer to help them write one.[38] The law made sense, as did any effort to educate patients and their families about the true costs and benefits of end-of-life treatment. Patient who made living wills tended to think proactively about their own deaths and discuss their wishes with their children and spouses. But data from the early 1990s suggested that living wills and clinical directives did little to reduce medical bills, laudable though the efforts might be. One study of eight hundred patients showed that those with living wills and advanced directives produced hospital bills in end-of-life admissions that were, on average, several thousand dollars more than patients who lacked such documents.[39]

One answer was hospice. The movement, grounded in the pioneering work of Cicely Saunders in England and Elizabeth Kübler-Ross in Switzerland, had started in the voluntary hospices of the Cleveland Clinic and the Medical College of Wisconsin in the 1980s. The movement took off with Medicare funding in the early 1990s. By 1995, the nation had over 1,800 programs, which were funded at nearly $3 billion.[40] Even with the growth, however, only 17 percent of dying patients sought hospice care, and few residents in internal medicine and geriatrics received formal hospice training. Hospice was still viewed as a marginal option for the handful of patients who actively sought it, rather than a central component of end-of-life care. HCFA approved a DRG classification for hospice in 1996, but the move seemed to trail rather than lead the movement. Sound economics dictated a more formal approach to hospice care, but few doctors or patients' advocates were eager to push for it.

In contrast, advocates pushed aggressively to legalize physician-assisted suicide. Doctors had probably quietly counseled terminal patients on lethal drugs and doses for decades, but virtually all of these efforts were technically illegal. In 1989, Jack Kevorkian, a Michigan pathologist, made the issue unavoidable by developing a suicide machine in which he hooked patients up to a series of lethal drugs and allowed them to activate the injections. The public was both fascinated and outraged by Kevorkian's activities, but state law refused to accommodate his pleas for sanctioning a more active role for physicians in euthanasia. He was eventually convicted of second-degree murder and spent time in prison.

In 1995, two federal appellate courts struck down state laws forbidding physician-assisted suicide, and a Dutch study of physician-assisted suicide indicated that physicians were unlikely to abuse the procedure.[41] The United States debated the issue over the next few years. The Supreme Court found no constitutional right to physician-assisted suicide, but Attorney General Janet Reno endorsed Oregon's efforts to allow physicians to prescribe illicit substances in the course of assisting a patient's suicide. In response, the US House of Representatives voted in 1999 to outlaw doctors from prescribing drugs for aid in suicide, and explicitly forbade the attorney general from doing otherwise.

Physicians admitted privately that many of them aided patients' suicides surreptitiously. One study showed that 43 percent of physicians treating terminal patients were willing to raise doses of painkillers to lethal levels. Samuel Klagsbrun, a New York physician, asserted that the law "forces doctors to kill secretly, and this happens much more often than we acknowledge."[42] Terminal patients welcomed their physicians' advice on suicide, hoping to end their lives cleanly and painlessly. One man wrote, "When my continued survival is no longer meaningful to me, I hope that a caring physician will make the transition as easy as possible."[43]

The nation seemed caught in a bind. On one hand, many people agreed with Judge Roger Miner of the Second Circuit who wrote that the state "has no interest in prolonging a life that is ending." On the other hand, physician-assisted suicide became a rallying cry for the Christian right, which hoped to exploit the issue for political gain.[44] One theologian wrote, in disgust, that support for the measure demonstrated that "our post-modern, technological culture cannot find meaning in suffering."[45]

Doctors themselves were divided. The issue seemed to lie on a fault line between doing the patient no harm and serving the patient's needs as the patient demanded. Did doctoring privilege patient autonomy, patient well-being, health, or longevity, or did it seek to find a workable compromise? Marcia Angell wrote a revealing description of her father's suicide as he faced death from prostate cancer at age 81. He feared losing his personal agency over the succeeding months of treatment and shot himself shortly before he was to be admitted to the hospital. She wrote, "Was he depressed? He would probably have freely admitted that he was, but he would have thought it beside the point. In any case, he was an intensely private man who would have refused psychiatric care. Was he overly concerned with maintaining control of the circumstances of his life and death? Man people would say so, but that was the way he was. It is the job of medicine to deal with patients as they are, not as we would like them to be."[46]

Countervailing debates over physician-assisted suicide and hospice care exposed the most unresolved tensions in US medicine. Even as patients demanded the right to die, they resisted efforts in teaching them how to eschew heroic treatment. Doctors, hospitals, and payers were demonized for threatening to end life support or assist in efforts at self-destruction, yet were equally demonized in counseling patients about the relatively poor chances for recovery in end-of-life treatment. Americans demanded control over their treatment and demise, but seemed unwilling to allow clinicians to play constructive roles in either. As usual, suggestions that financial considerations should play a role in any of these questions were rebuffed by both physicians and patients.

10

Medicare and Medicaid

Evolving Government Programs

Changes to Medicare: The Balanced Budget Amendment

Medicare was confronting challenges in the 1990s. The program was funded through a combination of payroll taxes, monthly premiums, and general tax revenues, and was funded on a pay-as-you-go basis: that is, current taxpayers funded current beneficiaries. The program had been exceeding cost projections almost from its inception, but the overruns had been manageable with a combination of higher monthly premiums and higher payroll taxes. Since 1990, however, payments had exceeded income. The program posted a $2.6 billion shortfall in 1995; a $5.3 billion shortfall in 1996, and a $12 billion shortfall in 1997. Although the federal government could cover the shortfalls temporarily by drawing on the Medicare trust fund, the trend was unsustainable. At that rate of growth, the trust fund would be exhausted by 2010.[1]

Medicare was growing insolvent for a number of reasons. Usage rates among the elderly were up, as were physician fees. New technologies made new procedures possible, and improved longevity allowed more people to live to collect Medicare benefits. At the same time, birth rates had fallen since the program's inception in 1966, meaning that the ratio of current workers paying into the system through payroll and income taxes was proportionally smaller to the retired population than had been true a generation earlier. The monthly premiums that funded a portion of physician services stayed static. By 1997, the monthly premium for Part B was a shockingly low $44, although Part B costs had risen by 45 percent over the previous five years.

Part of the problem was born of rising expectations. Elderly people in 1995 expected to live more comfortably and functionally than their parents and grandparents had. Many now expected to remain mobile, cogent, alert, and energetic into their ninth decade. Flush with corporate and government pension benefits and monthly Social Security income, the elderly in the 1990s traveled the world on elder-cruises and elder-hostels, hiked, took in shows and sights, played golf, and strived to live independently. One observer noted, "Health care is an ever-expanding concept." A generation previously, an elderly person who had become forgetful would have been defined as "aging" rather than "ill."[2] But newer drugs, interventions, and therapies had medicalized the aging process and raised hopes for delaying the ravages of aging.[3]

The newfound zest for elder living placed enormous demands on ambulatory medicine. Medicare spending on physicians' fees had grown 13.7 percent a year from 1981 to 1990. By 1990 the average US physician was receiving 2.5 times more in Medicare reimbursement than she had a decade before (in constant dollars), and the total size of Part B had grown threefold during the same period.[4] Eighty percent of Medicare beneficiaries used Part B benefits in any given year (as opposed to only 20 percent who used Part A), and little in the program worked to dissuade beneficiaries from consulting a doctor for even minor ailments.

Even with this growth, Medicare payments were not staying competitive with private insurance payments, and many doctors limited the portion of their practices they devoted to Medicare patients. Although fees varied regionally (as did Medicare payments), across the country Medicare paid 59 percent of the reimbursement paid by private insurers. A survey conducted by the Consumers' Union in 1994 found that nearly a third of doctors in three disparate counties had closed their practices to new Medicare patients. Few elderly were failing to get care, but the trend was worrisome.[5]

One of the odd problems that confronted Medicare in the late 1990s, and indeed the entire healthcare system, was a glut of physicians.

Between 1956 and 1980, the number of US medical schools had increased from 84 to 127, effectively doubling the size of the first-year class to sixteen thousand. The number of entering osteopathic students had doubled over this period as well, to just over two thousand. Four years later, these eighteen thousand graduates were joined by approximately five thousand graduates of foreign medical schools (FMGs) to create a class of twenty-three thousand first-year residents in the nation's graduate medical education programs. While the US population had grown over time, growth in the supply of new physicians had exceeded general population growth. In 1950 the United States had had 112 practicing physicians per 100,000 people; in 1990 the nation had 182 physicians per 100,000.[6]

In response, the Council on Graduate Medical Education recommended in 1994 that the number of first-year residency slots be cut by 20 percent, effectively eliminating the slots previously filled by FMGs.[7] Simply maintaining level physician coverage from 1994 would require a 29 percent reduction in overall physicians, and optimizing the ratio of generalist to specialists would probably require reducing the number of specialty training slots by 33 percent.[8] This could be best accomplished by reducing the $6 billion annual subsidy paid to teaching hospitals to train medical residents, or at the very least capping subsidies to certain specialty training programs or denying green card status to FMGs emerging from the residency programs. Health economists argued that part of the problem lay with the fact that government subsidies distorted market incentives and thus produced surpluses with no market forces to discipline the training programs.[9]

But simply reducing training slots indiscriminately would solve little. The nation continued to be plagued by excessive numbers of specialists and a paucity of primary care physicians, and many rural areas continued to suffer from poor physician coverage. Numbers bore out anecdotal evidence. Even as the physician-to-population ratio had risen by 63 percent over three decades, the primary care physician-to-population ratio had risen by only 13 percent. The solution was, rather, to selectively reduce training slots in the specialty areas, or induce young doctors to train in primary care through loan forgiveness programs. Congress had little appetite for either. Training slots were created and maintained through independent specialty training boards in conjunction with the nation's independent teaching hospitals, and Congress had long eschewed involving itself with administering the process. Moreover, loan forgiveness programs were generally unpopular. Doctors who served in the national health service corps rarely stayed after their initial obligation, and frequently returned for more training later.[10] Without exercising a very heavy regulatory hand, neither Congress nor HCFA had much control over the number and type of residents trained.

One possibility to alleviate shortages in primary care and rural physicians was more aggressive use of nurse practitioners, who continued to insist on their professional competence and potential for autonomy. By 1994, twenty-five states had authorized insurance reimbursement to independent nurse practitioners, and fifteen had granted them authorization to write prescriptions.[11] Nurse practitioners in other states, however, continued to work and write prescriptions under physicians' supervision, and nurse practitioners in all states lacked the ability to admit patients to hospitals. Nurse practitioners bristled under these restrictions and demanded an end to the medical monopoly. "How can the issue be anything else but turf?," demanded one nurse practitioner. A colleague declared, "Nurse practitioners and nurse-midwives seek the independence to complete the delivery of therapeutics that we have been trained to give."[12]

Physicians resisted the call of the nurse practitioners, correctly seeing that most would choose to practice not in underserved rural and inner-city areas but in the same demographically desirable suburban areas as they, themselves, migrated to.[13] The issue was indeed turf, and physicians felt that they had paid their dues many times over to earn exclusive prescribing, admitting, and diagnostic privileges. Nurse practitioners underwent one-tenth the total number of clinical training hours as a board-certified internist and absorbed substantially less biochemistry, molecular biology, and pharmacology in the basic science portion of their training. Doctors who pointed out these facts sounded hostile and snarky, but the facts were persuasive. One angry physician noted that nurse practitioners simply lacked the training to think subtly and insightfully "beyond the immediate, simple-appearing illness to the deeper, possibly serious root cause," and suggested that if they felt so inclined they could simply apply to medical school.[14] Another, more sympathetic physician agreed that nurse practitioners had a great deal to contribute but, damning with faint praise, noted that this was "despite their lack of training in pathogenetic mechanisms and differential diagnosis."[15] The message was ambiguous. Nurse practitioners had a role to play, but likely it was not in replacing primary care physicians in front-line diagnosis.

Ironically, even as nurses pushed for greater opportunities in primary care, the nation experienced a severe shortage in bedside nurses. Vacancy rates for RNs in a number of states neared 10 percent, and in some high-demand areas (critical care nursing for example) vacancy rates topped 15 percent. At the same time, the nursing workforce was aging rapidly; fewer than 33 percent of the nation's practicing nurses were under age 40 in 2000, down from 50 percent in 1980. One study showed that women graduating from high school in the 1990s were 35 percent less likely to choose nursing than women high school graduates of the 1970s.[16] Many factors contributed to the problem, among them greater opportunities for women, stagnant wage scales, high stress, and little opportunity for professional growth. Nursing homes in 2000 reported an astonishing 51 percent turnover rate for both RNs and LPNs annually.[17]

These discussions were overtaken by the Republican landslide of 1994, in which Republicans gained a majority in the House of Representatives for the first time in thirty years. Republicans in the House pledged themselves to uphold a "Contract with America," which included a commitment to balancing the federal budget within 100 days of the party taking power. At over 10 percent of the federal budget, Medicare became an attractive target to cut and reformulate.

Republican lawmakers, under the leadership of the new Speaker of the House, Newt Gingrich (R-GA), hoped to reduce the annual cost of Medicare by $270 billion over seven years. They would accomplish this by reducing payments to physicians and giving Medicare beneficiaries vouchers to purchase managed care policies in the private market. The movement would force beneficiaries to pay the balance of premium costs out of pocket, effectively transferring the cost of Medicare from the public to its recipients. The program was sure to create hardships for elderly citizens living just above the poverty line who failed to qualify for state-funded gap insurance and was almost certain to diminish the quality of care which many elderly people could afford. Michael Kinsley, an acerbic political commentator, called the program the "King Canute solution" for being predicated on Congress simply ordering the "tide of Medicare spending to stop."[18]

Republicans presented the proposed voucher program as promoting "choice" for elderly people, who would now be able to choose which private health plan to purchase with their Medicare funds. The "choice" argument was predicated on the conceit that Medicare was effectively a single-payer social insurance model which bound all Americans over

65 to a centrally controlled government program. "Every citizen has the right to choose," remarked Gingrich. "They shouldn't be trapped in a one-size-fits-all government monopoly."[19]

In contrast, opponents of the proposal tarred the notion of choice as disingenuous, noting that beneficiaries already had the choice to enroll in a Medicare managed care plan and could choose, as well, from among ten different approved Medigap policies to fill in the holes in their Medicare coverage. "If anything, Medicare already offers too many confusing and complex choices," wrote Trudy Lieberman, a longtime consumer health advocate.[20] More choice was more likely to promote fraud and abuse for bewildered consumers who frequently fell prey to glib insurance brokers and benefits agents.

More fundamentally, choice would fracture the united elderly risk pool that underlay the integrity and success of the Medicare program. By requiring all of America's elderly to participate in the program through their mandated tax contributions, Congress had created within Medicare an enormous interest group which ran across lines of race, class, and wealth. Due to the size of the risk pool, Medicare could distribute the cost of ill-health, bad genes, and bad luck across the entire nation, and thus create the nation's most successful social leveling mechanism. The choice touted by Gingrich and his allies would rupture the mechanism and create pools of risky and uninsurable people who would either be left to die or be forced to take coverage in the US welfare system.

Republicans drew strength from the ugly realities of the Medicare program. Although insured through Medicare, the elderly faced substantial financial challenges in accessing medical care. Part B premiums, deductibles, co-pays, and uncovered prescription drugs and medical devices ate up 55 percent of all healthcare spending by the elderly. The Medicare program covered only 45 percent of the $83 billion the elderly spent annually on healthcare. These costs were rising yearly, and 45 percent was slated to drop to 40 percent over the next decade. Out-of-pocket costs for the elderly included a $356 deductible for each hospital stay; $89 a day co-payment for each day in the hospital after the first sixty; $178 a day after ninety days; the complete cost for all hospital care after day 150; $44 a day for skilled nursing care after twenty days; $175 a year in part B premiums; a $75 annual part B deductible; a 20 percent co-pay on all part B services after the initial $75 deductible; and all prescription and over-the-counter drugs used outside of a hospital, as well as home healthcare, nurses aids, the marginal cost of a private room, and other ancillary add-ons.

The elderly looked to private insurance policies, known as "Medigap" policies, to supplement their Medicare benefits. Gap policies took a variety of forms, but all worked to backstop catastrophic losses among elderly patients facing very long hospital stays and expensive drug regimens. The problem with the gap policies was that they were often either actuarially overpriced or grossly inadequate. The elderly presented a vulnerable and tempting market to unethical insurance providers, and many found themselves paying far more for the gap policies than they would have had they paid out-of-pocket expenses in cash. Congressman Claude Pepper (D-FL) called the market for gap policies a "colossal racket," and told of companies marketing as many as thirty different gap policies to an audience that could not possibly differentiate one from another.[21] Pepper ultimately led a reform effort to designate qualifying gap policies in one of a half-dozen qualifying categories and make the entire market more transparent. Even so, substantial numbers of elderly patients found themselves underinsured and vulnerable to catastrophic healthcare costs, even when subscribing to Medicare part B.

The elderly also looked to Medicaid to fill gaps in their Medicare coverage. A sizable number of Medicare beneficiaries qualified as "dual eligibles" who collected both Medicaid and Medicare benefits, with the Medicaid programs acting as their gap policies. Medicaid covered deductibles, part B premiums, and (most important) prescription drugs, although again holes in Medicaid coverage left a certain number of elderly persons uncovered. In addition, various federal grants funneled funds to states and municipalities, although virtually all of these programs were porous in one way or the other. All of the programs were under pressure to contract, even as prices for medical care went up.

By 1995, elderly Americans were actually spending a higher portion of their income on medical care than they had before the enactment of Medicare thirty years previously, due to the costs of their Medigap policies, co-payments, deductibles, and (uncovered) prescription drugs. The program was rife with waste and mismanagement, as well as fraud, abuse, and corruption. Moreover, the underlying idea of vouchers— forcing a certain amount of financial exposure onto the beneficiaries in an effort to make them more discriminating consumers of healthcare— was the motivating idea behind President's Bill Clinton's failed Health Security Act. One could not simultaneously fight for managed competition while opposing Medicare vouchers; the two plans had grown from the same shoot.[22]

Many of the Republican leadership's plans for Medicare reform were included in the Balanced Budget Act (BBA) of 1997. Included in the BBA was a new Medicare+Choice program that would allow (but not force) Medicare beneficiaries to use their Medicare funds to purchase a policy in a capitated plan, which could be either an HMO, a POS, a PHO, or a private, capitated fee-for-service plan. (Previously, Medicare enrollees who had opted out of traditional Medicare had to use a strict HMO plan.) The BBA also allowed Medicare enrollees to purchase catastrophic (high-deductible) plans and establish tax-deductible medical savings accounts, which they could use to purchase medical care up to the point that their catastrophic coverage would take over. Last, the BBA forced Medicare to pay capitated plans on a risk-adjusted basis, rather than simply paying them 95 percent of the cost of a traditional Medicare enrollee. This last change was made in an effort to capture some of the profits that HMOs were making on low-risk Medicare enrollees.

BBA provisions were not quite the voucher system that hard-right Republicans had worked for, but they did offer Medicare enrollees significantly more choice in how they used HCFA funds to purchase health insurance. One concern was whether the new risk-bearing arrangements would provide adequate care to elderly, difficult-to-treat patients who had long purchased their care from an array of internists and specialists. Research on the quality of care provided by HMOs tended to rank it equal to that proved by indemnity policies, but the parity seemed to wither in cases where patients were elderly, sick, and suffering from multiple complications.[23] A second concern was that the sickest Medicare beneficiaries would take refuge in traditional Medicare and Medigap programs, creating a problem of adverse selection. A third concern, a recurrent one, was that the changes wrought by the BBA failed to fix underlying inefficiencies in the production and distribution of health services in the United States.

Medicare+Choice succeeded in inducing millions of Medicare beneficiaries to enroll in risk-capitated plans, but also drove nearly one third of the 346 plans that had contracted with Medicare before the BBA to either stop taking Medicare patients or reduce the geographic areas from which they drew. The new risk-based payments were substantially smaller than the old payments, and were thus substantially less attractive to contracting plans. Plans located in rural areas or in small cities were more likely to withdraw from Medicare contracting than were plans in larger cities (due to lower capitated rates), meaning that the BBA was accomplishing exactly what Trudi Lieberman had so fearfully warned of: fracturing the united elderly risk pool into geographically and demographically isolated subpopulations.[24]

At the same time, Medicare+Choice failed to remedy two of the larger complaints about Medicare: lack of a prescription drug reimbursement program and rising rates of fraud and abuse. Although some of the risk-bearing plans did include limited drug coverage, many did not, while all Medicare beneficiaries who stayed in traditional Medicare lacked drug coverage if not purchased through Medigap plans. Congress had struggled for years with prescription drug coverage, but had never come to consensus. A number of wealthier socially progressive states in the Northeast and Upper Midwest implemented their own pharm-assistance programs for the elderly during the 1980s, but all of these were means-tested and more rightfully extensions of Medicaid programs rather than Medicare.[25] At the same time, most Medigap drug plans demanded a 50 percent co-pay after a deductible of $250 a year, and capped all benefits above $1,250 annually. For the 7 percent of Medicare beneficiaries considered high drug users (above $2,000 a year) the plans did little.

The Clinton administration proposed a drug benefit as part of its 2001 budget proposal, but the plan, like the Medigap plans, would pay for only half the cost of drugs up to a cap of $1,000 (to rise to $2,500 by 2009). The beneficiary would pay $575 extra in premiums to enroll in the program (called "Part D"), meaning that the average Medicare beneficiary would wind up shouldering 75 percent of the cost of his or her drugs. The program would cost the federal government $160 billion through 2010.[26] Responses from the AARP and other Medicare advocates were tepid, and Congress refused to fund the proposal.

More discouraging was the failure of the 1997 reforms to address systemic abuse and fraud in Medicare. The level of fraud was immense. In 1992 the Government Accountability Office had estimated annual losses to Medicare fraud at $100 billion, and some GAO staffers thought that the true number might be as high as $250 billion. One cardiologist who had bilked the government repeatedly by sending in bills for as much as $5,000 for a single patient visit testified to a Senate special committee, "The problem is that nobody is watching. The system is extremely easy to evade. The forms I sent in were absolutely outrageous. I was astounded when some of those payments were made."[27]

More troublesome than outright fraud were the efforts that many clinicians and hospitals made to bend regulations to overbill, double-bill, or fracture single procedures into multiple bills. Providers billed for procedures done in error; admitted patients to the hospital to cover prescription drugs that would not be covered in an outpatient setting;

referred patients for follow-up visits when none were indicated; and ordered tests and scans when a diagnosis did not demand them. Doctors and hospitals found ways to bill for procedures still considered experimental (and thus not approved for reimbursement) by listing them as approved procedures, or performing an approved procedure to back up the experimental one.[28]

To counter these claims, HCFA employed only 125 investigators (soon to drop to 100) which came to several million claims annually per investigator.[29] Although money saved through fraud detection more than paid for the cost of the investigations, the enforcement apparatus was inadequate to the challenge at hand. One state attorney general, responsible for investigating Medicaid fraud just in his state, noted, "We have no idea how much fraud falls through the cracks. I just doubled the number of my investigators, and my caseload doubled. If I tripled the investigators, the caseload would triple."[30]

Medicare challenged Congress's oversight along many axes. Enormously popular with the nation's elderly voters and aggressively protected by the lobbying power of the AARP, Medicare was politically untouchable. At the same time, its costs threatened to overwhelm the federal budget in coming decades, and politicians of all stripes understood the need for reform and retrenchment. The nation's elderly could not continue to consume healthcare at the rate, and in the form, which they had become accustomed to, but opposing the elderly carried an intolerable political cost for most elected leaders. The 1997 BBA reforms were a first step in reining in the program and aligning it with established managed care incentives, but lack of co-payments and oversight for the millions of elderly people who elected to remain in fee-for-service Medicare threatened the efficacy of those reforms. The reforms had done virtually nothing to reduce the amount of fraud and abuse in the system, and the need for some sort of universal prescription drug benefit still needed to be addressed.

Changes to Medicare: Prescription Drugs

Toward the end of his first term, President George W. Bush turned his attention to expanding the roster of Medicare benefits to include a prescription drug benefit. The enabling Medicare legislation of 1965 did not include a prescription drug benefit in Part B, and no such benefit had been added over the following four decades. During that time, the financial burden of prescription drugs for the elderly had increased tenfold as new generations of drugs had become indispensable aids to extending life and treating the symptoms of chronic disease. By 2002, Medicare beneficiaries were using $87 billion in prescription drugs annually, and the number was slated to rise to $128 billion in just a few years.[31]

Congress had excluded prescription drug coverage from Medicare originally because the cost of prescription drugs in 1965 simply did not pose a substantial burden to the elderly. The ensuing decades had brought drugs to control depression, anxiety, acid reflux, arthritis, cholesterol, blood clotting, stroke, heart disease, systemic inflammation, psychosis, and sleep disorders—to mention only a few. Access to these drugs, many sold under patent at high prices—had greatly improved life for the elderly, but at a considerable cost. The elderly consumed 40 percent of prescription drugs (despite making up only 15 percent of the population) and a not insignificant minority consumed more than $5,000 of drugs annually.[32]

Although Medicare Part B contained no prescription drug coverage, many beneficiaries purchased drug coverage through ancillary gap insurance, which covered part of the cost of prescription drugs. Other beneficiaries received partial drug coverage by enrolling in Medicare Part C (Medicare+Choice) or by qualifying for Medicaid, which served as a secondary insurer to Medicare and paid nearly the entire cost of prescription drugs. Nonetheless, in 2002 roughly 25 percent of all Medicare beneficiaries had no prescription drug coverage, and many either eschewed necessary drugs, took suboptimal doses of medication, or reached deep into savings to purchase drugs. The cost of prescription drugs was the single greatest medical burden to most Medicare beneficiaries, and the beneficiaries repeatedly called on Congress to amend the Medicare program.

Congress had resisted calls for prescription drugs for the simple reason that any such benefit would be very expensive. A new benefit would cost between $400 and $800 billion over ten years, at a time when congressional budget hawks were actively looking to reduce the cost of Medicare. At the same time, such a program violated philosophical tenets of insurance, as it would fail to distribute catastrophic risk. Congressional leaders feared making any such benefit means-tested. That is, any politically palatable prescription drug program would require a massive transfer of funds from the working population to retirees, most of whom were not facing catastrophic costs, and most of whom successfully paid for their own drugs. Political pressure to create a new program came largely from the AARP—the large and powerful lobby that spoke for the concerns of the elderly. Daniel Greenberg, a Washington-based writer who frequently wrote on health and medical issues, noted that the rising consensus in Congress for a prescription drug existed in "joyless harmony across the political spectrum."[33] Congress hated the idea, but hated opposing the idea even more.

One problem with any prescription drug program was that of adverse selection: the tendency of the cheapest beneficiaries to delay enrolling until they got sick and faced substantial drug costs to treat chronic diseases. Medicare Part B similarly faced adverse selection, but thwarted it by imposing a substantial penalty on elderly citizens who did not enroll in the program promptly at age 65 and by heavily subsidizing the program with general tax funds.[34] A prescription drug program could use a number of different techniques to prevent adverse selection, ranging from a mandated buy-in (as was done with Medicare Part A), to a penalty system for late enrollment (Part B), to a risk-adjusted premium based on historic or expected drug use (experience rating as opposed to community rating). Congress could also bias the program toward the sickest and poorest Medicare beneficiaries by offering subsidies to pay for the premiums in a scale adjusted for household income.

Between 2000 and 2002, members of the Clinton administration and Congress proposed four different prescription drug programs requiring different deductibles, premium subsidies, and risk adjustments. The proposals, introduced by the White House,[35] Senator Charles Robb (D-VA), Representative Bill Thomas (R-CA), and Senator John Breaux (D-LA), contained annual deductibles ranging from $0 to $250 and capped annual benefits at $1,000 (although the Robb proposal had no annual cap). All of the plans included a "stop-loss" amount above which the plan would pick up all drug costs (ranging from $4,000 to $6,000 annually), and all included either a premium subsidy for low-income elderly beneficiaries or a reinsurance mechanism which would effectively provide a 35 percent subsidy. All would pay for between 25 and 50 percent of the cost of the drugs within the active range of the benefit.

The proposals succeeded in making nobody happy. None provided the sort of comprehensive drug benefit the elderly craved, yet all were quite expensive and promised to become even more so as the size of the elderly population swelled in future years, and as Medicare beneficiaries demanded access to new generations of expensive, branded drugs. None passed.

In 2003, the Bush White House succeeded in passing the Medicare Prescription Drug, Improvement and Modernization Act, which successfully built on some of the congressional consensus developed in debate over the previous four efforts. The Bush administration promised that the plan would cost no more than $700 billion over ten years and held the program to that level by inserting a conspicuous "donut hole" in coverage between $2,250 and $5,100 per year, after which a stop-loss mechanism kicked in. Under the Bush plan, the elderly were responsible for a $250 deductible, and then paid 25 percent of their drug costs between $250 and $2,250. All figures would rise with inflation, such that by 2013 the annual deductible would be $445 and the stop-loss would activate at $9,000. Despite broad dissatisfaction with the donut hole, the Congressional Budget Office estimated that 87 percent of all Medicare beneficiaries would participate in the plan, although nobody could predict how Medicare Part C plans would respond to the new benefit.[36]

Opponents of the program voiced confidence that it would soon exceed its estimated costs, and that future generations of beneficiaries would place enormous pressure on Congress to eliminate the donut hole and increase the benefit. Moreover, opponents argued that in contracting with private insurance companies to deliver the benefit, the government was forfeiting the ability to negotiate discounted prices for most popular drugs while surrendering profits to the insurance companies.[37] Last, opponents questioned whether such a benefit could be better delivered through state programs in the style of Medicaid, where local administrators could tailor the programs to the specific needs of local impoverished elderly populations. That is, if the point of the drug program was to prevent penury in the elderly, then it should be treated as welfare rather than an insurance benefit and be funneled through state agencies. Notably, at the time that Congress passed the Bush drug benefit, seven states already had in place pharmacy-assistance programs for the elderly, which used means-testing to identify elderly who were at risk of foregoing prescription drugs due to financial constraints.[38] The programs worked well, and congressional skeptics wondered why the efforts could not be repeated in other states.

The new program, called Medicare Part D, was inaugurated January 1, 2006. The program immediately stumbled. Beneficiaries complained about the complexity of the different drug programs they faced and were uncertain of the ways the drug benefit interacted with their existing gap coverage. Enrollees in Medicare+Choice plans (Part C) found that their benefits changed in response to the new Part D benefits. Poorer citizens faced difficulties in applying for subsidies. Computer systems failed to communicate with retail pharmacies, leaving consumers with high bills for which they felt entitled to reimbursement. As the bizarreness of the donut hole became apparent, millions of Medicare beneficiaries seethed with anger over the essential randomness of the benefit. The spokesperson for Centers for Medicare and Medicaid Services (CMS) announced to the press, "This is going very well," on January 4. Other government spokespeople admitted to hitting initial "bumps" in implementing the large and complex new program.[39]

The program was the product of political and budgetary compromise, and the government could hardly be blamed for taking time to master the intricacies of the program. The program differed from the original Medicare program significantly in the level of choice it foisted on the elderly. Beneficiaries faced dozens of options in the precise level of coverage they purchased, with different plans covering differing drug formularies at different rates. In contrast, the original Parts A and B of Medicare were standard throughout the country when they were introduced in 1966. The lack of choice in original Medicare had been deliberate, for fear of confusing beneficiaries. Robert Ball, the first director of the Medicare program and career social welfare professional, reflected at the start of Medicare Part D, "I would not have dreamed of going about this in a way that meant individuals had to choose from among all these possibilities. I would have expected chaos."[40] No wonder, then, that when the first retrospective studies of Part D emerged a few years later, scholars acknowledged the potential good wrought by the programs but the tempering effects of its arcane rules. The general view of the program was, in the words of two policy scholars, that it was "enormously important but complex."[41]

Changes to Medicaid: Closing the Holes

Medicaid had provided tremendous benefits to the nation's poor over the preceding four decades, and the new State Children's Health Insurance Program (S-CHIP) was proving helpful in delivering healthcare to millions of near-poor children. But challenges remained for minorities seeking healthcare. A person's wealth or race continued to be stubbornly predictive of health status and life expectancy in 2005, despite decades of social programs aimed at the poor and affirmative action programs aimed at racial minorities. In fact, disparities between groups were actually growing in the early years of the twenty-first century, erasing gains of decades past. Between 1980 and 2000, for example, the gap in life expectancy (at birth) between the richest and poorest Americans widened from 2.8 to 4.5 years, and the gap in life expectancy at age 65 had gone from nil in 1980 to nearly two years by 2000. The case of Deamonte Driver, a twelve-year-old boy who died from a brain infection that spread from an ordinary tooth cavity, exemplified the problem. Although Driver's Medicaid policy had covered dental care, like millions of others in poverty he had failed to see a dentist for over a year. In fact, data confirmed at the time that Medicaid patients were twice as likely as children with private insurance to have untreated cavities.[42]

The gap in health status and life expectancy between rich and poor was increasing for a variety of reasons. Over the previous decades, highly educated (and thus wealthier) people had disproportionately quit smoking and turned to lower calorie diets, opening up smoking and obesity gaps between the rich and poor. The wealthier were far more likely to see doctors earlier in a disease cycle and more likely to comply with physicians' treatment directives. The wealthier were less likely to die from a car crash or gunshot wound than were the poor. The gap reflected not so much access to medicine as differences in underlying life choices, which had become more pronounced in the closing decades of the twentieth century. Moreover, isolated pockets of extreme poverty perpetuated unhygienic cultures, which proved resistant to health education efforts. When a child grew up in an area where most adults smoked, it was far more difficult for the child to choose not to smoke.[43]

Disparities between blacks and whites were, if anything, even more pronounced. Black men lived, on average, seven years less than white men and were more than twice as likely to die from cardiovascular disease. They contracted AIDS at five times the rate of white men, had substantially higher rates of oral cancer, and tended go far longer than white men in having cancer undiagnosed. Higher rates of smoking and obesity in African Americans contributed to higher rates of heart disease, but so did higher rates of poverty among this population. A pair of public health researchers deemed black men the "proverbial canary in a coal mine" insofar as their poor state of health presaged the declining state of the health of poor men of all races.[44]

Not only did black men suffer more than white men from most contagious and chronic diseases, but the disparity between the two racial groups was growing. From 1979 to 1998, for example, the ratio of black to white victims of cancer increased from 1.4 to 1.45; of obstructive pulmonary disease from 1.74 to 1.8; of asthma from 2.38 to 3.27; and of diabetes from 1.83 to 2.1. In fact, one of the few bright areas for black men was mental health; although the groups suffered equally from depression, white men committed suicide at nearly twice the rate of black men.

Beyond the disparities in health status between white and black Americans lay disparities in healthcare treatment when black patients sought care. For example, among patients with cancerous tumors in their lungs, 77 percent of white patients had the tumors surgically removed versus only 64 percent of black patients, leading to an 8 percent differential in survival rates.[45] Black patients were significantly less likely than white patients to receive many organ transplants, endoscopies, and joint replacements, and significantly more likely to undergo hysterectomies and amputations. In the VA system, black patients with heart disease were 54 percent less likely than white patients to undergo coronary artery bypass grafting (CABG) and a third less likely to receive cardiac catheterization. Nationally, black cardiac patients underwent CABG at one-fourth the rate of white patients.[46] Even the distribution of prescription drugs was racially biased. A study in the late 1990s found that pharmacies in predominantly black neighborhoods were less likely to stock opioid painkillers than were those in white neighborhoods.[47] In another study, researchers used audiotape and questionnaires to elicit information about physician behavior toward 458 black and white patients to discern differences displayed toward patients of different races in empathy and communication style. The researchers found that doctors were 23 percent more "verbally dominant" and 33 percent less "patient-centered" when treating black patients—suggesting latent paternalism on the part of the doctors.[48] With black physicians scarce and white physicians demeaning, black citizens had little chance to improve their relative health standing.

Racial disparities were rooted in part in disparities in income, insurance coverage, smoking rates, diet, and education. Black Americans were more likely to smoke, be obese, drop out of high school, be poor, and lack private health coverage. But even within controlled groups—Medicaid recipients, for example, or veterans seeking care in the VA system—the disparities remained. Doctors treated black patients differently than they did white ones, using less aggressive interventions and less complex formulations. As the pharmacy data showed, even when doctors prescribed similar regimens across the racial spectrum, black patients faced additional barriers in availing themselves of the remedies.

A major part of the problem continued to be a paucity of black and Latino physicians. After increasing slowly in the 1960s, the percentage of all US physicians who were either black or Latino had settled at 7 percent, despite the fact that these groups represented 23 percent of the general US population. Although medical schools had made substantial efforts to increase the number of minority students in their classes, they found that high-performing minority undergraduates disproportionately eschewed scientific and medical careers for law and business. Efforts to identify talented minority students at earlier ages, through gifted-and-talented programs and college preparatory outreach programs, failed to boost the number of qualified medical school applicants years later.

A paucity of minority physicians hurt minority communities. Besides disproportionately caring for minority patients, black and Latino physicians were disproportionately likely to practice in underserved areas (12 percent of graduating minority medical students, versus 6 percent of white medical students), to choose primary care (60 percent versus 24 percent), and to treat patient groups who were largely insured through Medicaid.[49] One study showed that Latino physicians practiced in neighborhoods that were, on average, populated with twice the density of Latino residents as neighborhoods cared for by non-Latino doctors; black doctors made similar practice choices.[50] It appeared that the route to providing better care for Latino and black patients was through training more Latino and black doctors.

Health planners in the federal government, working with the AAMC, inaugurated Project 3000 by 2000 in the early 1990s: an effort to boost the nationwide enrollment of minority medical students to three thousand. The program built partnerships between medical schools and college and high schools in an effort to recruit and motivate talented minority youth to apply to medical schools. Early results suggested some success (the entering class grew to 12 percent minority by 2000), but in part this simply reflected growing numbers of Latino students in the US school system.[51]

A number of health planners pointed to the Supreme Court's *Bakke* decision two decades previous as decisive in discouraging minorities from applying to medical school. Allan Bakke, a white applicant rejected by the medical school of the University of California at Davis in 1973 and 1974, despite having higher grades and MCAT scores than a number of admitted black applicants, had sued the university's regents for racial discrimination. The trial court found for Bakke and ordered the medical school to cease using race as a factor in admissions. The California Supreme Court upheld the lower court's decision. The regents appealed to the US Supreme Court, which issued a series of convoluted opinions in 1978 allowing the university to use race as a factor in admissions, but prohibiting it from setting aside specific numbers of seats for minority students. That is, universities could consider race but could not set explicit racial quotas.[52]

Despite the infamy of the decision, data did not support the notion that the Bakke decision had demoralized potential black applicants or otherwise dissuaded talented minority youth from pursuing medicine. Applications from minorities had already peaked several years before the *Bakke* decision and did not noticeably fall afterward. Rather, the problem seemed to lie in the pipeline of scientifically oriented minority students coming out of high school and college. Too few pursued majors in the hard sciences in college or sought summer research internships. Black and Latino students disproportionately attended lower-ranked, less research-intensive colleges where fewer faculty pursued research, fewer had grant support with which to pay college students for summer work, and fewer had contacts in the scientific community. The long-term remedy for racial disparities in medical care lay with the hard, grassroots work of improving minority high school achievement to prepare students for more competitive undergraduate institutions, which could better funnel them toward medical school. The road was long.[53]

Perhaps the most catastrophic health event for black men at the turn of the century was AIDS. The disease, which had started in the United States in the gay community, had migrated into the IV drug–using community and had come to rest heavily in the black community. By 2000, AIDS was hardly a disease of everybody, but it was very much a disease of the subset of people who regularly used IV drugs or slept with people who did. In 1979, just under two black men died of infectious disease for each white man; by 1998 the ratio was nearly six to one.[54]

One bright spot in erasing the many health disparities in the United States was the continuing success of Medicaid and S-CHIP. Medicaid patients had begun to migrate into managed care plans en masse in the early 1990s; by 2003 nearly 60 percent of all Medicaid beneficiaries were enrolled in the plans (versus less than 10 percent in 1990). The plans tended to offer better quality care to Medicaid beneficiaries, as they were tightly regulated and required to offer comprehensive benefits, care coordination, regular primary care, and a full drug formulary.[55] Moreover, in pushing Medicaid toward managed care, Congress had mandated that the managed care contractors locate themselves along public transportation lines to ensure access to patients without private cars.[56]

The S-CHIP program, begun in 1997, gained momentum over the succeeding years and by 2006 was serving 6.6 million children. The program gave states latitude in designing health insurance programs for children from families between 100 and 200 percent of poverty (most states simply expanded their Medicaid programs to serve these children) and contributed federal matching funds to cover up to 83 percent of the cost of the programs.[57] Among children between 100 and 200 percent of poverty, the uninsurance rate fell from 22.5 to 16.9 percent during this time, and new outreach programs conducted by the states promised to accomplish more. Although the program was not an entitlement—Congress had capped it at $40 billion and needed to reauthorize it periodically—it had bipartisan support in Congress and in the state legislatures and seemed to be one of the few bright points in poverty alleviation in the nation at the time.[58]

Not all was rosy with Medicaid, however. Governors feared the ever-increasing cost of the programs and the growing ranks of physicians who refused to treat Medicaid patients, while patients continued to suffer from the systemic health problems of poverty. The state of Tennessee, which had pushed Medicaid to the progressive edge with TennCare in 1994, announced in 2005 that it would need to make drastic cuts in the program. Physicians could not get reimbursed by TennCare, and managed care contractors began to close their enrollments. The state's fiscally conservative governor, Phil Bredesen, proposed shrinking the state's Medicaid rolls by 323,000 (out of 1.3 million), which would mean a loss of $1.1 billion in federal matching funds, hospital closures, physician out-migration, and possibly fifteen thousand jobs. The program was, in the words of one savvy reporter, "the monster that might eat Nashville," and the only recourse was to slay it.[59]

Medicaid programs worked, but seemed always underfunded. Part of the problem was that Medicaid patients tended to be expensive—the typical Medicaid patient filled thirty prescriptions a year, consumed substantial hospitalization, had a high rate of recidivism in chronic illness, had higher-than-average problems with substance abuse, and had a poor record of medical compliance. At the same time, the states could only fund the programs at a fraction of the rate, per patient, as did private insurance companies, and thus doctors and hospitals were forced to endlessly do more with less. For many doctors and hospitals, serving the poor was consistent with their pro bono community commitment, but nearly all eventually reached a point of exhaustion. Medicaid could not endlessly raise enrollment without sweetening the reimbursement formulas, and no state could afford to do both.

11

(Un)Affordable Care

The Suffering Middle Class

Americans have always complained about hospital bills, but in the years following the widespread adoption of managed care practices, these bills grew exponentially worse. Managed care companies saved money in a variety of ways, but one of their most powerful tools was aggressively negotiating discounted rates with hospitals. Hospitals responded by sharply raising their stated rates on virtually all services and implementing a dizzying array of fees, supplementary charges, and itemized add-ons. For the well-insured, the extras were onerous but tolerable; for the uninsured, who had no third party to negotiate discounted rates on their behalf, the inflated rates were disastrous.

Through the early years of the 2000s, horror stories emerged about $10 aspirin tablets, $150 bags of sucrose solution, and $60 nebulizer ampules. A study by the Institute for Health and Socio-Economic Policy revealed that hospitals, on average, marked up items by some 300 percent, and that mark-ups of 700 percent were not uncommon.[1] Self-paying patients arrived home to find pages of bills that defied comprehension with hundreds of coded itemized services at fantastical prices. Even within the tortured system of prices, patients found that hospitals frequently made errors, double-billed for some services, or billed for physician visits that had never taken place. One couple pondered the charge for a wheelchair that included itemized charges for the chair's brakes, footrests, armrests, seat, and seatbelt, in addition to the basic (and inflated) charge for the wheelchair itself.[2]

Even well-insured people were vulnerable. Many insurance policies had substantial required co-payments—often 20 percent of total billings—which could add tens of thousands of dollars for relatively short and mundane hospital stays. At the same time, a growing number of insurance policies increased the annual associated deductibles from relatively nominal fees (between $0 and $500) to several thousand dollars. Last, as more people found themselves limited to tight provider networks by their managed care companies, the cost of going out of net-work rose precipitously. When patients left the network, they also left behind the discounted rates their insurance had negotiated. Leaving the network for an MRI meant not only paying the 30 percent out-of-network charge but paying that 30 percent on a grossly inflated rate—often double the discounted rate. An in-network MRI might cost a patient 10 percent of a negotiated $800 fee ($80) whereas an out-of-network MRI might cost a patient 30 percent of a nonnegotiated fee of $2,500 ($750).

Inflated hospital rates, high deductibles, high out-of-network charges, and even predictable 20 percent co-payments on extremely high hospital charges all contributed to a spate of medical bankruptcies in the early 2000s. One research team found that medical bankruptcies—personal bankruptcies driven wholly or largely by unforeseen medical expenses—rose 2,200 percent between 1981 and 2001.[3] Medical bankruptcies tended to hit hardest at working-class people who failed to qualify for Medicaid or S-CHIP programs and either lacked insurance entirely or were underinsured. Layoffs tended to drive the trend as former mid-level managers and white-collar professionals renewed their previous work as noninsured consultants or contractors. Elizabeth Warren, a professor at Harvard Law School, noted, "The people we found to be profoundly affected are not some distant underclass. They're the very heart of the middle class. These are educated Americans with decent jobs, homes and families. But one stumble and they end up in complete financial collapse, wiped out by medical bills."[4]

Increasing co-payments, deductibles, out-of-network charges, and out-of-pocket payments for drugs weighed heavily on US consumers as the decade progressed. Where once a comprehensive health insurance policy shielded a family from substantial medical bills, increasingly this was no longer the case. People found themselves underinsured, rather than uninsured, and a single hospitalization or monthly drug bills for a chronic condition could unmoor a middle-class family. Free market advocates tended to argue that increasing pressure on a family's purse could induce individuals to make more informed and responsible healthcare purchasing decisions, but policy analysts responded that normal consumer behavior simply could not take place in the health-care environment. Often prices were opaque at the point of purchase, and few people had the wherewithal to negotiate rates while seeking urgent or critical care. People did not purchase healthcare the way they purchased other services. They had little ability to discern their own demand (patients could not self-diagnose without substantial training) and less ability to formulate a cost-effective therapeutic response. The essence of the patient–doctor relationship was one of dependency, if not outright helplessness.

Traditionally, health insurers had acted as purchasing agents and patient advocates. But as health insurance moved to a managed care model and shifted substantial costs onto patients, the old advocacy model withered. Patients who thought themselves well-insured found themselves vulnerable to bill balances totaling tens of thousands of dollars. As middle-class horror stories proliferated, and as middle-class concerns percolated through the political process, the call rose again for some sort of broad governmental intervention in the healthcare markets.

Obama's Approach

President Barack Obama chose health reform as the keystone of his do-mestic policy agenda, despite early indicators that growing unemploy-ment, financial breakdown, and housing default were the more critical challenges facing his administration. Taking lessons from the failings of the Clinton planning process, he charged congressional leaders with designing a new plan, building off of the managed competition core of the Clinton approach. In so doing, he hoped to maintain an air of trans-parency in the planning process while gaining commitment from the large congressional majority he had inherited on taking office.[5]

Obama did dictate a number of requirements for whatever plan would eventually emerge. It should provide coverage for all citizens with a comprehensive array of benefits; it should contain cost-control mechanisms to help bring healthcare inflation under control; and it should allow those with private insurance to keep their current coverage. He also charged Congress with creating a public plan that would compete alongside private plans while serving as an insurer of last resort to those who could not afford private health insurance. The president hoped that the public plan, with its low administrative overhead, would provide downward price pressure on the private plans and force cost savings into the system.[6]

The public plan was the most contentious single aspect of the proposal. Supporters viewed it as a natural safety measure for a population with broadly different employment situations and financial resources, not unlike state universities and public swimming pools, which coexisted comfortably with private competitors. Opponents viewed the public plan as the "camel's nose under the tent."[7] The seemingly innocuous public plan threatened to underprice private plans and ultimately drive them out of business, leaving the public dependent on a government monopoly for health insurance. Even progressive citizens expressed concern over the long-term balance of government and private health insurance, while more conservative members of the electorate rejected the idea of a government health insurer beyond that serving the elderly.[8]

Politically, a successful plan depended on the support of the pharmaceutical industry, the physicians' lobby, and the private health insurance industry. Forced to contend with ever-diminishing private insurance reimbursement and increasingly dense bureaucratic systems, physicians had changed their view substantially over the previous decades. One wag noted, "physicians were now poor enough to start voting Democrat."[9] The American Medical Association notably did not oppose the reforms from the start, although it viewed the public option skeptically. Similarly, both the pharmaceutical industry (represented by the Pharmaceutical Research and Manufactures of America) and the insurance industry (represented by the Health Insurance Association of America and the American Association of Health Plans) were willing to work with the effort provided they could be guaranteed protections from government regulation, price negotiation, and public agency competition.[10]

The end result of these pressures was a plan that drew from managed competition insofar as it leveraged the existing private insurance market while creating health purchasing cooperatives, expanding Medicaid, mandating employer and individual buy-in, and protecting drug reimbursement. When enacted, the plan would all but guarantee all legal citizens health insurance. At the same time, it would do little to hold down costs and would fail to create a competing public option that might impose discipline on the private plans.

As President Obama had hoped, most of the planning and negotiating for the health reform took place within House and Senate committees, with Democratic leaders Harry Reid (D-UT) and Nancy Pelosi (D-CA) taking the lead in creating planning bodies. At the outset, Obama worked to find Republican supporters for the bill, wanting to present the finished product to the people as a result of bipartisan agreements. He focused particularly on the two moderate Maine Republican senators (Olympia Snowe and Susan Collins) but ultimately realized that few GOP members would back the plan. Critical to the plan's success was the Democrats' filibuster-proof sixty-seat majority in the Senate: the precise number needed to close debate and allow a bill to come to vote.

In October 2009, the House of Representatives passed one version of the bill, and two months later the Senate passed a similar but not identical version of the bill. Only one Republican member of the House voted in support of the bill, and not a single Senate Republican did so, meaning that the Democrats depended on every one of the sixty votes (fifty-eight Democrats and two independents) to be able to close debate and avoid a Republican filibuster. All that remained was to create a conference committee to reconcile the bills and pass the new law.

Tragedy had struck the month before, however, with the death of Senator Edward M. Kennedy of Massachusetts, one of the liberal lions of the Senate who had served since taking his brother's seat in 1963. Most people assumed that the dependable but unexciting state attorney general, Martha Coakley, would win the special election to fill out the remainder of the term held that December. However, in a remarkable upset, Republican Scott Brown beat Coakley, who had run a lackluster campaign and failed to pull the Democratic base to the polls. Brown had made the health reform package the centerpiece of his campaign, noting that electing him would effectively kill the new law as it would allow for a Republican filibuster on the reconciled bill.[11]

In a piece of legislative legerdemain, the Democrats preserved their victory by retaining the Senate bill's language in the conference committee, meaning that the bill would not have to return to the full Senate for a vote and thus could not be filibustered. The Senate version was given to the House, which passed it in March. Obama signed the bill into law the next day as the Patient Protection and Affordable Care Act (ACA) of 2010, quickly nicknamed "Obamacare." In his signing statement, the president noted, "Today, after almost a century of trying;

today, after over a year of debate; today, after all the votes have been tallied—health insurance reform becomes law in the United States of America."[12]

Terms of the ACA

The ACA contained a number provisions slated to be implemented over a staggered schedule over seven years, with the critical pieces becoming operative in 2014. The main provisions were as follows.

Expansion of Coverage to Age 26

This was a minor part of the bill, but a welcome component for middle-class families watching their children get taken off their family health policies at age 22. The move intelligently targeted one of the most under-insured demographic groups in the nation—young single adults—and was thus welcomed by a large group of voters who would see an immediate benefit yet would receive nothing new in federal funds. The main cost would be borne by employers and employees who would pay the increased premiums associated with the coverage. This provision became effective in 2010.

Regulating Away Preexisting Conditions

This was the single most important part of the bill and possibly the most welcome for legions of uninsured people. Starting in 2014, no health insurer in the United States would be allowed to deny an applicant coverage for a preexisting condition, nor would an insurer be allowed to carve out coverage for that condition from the overall menu of benefits. Moreover, although insurers could modify premium rates to some degree to comport with the risk profile of the patient, such modifications would be greatly limited, such that the most expensive policy for a given age group could not cost more than four times the price of the least expensive.

Healthcare observers had mixed feelings about this stipulation. On one hand, for the first time millions of people who were essentially un-insurable because of their health histories would be able to buy insurance on the open market. On the other hand, some more progressive advocates felt that by allowing the ceiling to go as high as four times the rate of the base, many would continue to be priced out of the market. Although Congress established a sliding scale of subsidies to allow the poor to purchase private insurance, the scale topped out at household income of approximately $80,000, meaning that anybody above that would need to pay the full rate or be forced to do without. Moreover, the provision exposed insurance companies to substantial risk, as the costly new beneficiaries would need to be subsidized by newly enrolled healthy young people. If young people opted out of insurance markets in large numbers, premiums would rise rapidly and create the opportunity for a death spiral, in which rising rates forced ever-more relatively healthy people out of the insurance market.

Mandating Buy-in

All people would be forced to purchase health insurance—through their employer, through Medicare, through Medicaid, or on an individual basis through the newly established insurance exchanges. This universal mandate flowed naturally from the proscription of preexisting condition carve-outs, for without the mandatory buy-in people would simply wait until they were sick or injured to purchase insurance. The two stipulations worked conjointly.

The mandate was the most controversial part of the ACA, since it appeared to extend the federal government's purview beyond its constitutional limits. Never before had Congress made a law requiring citizens to buy a product on the private market, although various states had made laws requiring helmets, auto insurance, and flood insurance conditional on certain other types of ownership.

In disallowing preexisting condition consideration, the law needed the mandatory buy-in provision. If the government was to require insurance companies to sell insurance to all comers, no matter how sick, then it also needed to require all people to buy health insurance, even when they were healthy. Otherwise, nobody would buy health insurance until they were sick, and the system would quickly collapse. A parallel scenario would be requiring insurance companies to sell all people homeowner policies, regardless of the condition of their houses. If it did not require everybody to buy a homeowner policy, then people would simply wait until their house caught fire to buy a policy, knowing that the insurance company would not be allowed to refuse coverage.

People who failed to comply would be fined up to $700 per person or up to $2,000 per household (on a sliding scale relative to income). Policy analysts expressed concern that these fines were not substantial enough to induce everybody to purchase insurance. Young single people in good health might choose to simply pay the $700 fine rather than purchase coverage costing many times that. The true resolution to this moral hazard—that of closing emergency room access to the uninsured—was never seriously considered as a policy option. Unsympathetic though Americans might be to their poorer citizens, no politicians of either party suggested that uninsured sick people be locked out of the charity care system, either formally or informally.

Mandating Employer Provision

The new law largely leveraged the existing system of private health insurance through the workplace and extended coverage by mandating that all employers of at least fifty people purchase coverage for their employees and families, or pay a steep fine that would be used to subsidize workers who would then have to purchase individual policies. The law further stipulated the comprehensiveness of the insurance packages and capped rates at which employees could be made to pay in. The use of employer-sponsored insurance with the risk of a fine had historically been called a pay-or-play system, and formed the core of many other nations' insurance systems, including those of Germany, Switzerland, the Netherlands, and France.

By preserving and expanding the existing employer-based system, the law preserved the massive $1 trillion private insurance system and leveraged the natural risk pooling that occurred in employee groups, removing the burden of risk pooling for millions from the new insurance exchanges. By preserving the private health insurance system, the law also promised to preserve the heavy administrative burden, inefficiency, bureaucratic inconsistency, and frustrating opacity of the existing payment system. Providers who complained bitterly over waiting hours on the phone for sign-off from utilization review nurses or for permission to admit, refer, or treat were offered no relief. Moreover, in preserving the existing insurance system, the new law effectively rejected substantial anti-inflationary provisions that might tame the extraordinary fiscal burden healthcare was posing to the US economy. A dangerous adversary had been placated, but at a very high cost.

Critics of the law, particularly owners of small businesses, singled out this provision for attack. They noted that by setting the threshold at fifty full-time workers (that is, employees working at least thirty hours a week), they were effectively thwarting job creation. Business could try to get around the provision by capping employee hours at twenty-nine a week or by outsourcing work to contract firms rather than legally employing people to do their work. Critics of this stripe tended to call the ACA a "job-killing" bill: a moniker that found particular reception with Republican primary voters during the 2012 presidential race. The Republican presidential nominee, Mitt Romney, articulated this point of attack in saying, "With unemployment stuck over 8 percent for forty months, we can't afford policies that kill jobs and stifle innovation in one of America's most dynamic industries."[13] Funding mechanisms encapsulated in the bill, such as taxes on medical devices and brand-name pharmaceuticals, gave further credence to these accusation of the law as a drag on economic growth. Given the slow recovery from the disastrous 2008 recession, such sentiments found receptive audiences.

Establishing Health Insurance Exchanges

The law required states to establish new health insurance exchanges by 2014, which would contract with private insurers to set group rates, and then add individual insurance purchasers into purchasing pools. This would lower administrative costs for insurance companies, reduce rates for private individuals purchasing insurance, and allow a person to achieve the same market leverage as could be gained by a large employer purchasing a group policy. Although the theoretical underpinning of these exchanges was clear—they essentially allowed individuals to buy in bulk and realize the cost savings—the actual implementation was problematic. Only one state, Massachusetts, had ever created such an exchange before, and the administrative challenges appeared to be formidable. Many people were concerned about what appeared to be an added layer of bureaucracy between themselves and an insurance agent.[14]

In a political miscalculation by congressional Democrats, the law's authors allowed states to opt out of creating state-level health exchanges by offering them access to a new federal exchange instead. The bill's designers assumed that most states, particularly the politically conservative (so-called red) states, which argued most tendentiously for expanded state rights and limited federal government, would reject federal control of their exchanges. But in a strange example of unintended consequences, over the next few years many governors who most vociferously opposed the law refused to create state-level exchanges, requiring the federal government to come in and run their exchanges for them—essentially operating in hostile territory. By fall of 2013, when the exchanges actually began to register new beneficiaries, the federal government found itself responsible for operating health exchanges in thirty-four states, creating a far larger administrative challenge for the

Obama administration than it had anticipated.[15] This massive and unforeseen obligation of the federal bureaucracy led to the disastrous
launch of the website for the federal health exchange in October 2013,
inviting ridicule and accusations of administrative incompetence.

Why did so many states reject the opportunity to build their own
websites? The decision seemed born out of broad rejection of domestic
initiatives coming from the Obama White House. Many Republican
leaders never seemed to accept the legitimacy of Barack Obama's presidency, questioning the fairness of the election and (more perniciously)
his claims to be a US citizen. At the extreme, a movement of "birthers"
accused the president of being born in Africa or being a citizen of Indo-
nesia and thus constitutionally unqualified to hold the presidency. These
accusations, given voice by the real estate developer Donald Trump,
ultimately forced the president to post his long-form birth certificate
on the White House website in 2012: a humiliatingly defensive posture
for the nation's foremost political leader.[16]

The refusal of many Republican governors to establish state health
exchanges also reflected a desire to distance themselves from a program
they feared voters would credit to the sitting administration. That is,
the refusal to set up websites was an effort to sabotage the program from
the start.[17] Notably, the decision to establish state health exchanges or
to use the federal exchange fell cleanly along political lines, with most
state exchanges being set up in states with Democratic governors or
Democrat-controlled legislatures (or both). The historic Republican
support for increased federalism and states' rights might have dictated
precisely the opposite effect.[18]

Expanding Medicaid

The ACA expanded coverage by leveraging the existing Medicaid
plans of the states that had demonstrated themselves able to provide
effective insurance coverage over four decades to poor Americans.
Medicaid, previously available only to those at or below the federal
poverty line, would now be available in all states to individuals and
families with incomes up to 133 percent of the poverty line. Though
few children would be affected by this new provision, many working-
class men, previously shut out of the insurance market, would now be
able to get coverage this way.

In expanding Medicaid, the ACA was adding incrementally to a
long history of Medicaid expansion, starting almost immediately after
the program was inaugurated in 1966. Governments of both political

persuasions had expanded Medicaid to cover early screening, pregnant women, uninsured children above the poverty line (through the S-CHIP program), and permanently disabled adults. At every juncture, state governments had enthusiastically endorsed the mandated expansions, knowing that even as they would be liable for part of the cost of the expansions, the moves would bring billions in federal funds into state coffers to help offset the costs of caring for the states' neediest citizens. Democratic authors of the ACA never considered the idea that governors or state legislators would reject the Medicaid expansion provisions. They had not done so in the past, and few state leaders had expressed concern over the provisions during the debate over the bill.[19]

The federal government agreed to shoulder almost the entire cost of the Medicaid expansion. In the first two years of the expansion (2014–16), the federal government would pay 100 percent of the additional cost, and thereupon would drop its contribution in a series of steps to 90 percent by 2020. Governors and state legislators who rejected the expansion questioned the federal government's long-term commitment to it and professed concern that the states might ultimately be left to pay the full cost of the expansion up to the usual state contribution to Medicaid.

Filling the Medicare Part D Donut Hole

Medicare Part D, enacted in 2005 to provide prescription drug coverage to the elderly, had left a bizarre donut hole for that population for which annual prescription billings between $2,500 and $5,000 were wholly uncovered. Expenditures below $2,500 were 75 percent covered, and expenditures above $5,000 were 100 percent covered, but the middle range of expenditures fell on the consumer in toto. The ACA closed the donut hole by covering prescription drug purchases up to $5,000 a year at 75 percent and purchases over $5,000 at 100 percent. This new provision was designed to win over any objections from the elderly and the AARP, as well as the pharmaceutical industry. The gap-closing coverage was to be enacted incrementally from 2010 to 2020.

The donut hole fix was more political foil than reform. The elderly, a critical constituency to both parties, had complained bitterly about the odd coverage gap when Part D was unveiled and questioned the rationale for it. The gap had been driven by an effort to cap the cost of the program over ten years at $700 billion: a threshold critical to President George W. Bush's goals at the time the program was designed. Almost everybody involved with the planning of Part D had agreed that the gap made no sense from a policy standpoint—neither progressive nor equitable—nor did it serve to cap demand for drugs. Moreover, it had antagonized the precise constituency Part D was intended to placate: elder voters. Around the nation through the second half of President Bush's term, senior citizens had demanded that the donut hole be rectified, with the AARP calling it a "top priority" and a "dangerous gap in prescription drug coverage that leaves more than three million seniors without affordable medications each year."[20] It had been an awkward compromise born of political necessity, which the Obama administration was eager to take credit for fixing. By implementing the fix over nearly ten years, the Obama administration could claim success while deferring payment for a decade.

Sliding Subsidies

By mandating that all people purchase coverage, but by only allowing those with incomes up to 133 percent of poverty to buy into Medicaid, the new law risked impoverishing middle-class and lower middle-class citizens by forcing them to buy insurance policies that could cost $15,000 a year or more: a serious liability for a family at the median household income of $63,000. In response to this concern, the new law provided a sliding scale of subsidies in the form of income tax rebates that would cover part of the cost of a policy for household with up to $80,000 of annual income. Conceivably, some families with income above that level would still find the cost of purchasing insurance onerous and choose to pay the fine rather than buy coverage, but the law's designers predicted that no more than 1 percent of people would make this choice.

The subsidies were critical to the program's success. The ACA forbade the continuing sale of minimalist "catastrophic" policies (with very high deductibles and low annual ceilings) meaning that a sizable number of working-class people who had purchased these policies because of their low premiums would find that they could no longer do so. Rather, they would be pushed into more comprehensive policies with higher annual and lifetime maximums, at considerably higher costs. This limitation ultimately proved to be a political liability at the program's roll-out as the administration was accused of reneging on its promise that people could keep their present insurance plan if they liked it.[21] Given the already limited budgets of the nation's middle-class families, the promised subsidies were a critical part of maintaining affordability.

In a bizarre footnote to the subsidy program, the reluctance of many states to expand their Medicaid programs created a new donut hole of uncovered near-poor citizens. The designers of the law had assumed that those with incomes between 100 and 133 percent of the federal poverty line would now be covered under expanded Medicaid programs and thus stipulated that subsidies for policies purchased on the exchanges would begin at 133 percent of poverty. Thus, residents of states that had refused to expand their Medicaid programs who earned between 100 and 133 percent of the poverty line were actually too poor to qualify for subsidies but too wealthy to qualify for Medicaid. This gap in coverage left an estimated four million people uncovered, with no recourse but to hope that their governors and legislators would choose to expand their Medicaid programs.[22]

Revenues

The cost of an expanded Medicaid program and federal subsidies to lower income families buying insurance through the new exchanges was to be offset in part by a 40 percent tax on "Cadillac" insurance plans (those costing more than $27,000 for a family per year) and in part on expanded taxes for couples with over $250,000 in annual income. Taxes were also assessed on providers, drug makers, and device makers, while the floor for the medical expenses deduction was raised from 7.5 to 10 percent of annual household income. All revenue sources together were expected to generate $410 billion over ten years.

Many critics of the plan noted that the promised revenues were unlikely to offset the ultimate cost of the subsidies and expanded Medicaid benefits. While projections for such a program could never be highly accurate (nobody could accurately predict wage and GDP growth, human behavior, health costs, and even general demographic trends more than a year or two out), even the loosest estimates and projections suggested that the ACA would quickly become another drain on the federal budget, as had other domestic entitlement programs in the past.[23] The modest cost containment provisions in the bill, largely in the form of the newly established Independent Payment Advisory Commission, were tarred from the outset as insubstantial and "lacking teeth."[24]

Results and Prognostications

The new ACA faced extensive opposition during its enactment and immediately following. Many Republicans vowed to find ways to repeal it, fail to fund it, undermine it, or simply ignore it. All of the major

Republican candidates for the presidency attested publicly in 2011 that they believed the universal mandate violated the constitution, and that if elected they would repeal it by executive order immediately on taking office (although it was not clear if they would have the authority to do this). In late 2013, several Republican congressional leaders, notably Senators Ted Cruz of Texas and Marco Rubio of Florida, vowed to undermine the law not by repealing it but by simply refusing to fund it. Garnering support in both Houses, these legislators led a sixteen-day government shutdown in an effort to pass a federal budget that denied all funding to the law, but ultimately capitulated in the face of declining public support.[25] On a more superficial note, by that time House Republicans had voted to repeal the law repeatedly over the five years following its passage, each time finding its efforts (predictably) stymied in the Democrat-controlled Senate. Unlike in the cases of many contentious pieces of legislation past, when minority party leadership had vigorously contested the legislation while under debate, but ultimately pledged loyalty to the law once passed, in the case of the ACA the debate seemed to never end.

More immediate were legal challenges to the law. At least six cases challenging its constitutionality were filed by state attorneys general, with half being found for the plaintiffs in the US appellate courts and half being found for the law. In other states, the legislatures attempted to ban the implementation of portions of the law. Most of these challenges, both legal and legislative, questioned whether the constitution's Commerce Clause could be used to justify the universal mandate and the creation of health exchanges. The US Supreme Court reviewed these challenges during the 2011–12 court term and decided, in a five to four decision, that the individual mandate was constitutional because it was effectively a tax in another form, which Congress had the right to impose. However, it ruled that the Medicaid mandate was unconstitutional given the parameters of the original Medicaid legislation, which offered federal matching funds to states that established Medicaid programs but did not mandate that states establish programs.[26] The decision, which preserved the most important component of the law, nonetheless proved disastrous for the donut hole families who were not covered by the exchange subsidies yet were locked out of the cheaper catastrophic policies many had previously availed themselves of. For this group, the ACA proved to be actually harmful. While twenty-eight states exercised their right to unilaterally expand their Medicaid programs, many of the states in which the poor resided disproportionately did not.[27]

By almost any measure, the ACA was the most significant health reform effort since the passage of Medicare in 1965. The ACA bound the United States to virtually all other industrialized nations in guaranteeing health coverage to all of its citizens. Although it would be misleading to say the United States now had "national health insurance," it would be correct to say that the nation had adopted a hybrid universal coverage model used by many European countries that combined employer coverage, purchasing cooperatives, poverty care programs, government insurance, private gap policies, and insurance regulation to mandate that all citizens be covered with some form of insurance in a fiscally realistic manner.

The new law greatly expanded coverage; largely ended the problem of job-lock; leveraged the existing power of the private insurance markets; preserved the autonomy of private physician practices, clinics, and hospitals; and exploited the proven efficacy of employee-based risk groups, which could be communally rated. There were several serious problems that it did not solve, however.

Expanding National Debt

A number of analysts suspected that the revenue mechanisms embedded in the law would not cover the full costs of expanded Medicaid and insurance premium subsidies. Estimates ranged from the law actually creating budget surpluses (as stated by the Congressional Budget Office) to costing the federal government $600 billion over its first ten years.[28] Those who expressed skepticism about the rosy budget numbers presented by the CBO cited the failure of past efforts to contain costs, including the many adjustments made to the prospective payment system. The ability of providers to find ways of manipulating reimbursement rules, expand diagnostic related group parameters, build capital investment costs into ordinary fees, and generally inflate prices and costs had been a consistent rule of healthcare delivery in the United States. Indeed, when *Time* magazine published a cover article on the rising costs of hospital care in spring 2013, the issue proved to be the best-selling one of the year.[29]

Cost Control

The new law did little to bring historic healthcare inflation under control. Its most important cost control provision was the creation of a new panel called the Patient-Centered Outcomes Research Institute, which would make nonbinding recommendations to the Centers for Medicare and Medicaid Services (CMS) in developing Medicare reimbursement policy (which would presumably serve as a market exemplar for private payers). The institute would have a nineteen-member board drawn from multiple stakeholders, independent from the government. The law also created a National Prevention, Health Promotion, and Public Health Council to advise the surgeon general on health promotion efforts. A number of health watchers questioned the authority invested in both boards. Michael Cannon, of the libertarian Cato Institute in Washington, noted in a speech in January 2009 that, "The graveyards in Washington are littered with agencies that have tried to use comparative effectiveness research to reduce government spending on low-value medical services, as well as schemes to contain Medicare and Medicaid spending that have later been undone by Congress."[30] Matthew Holt, co-chair of Health 2.0, wrote similarly in a blog, "The Federal Health Board, if it gets established, will get defanged by lobbyists immediately."[31]

Illegal Immigrants

The law did not expand coverage for undocumented residents in the United States, who continued to labor without benefits and were frequently locked out of the mainstream medical system. These immigrants sometimes paid cash to providers, sometimes exploited local emergency rooms, and sometimes returned to their home countries for care. Notably, the issue of covering illegal residents was never raised as a major point in the debates over the legislation. Few members of Congress wished to introduce the divisive topic of immigration reform into the debate. Most assumed that immigrant coverage would become part of a future, broader debate over immigration reform, possibly to be addressed in the president's second term.

Unfortunately, illegal migrants posed a substantial challenge to the US poverty care system. Numbering some twelve million, they routinely required healthcare in their stays in the United States and threw themselves, not infrequently, on the largesse of public hospitals and community clinics, where they would expand the rolls of bad debt and uncompensated care. One research group estimated the annual cost of illegal immigrants to California's public hospital system at $1.4 billion in 2004, while the Commonwealth Fund estimated that over half of the undocumented workers in California lacked any sort of health insurance and posted the highest rates of impoverished children of any group in the United States.[32] The ACA did nothing to alleviate this problem.

Opposition

Liberal critics of the new law felt that it did not do enough. While putatively expanding access to health insurance, the law did nothing to lower prices, reduce the role of for-profit insurance, encourage physicians to pursue careers in primary care, and push the populace toward wellness rather than illness. The law did not attempt to move healthcare delivery into a more coordinated system of care except in the most oblique ways. Arnold Relman, one of the fiercest and most vocal critics, penned a savage rejoinder to the tepid defense of the law given by Obama health advisers Ezekiel Emanuel and Victor Fuchs. He wrote: "No other health care system is as focused on generating income as ours, and in no other country is medical care marketed and advertised so aggressively, as if it were just another commodity in trade. This increases health costs, while hospitals concentrate on the delivery of profitable, rather than effective, services. It also favors those who can pay over those who need medical care but can't afford it."[33]

The law was redistributive, insofar as it actuarially smoothed premium prices and heavily subsidized premium costs for poorer people, but it preserved the existing system of independent providers reimbursed through for-profit payers. For expansive thinkers like Relman, the law was pernicious—it implied comprehensive reform while merely tweaking small gaps in the system of access. Nearly half of all newly insured people in the coming decade would come through the Medicaid expansion, which had hardly required the bloody political battles preceding the ACA's passage.[34] Relman and his allies deeply resented the fact that the new law would actually empower for-profit insurance companies by enlarging their role in the nation's health system, despite the fact that these companies had contributed disproportionately to making the system an "unjust and expensive shambles."[35]

Liberal critics were deeply skeptical of the law's tepid efforts at controlling healthcare inflation, whose unbridled growth threatened to erode the efficacy of medical care. Both stipulations in the law aimed at cost control—the Independent Payment Advisory Board (IPAB) and the mandate for Medicare to create incentives for physicians to form accountable care organizations (ACOs)—were weak. The fifteen-member IPAB, to be appointed by the president, was empowered to make recommendations to Congress should Medicare costs rise too rapidly, but physicians could probably counter the recommendations by raising the volume and intensity of their services. The newly envisioned

ACOs—multispecialty groups of physicians who would contract with
Medicare to provide coordinated care at reduced rates—were little different than HMO contractors already reimbursed through Part C.
Moreover, the regulations surrounding the ACOs were so tightly written
(taking up nearly 125 pages) that they were likely to dissuade interested
groups from participating.[36]

Conservative critics thought the new law went too far. In a certain
sense, a number of conservative opponents probably thought that any
effort at health reform emanating from a Democrat-led White House
would have been unacceptable. The rise of the Tea Party in 2008 had
ushered in an era of destructive vitriol aimed at the new administration
in which any legislative victory was seen to accrue to the advantage of
the left. Senator Jim DeMint (R-SC) spoke for many on the right when
he said publicly of the ACA, "If we're able to stop Obama on this it will
be his Waterloo. It will break him."[37] But aside from general opprobrium
toward Democratic initiatives, Republican opponents disdained the
regulatory overlay on what they perceived to be a functioning market-
based system of care and they opposed the expanded taxes required to
pay for some of the law's redistributive actions. The law required new
taxes, new arms of government, many new regulations, new mandates
on both businesses and individuals, and new federal oversight of vast
portions of the private sector: all anathema to Tea Party Republicans.

The part of the law that drew particular ire from the right was the
individual mandate requiring all people to purchase health insurance
by 2014 or pay the modest penalty. Democrats had resisted using the
word *tax* in describing the penalty (in an effort to dodge the accusation
of creating an unpopular new tax) but in so doing had entered constitutionally uncharted waters. The individual mandate would be the first
time that private citizens would be compelled to purchase a good or service in the private sector to comply with a federal law—requirements
for many other goods (such as motorcycle helmets and seatbelts) were
predicated on voluntarily choosing to engage in certain activities. Defenders of the law justified the mandate in the constitution's Commerce
Clause, which allowed Congress to "regulate commerce . . . among the
several states." In the past, Congress had used the clause to justify federal regulations around environmental protection, child labor, employment conditions, and drug labeling, to name a few.[38]

But never before had Congress used the Commerce Clause to mandate individual purchases of privately distributed goods. Republicans

seized on the inconsistency to challenge the law's constitutionality, and four state attorneys general brought suit in the year following the law's passage. In arguing the government's case before the US Supreme Court, the US solicitor general, Donald Verrilli Jr., agued that the mandate simply recognized the fact that virtually all citizens already had health insurance insofar as Medicare regulations required hospitals to stabilize all urgent care patients regardless of ability to pay, but this argument stumbled in that it suggested that people should be required to purchase a private product in an effort to secure public resources.[39]

Chief Justice John Roberts's deciding vote in the case in 2012 was grounded explicitly on deeming the penalty a tax, which Congress clearly had the right to impose.[40] Although the word *tax* had been avoided in drafting the legislation, certainly the punitive use of the tax seemed more similar to a fine than to a traditional tax. Court observers responded with surprise and confusion over Roberts's reasoning, but in the end explained his behavior as a tortured effort to recenter the Court, which was viewed by many to be increasingly partisan. Roberts defended his action by stating that the Court had "general reticence to invalidate the acts of the Nation's elected leaders."[41]

Even having escaped the legal challenges, however, the law seemed guaranteed to anger many while failing to deliver on its promises. Many young people would likely choose to pay the modest tax rather than purchase a catastrophic health policy costing many thousands of dollars, which would fail to reimburse them for most ordinary medical bills. Health insurers would have little incentive to streamline their operations or fold part of their ample profit streams into reimbursements. Doctors, hospitals, and other providers could continue their expansive and expensive patterns of medical care delivery with little fear of recourse from the new IPAB, and with little incentive to join cumbersome new ACOs. The nation as a whole would continue to spend hundreds of billions of dollars annually on healthcare, which was largely used in purchasing overpriced drugs and technology and superfluous procedures and physician visits.

Efficacy

The venomous opposition to the ACA oddly missed the law's essential failing: its inability to provide comprehensive coverage for most middle-class citizens. The law mandated a series of tiers in which all new policies listed on the exchanges must fall—platinum, gold, silver, and bronze—with plans placed into tiers depending on their price. Plans in the silver tier, for example, were required to pay for 70 percent of all expected health costs in a given year, and plans in the bronze tier were required to pay for 60 percent. Although this sounded generous, the reality was that the majority of all payments would go to pay for catastrophically high medical bills, meaning that the plans would fail to pay for ordinary medical expenses. Thus, the plans were designed with high deductibles and co-payments and very high annual maximum caps for each household. The initial silver plans, for example, had average annual household deductibles of $6,000, with $60 co-payments for physician visits and $11,500 in annual out-of-pocket caps. The bronze plans were even worse, requiring $10,500 annual deductibles, and 35 percent co-insurance fees on all doctor visits even after the deductible was reached. Given that the majority of people purchasing plans on the exchanges were expected to purchase silver or bronze plans, most newly insured people would find that their policies failed to pay for any but their most catastrophic healthcare costs.

These high out-of-pocket costs reflected the underlying inefficiencies of the US healthcare marketplace, which the new law had done virtually nothing to ameliorate. The nation's health bill in 2009 was expected to be $2.5 trillion, constituting over $8,000 per capita, and over 18 percent of the nation's GDP. Federal agencies estimated that the costs would rise to 20 percent of GDP within a decade, and top $13,000 per capita annually if substantial changes were not imposed.[42] These figures were 25–40 percent higher than figures for other industrialized countries (nearly 100 percent higher than those in the United Kingdom) and reflected years of excessive price and volume growth in a system with few incentives to move toward greater efficacy. True, the ACA had delivered on its mandate to provide the opportunity for all citizens to purchase health insurance, but in the absence of systemic reform the new health insurance policies could cover only a small portion of most families' health bills.

US health costs had been growing unbridled for years. By 2010, estimates of waste in the system ranged between $550 billion and $910 billion annually, constituting nearly a third of all monies spent.[43] Donald Berwick, a former administrator of CMS, along with Andrew Hackbarth parsed the waste into six categories as follows, with estimates of associated wasted funds:

- *Failure of care delivery*, which included errors, lack of appropriate preventive care, and absence of best practices treatment. Some healthcare scholars titled this category "undertreatment." ($102–154 billion)
- *Failures of care coordination*, which resulted from fragmented systems in which different providers failed to communicate with each other, resulting in redundant tests and procedures. ($25–45 billion)
- *Overtreatment*, which included tests and procedures that lay beyond those recommended by solid outcomes research. Though not necessarily harmful to the patient, overtreatment added little utility while drawing excessive funds from the system. ($158–226 billion)
- *Administrative complexity*, which produced excessive administrative costs associated with multiple payers, lack of care coordination, and lack of unified recordkeeping. The GAO had estimated the cost of these inefficiencies as nearly a fifth of all US health costs as far back as 1991. ($107–389 billion)
- *Pricing failures*: Overpricing resulting from lack of transparency and the inability of patients to shop competitively for services. In an effort to stem these failures, the CMS strongly encouraged all consumers of plans on the exchanges to shop anew for cheaper policies each year, despite the fact that research indicated that health insurance was an inherently "sticky" consumer product from which consumers were unlikely to switch. ($84–178 billion)[44]
- *Fraud and abuse*: Closely allied with overtreatment, this waste derived from explicit efforts from providers to sell bogus treatments and issue false bills. ($82–272 billion)[45]

In building health reform on such a wasteful system, the new law had reinforced many of the most wasteful practices of US healthcare, and forced millions of people to purchase shares in a leaky system. It was as if a nation that could produce only overpriced, shoddy automobiles now required every citizen to purchase one at "market" price. True, everybody would now have a car, but few would be happy with that car and many would find themselves poorer.

Worse, little in the law promised to rein in the excessive costs. Efforts to fight overpricing, overtreatment, and lack of coordination would all require the leverage of single or state-based payers (as was true in Canada) or global caps on training and investment (as was true in Western Europe). The much touted potential of electronic health records to provide coordination and efficacy seemed overblown; by 2008, only 12 percent of all hospitals and physicians had adopted them, and many of the systems in place could not communicate with each other.[46] The market system, which generally produced cost savings and efficiencies in other parts of the economy, failed along multiple axes in healthcare. Health insurance companies continued to draw off 25–30 percent of revenues for profit and administrative costs, leading to extravagant salaries for top executives.[47] Physicians, device manufacturers, pharmaceutical companies, hospitals, and insurers had tremendous incentives to maximize sales of new procedures, tests, pills, and products, and consumers had little ability to shop competitively to drive prices down. Most new procedures—such as joint replacement, angioplasty, and dialysis—actually produced greater costs, in contrast to other sectors of the economy in which innovative technologies reduced costs.[48]

The ACA did little to alleviate the growing problems of obesity and chronic disease, which relentlessly drove health costs higher. Since the 1970s, chronic disease had progressively displaced infectious disease as the primary driver of health costs in the United States. By 2000, nearly 80 percent of all health expenditures were directed to patients suffering from chronic disease, and nearly three-fourths of all physician visits involved treatment for chronic disease. The shift had been inevitable in the wake of postwar revolutions in antibiotics and virology, but medical care and medical training had not shifted adequately to accommodate the new reality. The result was sharply higher expenditures due more to demographics and underlying behavioral trends than to any specific pathogen.[49]

Thus, newly insured people under the ACA would have little to celebrate. Middle-class people could protect themselves against much-feared medical bankruptcies, but they would continue to have to weigh purchasing basic health services against other staples such as housing, transportation, food, clothing, and childcare. Reversing inflationary trends would require manifest changes in the ways the United States trained clinicians, financed hospital care, and worked to keep people healthy. In the absence of such change, the law could only expand coverage rates for marginalized citizens with suboptimal insurance that would do little to pay for care or keep them healthier. The law's promise—to make care "affordable" to all—was empty.

Threats

By late 2016, the major provisions of the ACA had been in place for nearly three years: time enough for people to experience the effects of the law and judge its merits for themselves. Twenty-seven states plus the District of Columbia had expanded their Medicaid programs, covering an additional eight million people. An additional fourteen million previously uninsured people had purchased plans on the exchanges, leading to a net gain of twenty-one million insured Americans. (One million buying plans through the exchanges had previously been insured through the individual market or by their employers.[50]) Fully 85 percent of the people who had purchased plans on the exchanges had used the federal subsidies available to them. Coupled with large numbers of young people who could stay on their parents' policies through age 27, the law had shrunk the percentage of uninsured people to the lowest rate in history.

All was not well, however. Large numbers of young healthy people refused to purchase plans, daunted by the high prices and high deductibles. The refusal of young people to "buy in" created a more expensive risk pool for insurers operating on the exchanges, forcing them to raise prices sharply in 2016. By October, when prices were posted on the exchanges for people wanting to renew their policies for the following year, the average price of the silver (second least expensive) plans had risen 21 percent *in one year*.[51] Such an increase in premiums was unprecedented; health inflation in the 1970s, at its peak, had never exceeded 13 percent in a year. Premium increases in individual states were even worse, with prices rising by 50 percent in Kansas, 51 percent in Alabama, and 125 percent in Arizona.

Although insurers in some states were keeping premium hikes close to general inflation, the majority raised prices to accommodate expensive risk pools or because lack of competition allowed for monopoly pricing. The price hikes were even more pronounced when compared with a general easing of the national healthcare cost curve. The combined effects of the 2008 recession, changes in Medicare reimbursement, and more aggressive price-making by large corporate buyers of insurance had succeeded in reducing the predicted 2019 national health bill from $4.5 trillion (before the passage of the ACA) to just over $4 trillion.[52] The ACA was gently "bending the cost curve," in President Obama's words, but was distributing its savings unevenly.

Donald Trump's election to the presidency in November 2016 boded poorly for the future of the ACA. For six years Republicans had promised to repeal the law when they were able to, and they now controlled the White House and both houses of Congress. Trump himself had repeatedly promised to repeal the law throughout his campaign, and the new Congress that convened on January 1, 2017, set repeal as one of their highest legislative priorities.

Republicans soon ran into problems, however. Although they had fervently promised to "repeal and replace" the law as soon as they were able, they quickly realized that creating a new law that would end the most disliked component of the ACA (the individual mandates) while preserving the most popular parts (the prohibition on excluding pre-existing conditions) would be impossible without severely disrupting insurance markets across the country. Several Republican leaders posed a roadmap in which they would repeal the law without a replacement, but delay the implementation of the repeal by several years to allow them time to come up with a good replacement. Insurance companies expressed distaste for this option; it would be very difficult to maintain a presence on the exchanges if they did not have a clear idea of the future risk pool they would be insuring.

The most concrete plan for replacing the ACA in fall 2016, was proposed by Paul Ryan (R-WI), the Speaker of the House of Representatives. Ryan had made his name as a conscientious deficit hawk on the House Budget Committee, and he continued to promote general austerity while holding the Speaker position. His plan retained large parts of the ACA while tweaking it in places: providing age-related tax credits to purchase individual insurance premiums, for example, and replacing the individual mandate with a severe financial penalty for delaying enrollment in coverage. The three most important components of the Ryan proposal, all endorsed by the Trump team, were the creation of high-risk pools at the state level, which would be subsidized with $25 billion in federal grant support; easing restriction on purchasing insurance across state lines; and capping the tax exclusion on employer-sponsored plans. The first of these three proposals would allow insurance plans to charge lower premiums for younger, lower-risk purchasers; the second would (hopefully) create more vigorous individual insurance markets, which would drive down prices; the last would essentially raise taxes on high-wage earners who at the time could deduct the entire value of their employers' contribution to their health plans.[53]

The Ryan plan maintained a number of components that were central to Democrat demands—substantial federal subsidies for low-income people to purchase individual plans, portability, and prohibition of carve-outs for preexisting conditions. At the same time, by technically (though not effectively) ending the individual mandate and easing regulations on insurance markets and policies, the plan promised to make at least some Republican voters happy. Nonetheless, the transition from the ACA to a new sort of plan would be immense and promised to upend insurance markets around the country. Two components of Ryan's plan that had nothing to do with the individual markets—transforming Medicaid to a block grant program and transforming Medicare to a "premium support system" wherein Medicare beneficiaries would purchase individual plans on the private market—promised to profoundly upset the nation's elderly plus nearly every governor in the country.

Repealing the ACA without replacing it promised to be even more disruptive. Most private insurance companies would likely withdraw from the individual insurance market entirely in the unpredictable environment that would result from a sudden repeal, or at least sharply raise their premiums to account for future uncertainties in the risk pool.[54] The government would lose an estimated $680 billion in tax revenue created by various components of the ACA, and large numbers of people trying to purchase individual policies would find themselves uncovered for their preexisting conditions or locked out of the insurance market entirely. A team at the Brookings Institution led by Alice Rivlin estimated that nine million people would lose coverage immediately under such a scenario, unable to afford a policy without federal subsidies, and that large numbers of people with preexisting conditions would be rejected shortly after.[55]

One variable for the incoming Trump administration was the popularity of the program as a whole. Nobody knew precisely how many Americans really liked the ACA, how many hated it, and how many were indifferent to it. The planners had made a strategic political mistake in allowing the bronze and silver plans to have such high deductibles; millions of middle-class people had unenthusiastically purchased plans with benefits that were hardly obvious given the enormous out-of-pocket deductibles they were required to pay. At the same time, others had lost their previous inexpensive, high-deductible catastrophic plans, which were now illegal because of their low annual and lifetime limits. Many hated the individual mandate without understanding that the only way to make insurance affordable for the sick and elderly was to require buy-in by the young and healthy. That is, the ACA had not been sold to people very effectively, even if many benefited from the massive federal subsidies and Medicaid expansions now in place.

Such unpopularity and misunderstanding made the reception of the ACA fundamentally different from the reception of Social Security in

1935 or Medicare in 1966. Both of those programs had also met with some fear and distaste, but skeptics had been quickly won over. Within just a few years of implementation, those programs were among the most popular of all federal programs. But the complex, weighty, and unloved ACA was ripe for repeal, even if its future was not clear. It had never had the support of large numbers of people, and even those who benefited from its provisions were skeptical of its true utility.

12

![black bar]

Afterword

US healthcare cannot be neatly wrapped up. The story is tremendously complex—winners and losers fight daily over the spoils of a $2.3 trillion enterprise. Many who have won are not even aware of the degree of their victory; others who are losing or have lost do not understand how far they have fallen behind. While the US health system can excise cancers and transplant organs, it can also deny its wares to millions of able-bodied adults who cannot easily access a physician, tolerate a deductible, or afford the price of a brand-new drug. Our lower life expectancies and higher rates of infant mortality (compared with other developed nations) are testament to the strange ways we squander our medical patrimony.

Many critics of US medicine use the word *broken* in describing the system, but the word is misleading. Aspects of the system work well, and as would be expected in a market-driven healthcare system, savvy entrepreneurs thrive. Perhaps a more apt descriptor for the system is *irrational*, insofar as we might expect our national medical enterprise to achieve certain agreed-on goals, much as we ask of our transportation and criminal justice systems. Irrationality suggests not so much broken healthcare as misallocated and cumbersome healthcare. Millions of people delight daily in the miracles of modern medicine and savor their access to drugs, procedures, images, and hospitals. But millions of others rue the system's impenetrable bills, arbitrary restrictions, impersonal professionals, and redundant procedures. The system is not so much bad as tragically suboptimal.

Rather than try to summarize the net merit of the system in a few lines, I offer the reader a catalog of the system's winners and losers.

Winners

Many individuals, industries, and professionals benefit tremendously from the peculiar state of US healthcare. I categorize winners as those people, firms, and sectors who are wealthier, healthier, happier, and better cared for as a result of either producing, consuming, or paying for healthcare in the United States than they would be elsewhere. The list of winners is long, and for this reason comprehensive change in US medicine is elusive. When millions benefit every day by embracing an established paradigm, the paradigm will prove highly resistant to change.

One often overlooked group of beneficiaries of US medicine is the nation's vaunted *medical schools*. The 141 schools that offer the MD degree in the United States (and their Canadian cousins) produce much of the world's leading biomedical research and partner with many of the world's leading tertiary care hospitals.[1] Funded by federal research largesse, Medicare training supplements, and grateful alumni, these schools continue to draw many of the world's most ambitious young biomedical researchers, who come to train with the leading basic and clinical scientists in unparalleled facilities. Other nations harbor first-rank research labs and offer excellent training, but no other nation supports the volume, depth, and excellence of the US research and training effort.

Unlike in other nations, *private health insurers* in the United States get rich. Although payers in almost all other nations are either nonprofit agencies or arms of government, in the United States payers are often extensions of for-profit insurance companies. The companies collectively draw off nearly 30 percent of all premiums for administrative costs and profits, leading to multimillion-dollar payouts for senior executives and collective industry profits of $12 billion.[2] Such wealth could only be generated in a medical sphere that invites entrepreneurship and rent-seeking behavior.

Similarly, *pharmaceutical companies* in the United States are uniquely profitable. Leveraging lengthy patent protection periods, liberal allowances for direct-to-consumer marketing, and monopoly pricing, the pharmaceutical sector has been consistently one of the nation's most profitable for half a century.[3] Although most other wealthy nations either use monopsony power to negotiate lower rates for drugs or pharmaceutical caps to mandate lower prices, the United States has failed to take these actions. Indeed, provisions in Medicare Part D explicitly prevent the Centers for Medicare and Medicaid Services (CMS) from negotiating discounted drug prices for Medicare beneficiaries.

Reports of the demise of *US hospitals* have been greatly exaggerated. Although the hospital industry underwent a painful period of consolidation in the late 1980s and early 1990s, few have closed in the past two decades. Most are today highly profitable (regardless of their designation as a for-profit or nonprofit), and the majority have expanded or upgraded their infrastructure relatively recently. Although occupancy rates are higher today than they were thirty years ago, the rates continue to be low by world standards.[4] US hospitals generally overinvest in technology whose high costs must be recaptured in extravagant billing practices, which have become almost legendary.[5] As I write this, the *Guardian* is reporting on a bizarre but quite predictable instance of a British tourist who unexpectedly had to give birth (eleven weeks early) in a New York hospital. The resulting bill of more than $200,000 would have meant insolvency for the woman and her family, had not their supplementary insurance company in the United Kingdom agreed to foot the bill.[6]

Procedure-oriented *specialists* continue to earn substantially higher incomes in the United States than they do in other countries. Average income for many specialty groups had declined over the past two decades, but it is still substantially higher than income for primary care physicians and more than compensates specialists for lost income in the additional years of required training. At present, median income for general surgeons in the United States is just under $200,000 a year, whereas the comparable figures for surgeons in Canada and France are about 25 percent lower.[7] (Means are substantially higher.) One telling indicator is that while the United States successfully imports more than five thousand foreign-trained physicians each year into its residency programs, it exports virtually none of its own MDs into other nations' residency programs. A specialty practice in the United States remains a highly attractive career for physicians around the world.

The *US armed forces*, covered by the TriCare system, and its many veterans who seek care through the Veterans Administration system, benefit from high-quality medicine dispensed for free or near-free prices. Servicemen and -women on active duty receive care for free through the excellent TriCare system which, though a closed system, benefits from its close associations with the civilian health sector. The VA health system, which has in the past drawn attention for its shortcomings, has improved significantly over the past decade. Error rates are low, efficacy is high, and most reports suggest that the quality of medical and nursing care is consistently high.[8] Ironically, while most Americans firmly support the government-provided model of care for soldiers, sailors, and veterans, relatively few feel that the extension of that model to the general population would produce high-quality care.

Perhaps the greatest winners in the current US health ferment are the nation's *elderly*. Covered by Medicare parts A, B, and D, and further insured through private Medigap policies and state Medicaid programs, senior citizens in the United States are among the best insured people on Earth. Drawing off the earnings of current workers, and benefiting from substantial advances made in treating chronic illness, cancer, stroke, heart disease, and joint ailments, the nation's elderly generally take from their invested savings in the Medicare trust fund by the time they reach age 72. Medical care consumed in the years after that are delivered courtesy of current taxpayers. The programs as currently structured cannot be sustained; the Medicare trust fund will run dry in the next two decades. For now, however, those who participate in the system are able to access some of the best of US healthcare while paying relatively modest premiums and fees.[9]

Last, *allied health professionals* have benefited from the current health care environment. Nurses, occupational and physical therapists, psychologists, social workers, and related clinical professionals are all able to bill third-party payers for services rendered or hitch themselves to hospitals which bill on their behalf. In this environment, these non-MD professionals are able to induce demand in a manner similar to their physician colleagues. Their clientele become insensitive to price and utility calculations and seek out care not because it is worth more than it costs but because it is worth anything at all. Unconstrained demand for their services has induced a glut in the professions, however, so virtually all are currently in the process of raising their entrance and training standards. In a nation with declining wages, these plum roles have become dependable points of entry to the middle class.

Losers

Losers in the US system are those who would probably fare better if the country moved toward a more coordinated and nationalized system of payment or care. Whether bearing the cost in higher taxes, higher payroll deductions, lost wages, poorer access to care, or poorer health, these are the many participants in the US health system whose continued decline undermines the system's claims to supremacy.

Those who pay the greatest price for the peculiar idiosyncrasies of the US health system are *middle-income patients*. Mostly insured through employer-funded policies, this group pays increasingly more for healthcare through higher premiums, deductibles, co-payments, and out-of-network fees. When lost wages are added (in the form of wage discounts to fund employer portions of the health premium), rising health costs have taken up almost all wage increases for this sector over the past two decades. Unexpected fees and billing errors, requiring substantial investments of personal time to rectify, add to the burden on this group.

Middle-income patients receive good but not excellent care. Their ability to spend substantial time with their primary care physicians has been truncated by administrative pressures in the system. Their medical records are unreconciled and scattered among multiple providers. Physicians in their provider networks can be summarily excluded, forcing these patients to find new providers. Patients covered through policies bought on state and federal exchanges shoulder very high deductibles which may preclude them from seeking preventive care. Although provisions in the Affordable Care Act have ended the scourges of job-lock and insurance denial, middle-class patients find that larger portions of their total income are going toward healthcare without providing additional quality.

Second to the middle class, the *nation's poor* are victims of vagaries in the US system. Insured largely through the state Medicaid programs, poor citizens find that their Medicaid coverage is frequently inadequate to ensure access to a broad range of high-quality physicians. While they are able to access hospital care at most US nonprofit hospitals, they have a much harder time finding private physicians willing to take them on as patients or even treat them on an episodic basis. The poor are substantially better off health-wise than they were before the advent of Medicaid in 1965, but they are falling behind the middle class in their ability to take advantage of the full capabilities of the health system.[10]

As the Medicaid rolls swell in those states that have chosen to expand their programs under the provisions of the Affordable Care Act, barriers to access are accentuated. Increasing numbers of physicians are closing their practices to additional Medicaid patients, and many hospitals are favoring privately insured patients over Medicaid patients. The poor, who already consume a lower tier of care, are finding themselves driven into a class of welfare medicine that echoes the charity care of earlier generations.

Among the most bitter victims of our delivery model are the nation's *primary care physicians*. Internists, general practitioners, pediatricians, and geriatricians who diagnose the majority of illness and treat, oversee, and refer patients to appropriate venues have seen their incomes decline as their workloads have risen. Nearly all primary care physicians in practice today feel substantial pressure to treat patients more quickly and impersonally, even as they contend with greater threats of malpractice litigation, more complex practice management challenges, and greater challenges to their judgment. Some internists have tried to reclaim their autonomy by establishing cash-based boutique practices, but most soldier on through fatigue and burnout in an effort to keep up with unrealistic patient loads. Greater levels of student debt from training only exacerbate the pressures on these professionals.

Closely allied with primary care physicians are the nation's *medical students*, who face rising training expenses, increasingly lengthy training regimens (for those who enter postresidency fellowship training), and declining incomes. Many doctors continue to earn generous incomes, and pay in the profession remains among the highest for all US workers. But combined undergraduate and medical school expenses can leave young doctors with hundreds of thousands of dollars of debt, even as they face years of modest earnings while they undergo residency training. These debts are unique to US medical students, as almost all other countries heavily subsidize medical training with general tax revenues.

Oddly, the *young* pay a price to live in the United States. In other countries, population health costs are smoothed through payroll deductions and general taxation, but in the United States the costs are being smoothed by inflated premiums for young people. As young adults purchase policies through the exchanges, they consistently pay more for their premiums than their risk profiles demand—part of the ACA's broader effort to distribute health costs more evenly through the population. At present, the young can opt out of the exchanges by paying a modest penalty, but in coming years the penalties will rise and the young will feel compelled to purchase policies. Given the high rates of unemployment among Americans in their twenties, and the poor prospects for future wage hikes for this cohort, the young will disproportionately feel the weight of an inefficient health system.

Last, *US taxpayers* are net losers in the current system. Nearly 43 percent of the US health bill is funded by the government in the form of Medicare, Medicaid, TriCare, Veterans Affairs, and various state programs. All of this nearly $1 trillion must come from US taxpayers in the form of state and federal income taxes and payroll taxes. Residents of other nations pay a higher portion of their incomes in taxes to fund national health programs, but in turn they have far fewer out-of-pocket costs. US taxpayers bear the substantial burden of tax funding these many programs while shouldering portions of their own premiums and co-pays, deductibles, and out-of-network costs. A more efficient health system would lighten this burden and open up government funds for other programs.

The Future

We opened a new chapter in the history of US medicine with the full implementation of the Affordable Care Act. The law is the single most substantial change to healthcare delivery in a generation, and appeared, at the time of its passing, to usher in a new era. At long last, the United States would have "national" health insurance, or at least a closely coordinated matrix of private health insurers to protect the population. Many of the worst abuses and excesses of a private insurance system would end, and one of the greatest threats to middle-class insolvency dispelled.

Alas, early reports have been middling. Citizens purchased fewer policies on the exchanges in their first years than had been anticipated at the law's passing, and the policies that were sold were overwhelmingly bronze and silver policies, which largely failed to properly insure the middle class. Large groups of people resented the perceived overreach of the law, particularly the individual mandate. After holding steady for two years, the price of premiums increased markedly in the third, even as many insurers abandoned the public exchanges. Many people found that they needed to switch plans regularly if they were to take advantage of cheaper premiums, requiring them to find new doctors included on their new rosters. More ominously, substantial numbers of physicians opted out of many plans, leaving newly insured Americans with few choices in actually accessing healthcare.

Our system of care is inefficient, redundant, and expensive, and the ACA has done little to ameliorate these problems. A system composed of overbuilt hospitals, overengineered devices, overmarketed drugs, and overtrained professionals is an expensive system. Most other nations rely on global budgets, regulated monopsony, or government-negotiated rates to rein in the worst rent-seeking behaviors. In the absence of the heavy hand of government, people will continue to pay more in premiums and out-of-pocket costs than they would otherwise need to. The ACA better distributes the costs of the system but does not actually reduce the sum total cost.

There is no one ideal health system. Different nations produce high-quality, universally available care using a variety of different delivery and payment mechanisms. All do it for substantially less than the United States does. All rely on regulation, mandates, global investment caps, universally negotiated rates, and strict restrictions on training slots. That is, every other nation plans its healthcare delivery, while the United States is more inclined to allow individual agents to shape the system.

US entrepreneurship and ingenuity has produced much in the past. At present, the United States has the most robust economy in the world, some of the world's lowest unemployment rates, a sound banking system, manageable national debt, healthy equity markets, and facilitated flows of investment funds. The nation continues to lead the world in basic and applied research, innovative high-tech products, media content, agricultural output, and energy. It has escaped the worst of the economic malaise that swept Europe after 2008, and recovered from its recession far more rapidly than did Japan. It is no wonder that Americans have an almost religious faith in the healing powers of free enterprise.

Healthcare, however, is different. More akin to education than to a consumer product, it demands third-party funding and external oversight. The redistributive quality of health insurance demands intense public investment and regulation. Markets largely do not work to produce and distribute high-quality healthcare; certainty few healthcare consumers can articulate which services and products they actually want.

A rosier future for US medicine will demand reconceiving the production, distribution, and financing of healthcare. Much as we depend on highly trained professional government servants to defend our borders and police our streets, so we may need a technically proficient health oversight force to vigilantly guide and manage our healthcare enterprise. Our healthcare delivery system has extraordinary components—world-class hospitals, brilliant physicians, prize-winning researchers—but the whole is less than the sum of its parts. To achieve its potential will require talented management to coordinate the efforts of thousands and rationally impose order on its disparate enterprises.

Acknowledgments

Thank you to Paul Ehrlich, friend and physician, who read the entire manuscript and helped me clarify points and avoid errors and redundancies. Thank you also to Samantha Ehrlich, my research assistant on three books, who tracked down hundreds of old articles and saved my eyesight from the microfilm reader.

I have made my professional home at the Marxe School of Public and International Affairs for a decade. Wonderful colleagues who have offered thoughtful insights and conversation include Jerry Mitchell, Floss Frucher, Michael Feller, Richard Hochhauser, Lewis Friedman, Jack Krauskopf, Dan Williams, Diane Gibson, Martha Stark, John Casey, Carla Robbins, Frank Heiland, Don Waisanen, Nancy Aries, and Neil Sullivan. Karl Kronebusch and Sandy Korenman offered particularly astute feedback at a faculty seminar where I presented an early draft of this work, and I am grateful to them. David Birdsell, dean of the Marxe School, has consistently supported my research with release time and supplementary funding.

Joshua Schor, Rajiv Kinkhabwala, David Gutstein, Andrew Engel, and Hillary Kruger are physicians in my life who remind me of the remarkable role the profession plays in our lives and in our society. Gwen Walker at the University of Wisconsin Press saw potential in this manuscript and encouraged me to improve and refine it. Thank you to Rozlyn, who lives in fear that I will give up my day job to open a delicatessen, and to my children, who are still not sure how I earn a living.

Notes

Introduction

1. TRB, "Sick," *The New Republic*, 1971.
2. Rashi Fein, "The Case for National Health Insurance," *Saturday Review*, August 22, 1970, p. 27.
3. The literature on the history of national health insurance and comprehensive health reform is extensive. See particularly, Ronald Numbers, *Almost Persuaded: American Physicians and Compulsory Health Insurance* (Johns Hopkins University Press, 1978); Monte Poen, *Harry S Truman versus the Medical Lobby* (University of Missouri Press, 1996); Daniel Hirschfield, *The Lost Reform: The Campaign for Compulsory Health Insurance in the United States from 1932 to 1943* (Harvard University Press, 1970); Jill Quadagno, *One Nation Uninsured: Why the US Has No National Health Insurance* (Oxford University Press, 2005); and Beatrix Hoffman, *The Wages of Sickness: The Politics of Health Insurance in Progressive America* (University of North Carolina Press, 2001).
4. Paul Ellwood and Michael Herbert, "Health Care: Should Industry Buy It or Sell It?," *Harvard Business Review*, July–August 1973, p. 102.
5. Quoted in William Kissick, "Health Care in the 80s: Changes, Consequences and Choices," *Vital Speeches*, September 26, 1985.
6. Numbers, *Almost Persuaded*, particularly chapters 1 and 2.
7. See the transcript of the oral argument in *National Federation of Independent Business v. Sebelius*, available at http://www.supremecourt.gov/oral_arguments/argument_transcripts/14-114_lkhn.pdf.

8. A wealth of these studies may be found in the Dartmouth Atlas of Healthcare, available at http://www.dartmouthatlas.org.

9. Dana Seiden, "Diminishing Resources: Critical Choices," *Commonweal* 112, March 8, 1985, p. 139.

10. Statistics are from Leda Judd, "Federal Involvement in Healthcare after 1945," *Current History* 72, May–June 1977.

11. CBO, "Opportunities to Increase Efficiency in Healthcare," June 16, 2008, p. 1.

12. For households, the bronze-tier exclusions were $11,000.

13. For a longer-term timeline of the impact of medical costs, see Ronald Numbers, "The Third Party: Health Insurance in America," in Judith Leavitt and Ronald Numbers, eds., *Sickness and Health in America* (University of Wisconsin Press, 1985).

14. Atul Gawande, "Something Wicked This Way Comes," *New Yorker* blog, posted June 28, 2012.

Chapter 1. A System Run Amok

1. "A Dose of Control for Health Costs," *Business Week*, March 14, 1970, p. 32.

2. Aaron Catlin and Cathy Cowan, "History of Health Spending in the United States, 1960–2013," unpublished paper, November 19, 2015. Also, Godfrey Hodgson, "The Politics of American Health Care: What Is It Costing You?," *Atlantic* 232, October 1973, p. 51.

3. Joel Kramer, "As Costs Soar, Support Grows for Major Reform," *Science* 166:3909, November 28, 1969, p. 1126.

4. See Joseph Newhouse, "Toward a Theory of Nonprofit Institutions: An Economic Model of a Hospital," *American Economic Review* 60:1, 1970, pp. 64–74. Also, Alan Sager, "Opiate of the Managers," *Society*, July–August 1986.

5. "Soaring Costs of Medical Care," *US News*, June 16, 1975, p. 52.

6. "Does Everybody Have to Drive a Cadillac?," *National Review*, March 9, 1971, p. 247.

7. "How to Improve Medical Care: Interview with the Head of the Blue Cross Association," *US News*, March 24, 1969, p. 46.

8. On this point, see John Griffith, Walton Hancock, and Fred Munson, "Practical Ways to Contain Hospital Costs," *Harvard Business Review*, November–December 1973.

9. Ibid., 138.

10. Lowell Bellin, "Changing Composition of Voluntary Hospital Boards," *HSMHA Health Reports* 6:8, August 1971, p. 675.

11. The literature on the history of poverty care and the role of hospitals in providing that care is substantial. See Sandra Opdycke, *No One Was Turned Away* (Oxford University Press, 2000), for a case study of public hospitals in New York; also, David Rosner, *A Once Charitable Enterprise: Hospitals and*

Healthcare in Brooklyn and New York, 1885–1915 (Cambridge University Press, 1982). More generally on public hospitals, Harry F. Dowling, *City Hospitals: The Undercare of the Underprivileged* (Harvard University Press, 1982). For a history of charity care generally and Medicaid specifically, see my own *Poor People's Medicine* (Duke University Press, 2006); and Laura Katz Olson, *The Politics of Medicaid* (Columbia University Press, 2010). For a broader history of social welfare in the United States, Edward Berkowitz, *America's Welfare State: From Roosevelt to Reagan* (Johns Hopkins University Press, 1991).

12. Sager, "Opiate of the Managers," 66.

13. "End of Hospital Shortage: Why the Turnaround," *US News,* September 6, 1971, pp. 72–74.

14. John Iglehart, "The American Health Care System: Medicare," *New England Journal of Medicine* 327:20, 1992, p. 1468.

15. On Medicaid spending during those years, see John Klemm, "Medicaid Spending: A Brief History," *Health Care Financing Review,* Fall 2000. For a contemporary report, Robert Michel, "Uncle Sam's Feverish Medical Spending," *Nation's Business,* October 1972, p. 25.

16. Klemm, "Medicaid Spending." See also Dorothy Rice, "Current Data from the Medicare Program," *Public Health Reports* 83:9, September 1968.

17. On this point, see Theodore Marmor, *The Politics of Medicare,* 2nd ed. (Aldine Transaction, 2000), and Jonathan Oberlander, *The Political Life of Medicare* (University of Chicago Press, 2003).

18. See "Plugged In," *Newsweek,* July 16, 1973, p. 93.

19. The Senate Finance Committee report was excerpted in "Medicare in Trouble: Senate Study of High Costs, Abuses," *US News,* February 16, 1970, pp. 70–72.

20. Ibid., 71.

21. Foline Gartside, "Causes of Increase in Medicaid Costs in California," *Health Services Reports* 88:3, March 1973, p. 225.

22. Quoted in "Medicaid: Granting a Reprieve," *Science News* 96, August 2, 1969, p. 98.

23. See "Medicare in Trouble," 72.

24. George Schieber, Ira Burney, et al., "Physician Fee Patterns under Medicare: A Descriptive Analysis," *New England Journal of Medicine* 294:20, May 13, 1976, p. 1090.

25. George Thelen, "Let the Patient Beware," *Nation,* April 17, 1972, p. 489.

26. George Crile, "The Surgeon's Dilemma," *Harper's,* May 1975, p. 31.

27. J. Bunker, "Surgical Manpower: A Comparison of Operations and Surgeons in the United States and in England and Wales," *New England Journal of Medicine* 282, 1970, pp. 135–44; also C. E. Lewis, "Variations in the Incidence of Surgery," *New England Journal of Medicine* 281, 1969, pp. 880–84.

28. John Mecklin, "Hospitals Need Management Even More Than Money," *Fortune* 81, January 1970, p. 97.

29. "Inside Critic," *Forbes* 107, 1971, p. 48. For more on the early history of the Blue Cross plans, see Robert Cunningham Jr. and Robert Cunningham III, *Blues: A History of the Blue Cross and Blue Shield System* (Northern Illinois University Press, 1997).

30. "What Controls Mean to Medical Care," *Business Week*, January 1, 1972, p. 38.

31. Ibid.

32. "Does Everybody Have to Drive a Cadillac?," 247.

33. For helpful statistics on broad categories of health spending through 1973, see Barbara Cooper, Nancy Worthington, and Paula Piro, "National Health Expenditures, 1929–1973," *Social Security Bulletin*, March 1974.

34. The litany of ailments is paraphrased from Helen Wallace, "The Health of American Indian Children," *Health Services Reports* 87:9, November 1972.

35. Hubert Humphrey, "The Future of Health Services for the Poor," *Public Health Reports* 83:1, January 1968, p. 1.

36. Ibid., 2.

37. "If You're Black and Sick," *Newsweek*, July 7, 1969, p. 83.

38. Humphrey, "The Future of Health Services for the Poor," 4–5.

39. Robin Cohen, Diane Makuc, et al., "Health Insurance Coverage Trends, 1959–2007," *National Health Statistics Reports*, US Department of Health and Human Services, July 1, 2009. Also, Alvin Rosenfeld, "Sick and Out of Work," *New Republic* 172, May 24, 1975, pp. 7–8.

40. Jerome Schwartz, "First National Survey of Free Medical Clinics, 1967–69," *HSMHA Health Reports* 86:9, September 1971. See also Geraldine Branch and Natalie Felix, "A Model Neighborhood Program at a Los Angeles Health Center," *HSMHA Health Reports* 86:8, August 1971; and Norman Gerie and Richard Ferraro, "Organizing a Program for Dental Care in a Neighborhood Health Center," *Public Health Reports* 83:8, August 1968. For a broader history, see Bonnie Lefkowitz, *Community Health Centers* (Rutgers University Press, 2007); and Alice Sardell, *The U.S. Experiment in Social Medicine: The Community Health Center Program, 1965–1986* (University of Pittsburgh Press, 1988). Lefkowitz used extensive interviews and oral histories in writing her history.

41. David Cowen, "Denver's Neighborhood Health Program," *Public Health Reports* 84:12, December 1969, p. 1028.

42. For a nice description, see Rosemary Corner, Kay Carlyle, et al., "Appraisal of Health Care Delivery in a Free Clinic," *Health Services Reports* 87:8, October 1972. For an early evaluation of the efficacy of the program, see Mildred Morehead, "Evaluating Quality of Medical Care in the Neighborhood Health Center Program of the Office of Economic Opportunity," *Medical Care* 8:2, March–April 1970. For historical background on early health centers, see George Rosen, "The First Neighborhood Health Center Movement: Its Rise and Fall," in Judith Leavitt and Ronald Numbers, eds., *Sickness and Health in America* (University of Wisconsin Press, 1985).

43. Karen Davis, "Achievements and Problems of Medicaid," *Public Health Reports* 91:4, July–August 1976.

44. Good details on the early Medicaid program and its antecedents can be found in Keith Weikel and Nancy Leamond, "A Decade of Medicaid," *Public Health Reports* 91:4, July–August 1976. Also, Rosemary Stevens and Robert Stevens, *Welfare Medicine in America* (Free Press, 1974); and Jonathan Engel, *Poor People's Medicine* (Duke University Press, 2006).

45. Davis, "Achievements and Problems of Medicaid."

46. See David Kindig, "Residency Training in Community Health Centers: An Unfulfilled Opportunity," *Public Health Reports* 110:3, May–June 1995.

47. See Samuel Bosch, David Banta, et al., "The Mount Sinai-HIP Joint Program," *Health Services Reports* 89:3, May–June 1974.

48. VISTA (Volunteers in Service to America) was one of the original anti-poverty programs funded by the 1964 Economic Opportunity Act. Early volunteers were placed in poor areas, rural and urban, to work on education and training programs. Although the program never garnered the media attention of the Peace Corps, it has continued to recruit volunteers; as of 2017 the program has eight thousand active volunteers. See the pamphlet, *Vista . . . In Service to America*, published by AmeriCorps Vista, https://www.nationalservice.gov /sites/default/files/documents/06_0523_americorps_vista_legacybook_0.pdf.

49. Penny Urvant, "Health Advocates," *Public Health Reports* 84:9, September 1969.

50. Allen Pond, "Role of the Public Health Service in Housing and Urban Life," *Public Health Reports* 83:2, February 1968.

51. Michael Michaelson, "Medical Students: Healers Become Activists," *Saturday Review*, August 16, 1969, p. 42.

52. Michael Halberstam, "The M.D. Should Not Try to Cure Society," *New York Times*, November 9, 1969.

53. Charles Hill and Mozart Spector, "Natality and Mortality of American Indians Compared with U.S. Whites and Nonwhites," *HSMHA Health Reports* 86:3, March 1971; Frank Norris and Paul Shipley, "A Closer Look at Race Differentials in California's Infant Mortality, 1965-67," *HSMHA Health Reports* 86:9, September 1971.

54. Robert Dietsch, "Care You Can't Buy," *New Republic* 166, May 20, 1972, p. 14; Helen Wallace, "The Health of American Indian Children," *Health Services Reports* 87:9, November 1972, pp. 869-70.

55. Wallace, "The Health of American Indian Children," 871. They died at nearly double the rates from murder, suicide, gastric disease, bronchitis, meningitis, and untreated sepsis.

56. Mata Nikias, "Trends and Patterns of Dental Care in an Urban Area before Medicaid," *HSMHA Health Reports* 86:1, January 1971, p. 59.

57. Bruce Rocheleau, "Black Physicians and Ambulatory Care," *Public Health Reports* 93:3, May–June 1978.

58. Sue Guyon, "The Challenge to the Indian Health Service," *Health Services Reports* 88:8, October 1973, p. 689.

59. Bernard Davis, "Academic Standards in Medical Schools," *New England Journal of Medicine* 294:20, May 13, 1976, p. 1119.

60. Robert Ebert, "Facts about Minority Students at Harvard Medical School," *New England Journal of Medicine* 294:25, June 17, 1976, p. 1402.

61. MCAT scores for black students who took the exam were notably lower than those for white students. See *Minority Students in Medical Education: Facts and Figures* (AAMC, 1983), and Steven Shea and Mindy Thompson Fullilove, "Entry of Black and Other Minority Students into US Medical Schools," *New England Journal of Medicine* 313:15, October 10, 1985. For more on the history of racial discrimination in US medical education and hospital care, see Vanessa Northington Gamble, *Making a Place for Ourselves* (Oxford University Press, 1995).

62. "New Medical School for Blacks Planned in New York," *Jet* 66, May 1984.

63. Tom Dorris, "The Doctor Shortage and Where It Hurts," *America* 131, October 5, 1974, p. 167.

64. Richard Henry, "Use of Physician's Assistants in Gilchrist County, Florida," *Health Services Reports* 87:8, October 1972, p. 687.

65. Dorris, "The Doctor Shortage," 167.

66. Pat Perry Gray, "National Health Services Corps Teams Filling Health Manpower Void," *Health Services Reports* 87:6, June–July 1972, p. 479.

67. "Country's No. 1 Health Problem: Interview with Top Presidential Adviser," *US News* 68, February 23, 1970, p. 68.

68. Philip Abelson, "Changing Climate for Medicine," *Science* 188:4192, June 6, 1975; R. C. Parker and T. G. Tuxill, "The Attitudes of Physicians toward Small Community Practice," *Journal of Medical Education* 42, April 1967, pp. 327–44; R. C. Parker, R. A. Rix, and T. G. Tuxill, "Social, Economic, and Demographic Factors Affecting Physician Population in Upstate New York," *New York State Journal of Medicine* 59, March 1, 1969, pp. 706–12.

69. See Abelson, "Changing Climate for Medicine."

70. Loudon Wainwright, "Dilemma I Dyersville," *Life* 68, May 29, 1970. Also, "Critical Shortage of Country Doctors," *US News*, April 14, 1975, p. 67.

71. Clifford Allen, "The Health of the Disadvantaged," *Public Health Reports* 89:6, November–December 1974, p. 501.

72. USDHEW, National Center for Health Statistics, *Health United States*, 1975, HRA 76-1232. Also, Paul Gastonguay, "The Cost of Medical Care," *America* 130, January 12, 1974, p. 13. Gastonguay cites Alan Chase, *The Biological Imperatives: Health, Politics, and Human Survival* (Holt, 1972).

73. Schools which adopted three-year programs could garner $8,500 for students in their third year.

74. John Walsh, "Health Manpower Training: Funding Levels at Issue," *Science* 174, December 3, 1971, p. 1003.

75. See John Walsh, "Health Manpower Bill: Catch Is Distribution of Doctors," *Science* 188, April 25, 1975, pp. 342–43.

76. See "Not Enough Doctors: What's Being Done," *US News*, February 19, 1973, pp. 53–55.

77. Dorris, "The Doctor Shortage," 167.

78. "Growing Crisis in Health Care: Interview with John Cooper, President, AAMC," *US News* 67, November 3, 1969, p. 71.

79. Ruth Roemer, "Legal Regulation of Health Manpower in the 1970s," *HSMHA Health Reports* 86:12, December 1971, p. 1053.

80. Ibid.

81. "Comeback of the Family Doctor," *Saturday Evening Post*, Summer 1972, p. 42. For a detailed study of healthcare in the United States in 1969, see "The Plight of the US Patient," *Time* 93, February 21, 1969, pp. 53–58.

82. See, USDHEW, National Center for Health Statistics, *Health United States, 1975*, HRA 76–1232. For a contemporary news account, see John Millis, "Diagnosing the Doctor Shortage," *Nation's Business* 62, October 1974, p. 71.

83. As quoted in "Ahead: A Comeback for the Family Doctor," *US News* 66, February 10, 1969, p. 89.

84. Kerr White, "Life and Death and Medicine," *Scientific American* 229:3, September 1973, p. 29.

85. Carl Cobb, "Solving the Doctor Shortage," *Saturday Review* 52, August 22, 1970, p. 24.

86. From Maynard Shapiro, president of the American Academy of General Practice, in "Ahead: A Comeback for the Family Doctor," 89.

87. The number of FMGs from Asian schools grew sharply after US immigration laws were changed in 1965, leading to fears of rising cultural influence of Asian physicians in US medicine. A group of public health scholars refuted some of the most panicked estimates of their numbers. See Rosemary Stevens, Louis Goodman, et al., "Physician Migration Reexamined," *Science* 190:4213, October 31, 1975, pp. 439–42.

88. Tom Dorris, "The Doctor Shortage and Where It Hurts," *America* 131, October 5, 1974, p. 168. Also Barry Stimmel and Thea Fuchs Benenson, "US Citizens in Foreign Medical Schools," *New England Journal of Medicine* 300:25, June 21, 1979.

89. "The Land of Opportunity," *Scientific American* 231, September 1974, p. 65.

90. Dorris, "The Doctor Shortage," 168.

91. Ibid.

92. For more on physician shortages, see Rashi Fein, *The Doctor Shortage* (Brookings Institution, 1967); and Bureau of Health Manpower, "Physician

Requirements Forecasting," US HEW, HRA 78–12, 1978. Also, George Silver, "Caspar Weinberger's Bitter Pill," *Nation*, October 24, 1973, p. 276.

93. Quoted in Silver, "Caspar Weinberger's Bitter Pill."

94. See Douglas Colligan, "Physician's Assistant: A New Career in Medicine," *Science Digest* 74, July 1973.

95. Janet Hughbanks and Donald Freeborn, "Review of 22 Training Programs for Physician's Assistants," *HSMHA Health Reports* 86:10, October 1971.

96. See "Physician's Assistants," *Public Health Reports* 85:11, 1970, p. 1012.

97. Richard Henry, "Evaluation of Physician's Assistants in Gilchrist County, Florida," *Public Health Reports* 89:5, September–October 1974, p. 432.

98. Walter Bornemeier, "Rx for the Family-Doctor Shortage," *Reader's Digest* 97, July 1970, p. 105.

99. Florence Ellen Lee and Jay Glasser, "Role of Lay Midwifery in Maternity Care in a Large Metropolitan Area," *Public Health Reports* 89:6, November–December 1974.

100. Ibid., 542.

101. An interesting study of nurse-midwifery is Barbara Ehrenreich and Deirdre English, *Witches, Midwives, and Nurses: A History of Women Healers* (Feminist Press at City University of New York, 2010), particularly pp. 27–60. See also Carl Cobb, "Solving the Doctor Shortage," *Saturday Review*, August 22, 1970, p. 25.

102. Jeanne Lemal Hurd, "A New Perspective on Head Start Health Care," *Health Services Reports* 87:7, August–September 1972, p. 581.

103. Roger Barkin, "Need for Statutory Legitimation of the Roles of Physician's Assistants," *Health Services Reports* 89:1, January–February 1974, p. 31.

104. Ruth Roemer, "Legal Regulation of Health Manpower in the 1970s," *HSMHA Health Reports* 86:12, December 1971, p. 1055.

105. See Winston Dean, "State Legislation for Physician's Assistants," *Health Services Reports* 88:1, January 1973.

106. See Helen Chase, "Ranking Countries by Infant Mortality Rates," *Public Health Reports* 84:1, January 1969. Also, see the speech by George Meany calling attention to this point: "National Health Insurance," *Vital Speeches of the Day*, September 7, 1970.

107. Chase, "Ranking Countries by Infant Mortality Rates."

108. Eric Cassell, "Death and the Physician," *Commentary*, June 1969, p. 73.

109. Ibid.

110. Richard Vanberg, "From the Thoughtful Businessman," *Harvard Business Review*, March–April 1972, p. 32.

111. See Kerr White, "Life and Death and Medicine," *Scientific American* 229:3, September 1973.

112. Interestingly, some of the early work on low-carbohydrate diet techniques was already being touted by the early 1970s. See "Latest Gains in Health Care," *US News*, July 10, 1972, p. 77.

113. The quote is from "Our Sick Medical System," *Life* 70, March 5, 1971. The literature on the national health insurance programs of Western Europe is immense. For an excellent history of the British National Health System, see Daniel Fox, *Health Policies, Health Politics: The British and American Experience, 1911–1965* (Princeton University Press, 2014).

114. "Cure-All?," *Newsweek*, October 27, 1969. See also John Walsh, "At the Center, the Problem Is Unreimbursed Costs," *Science* 166:3906, November 7, 1969.

Chapter 2. Medical Free Markets

1. "Growing Crisis in Health Care: Interview with Dr. John A. D. Cooper," *US News*, 67, November 3, 1969, p. 71. For more on the historical development of US medical culture, see John Duffy, *From Humors to Medical Science: A History of American Medicine* (University of Illinois Press, 1993). Also Ronald Numbers, *The Education of American Physicians* (University of California Press, 1980).

2. "The Plight of the US Patient," *Time* 93, February 21, 1969, p. 55.

3. Michael Halberstam, "The M.D. Should Not Try to Cure Society," *New York Times*, November 9, 1969.

4. J. D. Ratcliff, "A Way Out of Our Health-Care Crisis," *Reader's Digest* 100, April 1972, p. 232.

5. Michael Rothfeld, "Sensible Surgery for America," *Fortune*, 87, April 1973, p. 113. For early evaluations of managed care, see Doman Lum, "The HMO Delivery System," *American Journal of Public Health* 65:11, November 1975; Arnold Rosoff, "Phase Two of the Federal HMO Development Program," *American Journal of Law and Medicine* 1:2, Fall 1975; and Paul Starr, "An Experiment Designed to Fail," *New Republic* 172:16, April 19, 1975.

6. For an interesting institutional history of a specific HMO (Wisconsin's Marshfield Clinic), see Jan Gregoire Coombs, *The Rise and Fall of HMOs: An American Health Care Revolution* (University of Wisconsin Press, 2005).

7. "The President's Message on Medical Care," *US News* 70, March 1, 1971, pp. 70–74. Ellwood called the US healthcare delivery system an "anachronism" which had "escaped the industrial revolution," and lacked both vertical and horizontal integration. See Paul Ellwood and Michael Herbert, "Health Care: Should Industry Buy It or Sell It?," *Harvard Business Review*, July–August 1973, p. 102.

8. See Frank Seubold, "HMOs—The View from the Program," *Public Health Reports* 90:2, March–April 1975. For a very informative consumerists take on the new HMOs, see "HMOs: Are They the Answer to Your Medical Needs?," *Consumer Reports*, October 1974.

9. Starr, "An Experiment Designed to Fail," 15–16. Starr went on to write one of the most important extended analyses of the US health system. See Paul Starr, *The Social Transformation of American Medicine* (Basic Books, 1984).

10. Statistic from J. D. Ratcliff, "A Way Out," 236. The most comprehensive early analysis of HMOs was a compilation by William Roy, a physician/Congressman who had authored much of the HMO Act. See Roy, *The Proposed Health Maintenance Organization Act of 1972* (Health Communications Group, 1972).

11. Halberstam, "The M.D. Should Not Try to Cure Society."

12. Joel Kramer, "Medical Care: As Costs Soar, Support Grows for Major Reform," *Science* 166, November 28, 1969, p. 1128.

13. See Klaus Roghmann, William Gavett, et al., "Who Chooses Prepaid Medical Care?," *Public Health Reports* 90:6, November–December 1975.

14. Godfrey Hodgson, "The Politics of American Healthcare," *Atlantic*, October 1973, p. 41.

15. There are many sources for this statistic. See, for example, Wilbur Cohen, "The Development and Future of Group Practice Payment Plans," *Public Health Reports* 83:1, January 1968, p. 30.

16. Ellwood and Herbert, "Health Care: Should Industry Buy It or Sell It?"

17. "HMOs: Are They the Answer to Your Medical Needs?"

18. Lane Kirkland, "Labor's Point of View on HMOs," *Public Health Reports* 90:2, March–April 1975, p. 105. See also, "Lorin Kerr, "Medical Innovations of the United Mine Workers of America," *Public Health Reports* 83:7, July 1968.

19. For an excellent introduction to the politics of the Great Society programs, see Julian Zelizer, *The Fierce Urgency of Now* (Penguin Press, 2015). For a more general overview of the Johnson presidency, including much discussion of his domestic agenda, see John Andrew, *Lyndon Johnson and the Great Society* (Ivan Dee, 1999). For a firsthand account by Johnson's chief domestic policy advisor, see Joseph Califano, *The Triumph and Tragedy of Lyndon Johnson* (Touchstone, 2015).

20. Charles Wylie, "Schools of Public Health in 1972: Ivory Towers or Sites of Relevance?," *Health Services Reports* 87:10, December 1972, p. 887.

21. Lee Holder and Lynn Deniston, "A Decision Making Approach to Comprehensive Health Planning," *Public Health Reports* 83:7, July 1968, p. 559.

22. Harald Graning, "The Institution Needs of the Health Industry," *Public Health Reports* 84:4, April 1969.

23. Frank Carlucci, "The Future Outlook for Delivery of Human Services," *Health Services Reports* 88:10, December 1973, p. 891. Carlucci noted the odds of a welfare recipient becoming a "one-man epidemic of human service needs."

24. See Lynne Page Snyder, "Passage and Significance of the 1944 Pubic Health Service Act," *Public Health Reports* 109:6, November–December 1994.

25. Data on the Hill-Burton Act can be found in Center for Health Policy Studies, National Planning Association, *Federal Health Spending, 1969–1974* (and subsequent volumes) (Government Printing Office, 1974). See also "Bad Medicine," *New Republic* 167, July 8, 1972; and Michael Balter, "The Best Kept Secret Health Care," *Progressive* 45, April 1981.

26. See James Lee Dallas, "The HSA and the PSRO: Toward a Linkage," *Public Health Reports* 91:1, January–February 1976.

27. Eli Ginzburg, "What Next in Health Policy?," *Science* 188:4194, June 20, 1975, p. 1186.

28. "What Makes Doctors Sick?," *Newsweek*, December 17, 1973, p. 94.

29. For the breadth of the proposed tasks, see Carol Riddick, Sam Cordes, and Charles Crawford, "Educational Needs as Perceived by Community Health Decision Makers," *Public Health Reports* 93:5, September–October 1978.

30. See, among others, Ronald Numbers, *Almost Persuaded* (Johns Hopkins University Press, 1978); Monte Poen, *Harry S Truman versus the Medical Lobby* (University of Missouri Press, 2014); and Jonathan Engel, *Doctors and Reformers* (University of South Carolina Press, 2002).

31. Barry Borland, Franklin Williams, and David Taylor, "A Survey of Attitudes of Physicians on Proper Use of Physicians' Assistants," *Health Services Reports* 87:5, May 1972.

32. Paul Ashton, "The Health Security Program," *Vital Speeches*, September 9, 1970, p. 101.

33. Bill McCullough, "The Demise of Rural Medicine," *Vital Speeches*, February 20, 1971, p. 517.

34. Russell Gibbons, "Catching Up with Bismarck," *Commonweal*, November 21, 1969, p. 239.

35. Edward Saward, "Medicare, Medical Practice, and the Medical Profession," *Public Health Reports* 91:4, July–August 1976, p. 318.

36. "Keeping an Eye on the Doctors," *Forbes*, July 15, 1975, p. 57.

37. Miriam Shuchman and Michael Wilkes, "Body and Mind," *New York Times*, October 2, 1988.

38. "Keeping an Eye on the Doctors," 57. For an early evaluation of PSROs, see John Bussman and Sharon van Sell Davidson, *PSRO* (Addison-Wesley, 1981).

39. Chas Slackman, "What Doctors Think of Their Patients," *Life* 69, October 2, 1970, p. 68.

40. Ibid., 73.

41. Dwight Wilbur, "Health Care Costs," *Vital Speeches*, January 13, 1969, p. 264.

42. "Physician, What Ails Thee?," *Newsweek*, October 18, 1971, p. 84.

43. "Physician, Health Thyself," *Newsweek*, December 11, 1972, p. 80.

44. Harry Schwartz, "Health Care in America: A Heretical Diagnosis," *Saturday Review*, August 14, 1971, p. 17.

45. Malcolm Todd, "Are Doctors Doing Their Job?," *US News*, July 1, 1974, p. 30.

46. Ward Darley, "The Community Corporation and Its Implications for Education and Research in Health and Medical Care," *Health Services Reports* 87:8, October 1972, p. 681.

47. William Felch and Walter Ross, "An Internist Talks about His Work," *Today's Health*, February 1969, p. 26; Bill McCullough, "The Demise of Rural Medicine," *Vital Speeches*, February 20, 1971, p. 518. Also, more generally, Rosemary Stevens, *American Medicine and the Public Interest* (University of California Press, 1998).

48. Elizabeth DeVita, "The Decline of the Doctor-Patient Relationship," *American Health*, June 1995, p. 64.

49. See, for example, Anthony Moore, "Medical Humanities: A New Medical Adventure," *New England Journal of Medicine* 295:26, December 23, 1976.

50. J. Neal Greene, "Doctor's Apologia," *New England Journal of Medicine* 292:16, April 17, 1975, p. 867.

51. George Crile, "The Surgeon's Dilemma," *Harper's*, May 1975, p. 38.

52. It is important to note that there was no one Blue Shield program, but fifty-four separate ones (roughly one per state). The Blue Shield programs, along with the Blue Cross programs, were loosely coordinated by the umbrella Blue Cross/Blue Shield Association based in Chicago. For a comprehensive history of the plans, see Robert Cunningham III and Robert Cunningham Jr., *Blues: A History of the Blue Cross and Blue Shield System* (Northern Illinois University Press, 1997).

53. Samuel Their and Robert Berliner, "Manpower Policy: Base It on Facts, Not Opinions," *New England Journal of Medicine* 299:23, December 7, 1978, p. 1306.

54. The numbers are from D. W. Miller Jr., T. D. Ivey, et al., "The Practice of Coronary Bypass Surgery in 1980," *Journal of Thoracic and Cardiothoracic Surgery* 81, 1981, pp. 423–28. See also Benson Roe, "The UCR Boondoggle," *New England Journal of Medicine* 305:1, July 2, 1981.

55. The literature on professionalism is extensive. For a study on the development of professionalism in medical specialties, see Rosemary Stevens's excellent book, *American Medicine and the Public Interest* (University of California Press, 1998).

56. Donald Kennedy, "Creative Tension: FDA and Medicine," *New England Journal of Medicine* 298:15, April 13, 1978, p. 846.

57. On the history of hospitals in the United States, see Morris Vogel, *The Invention of the Modern Hospital: Boston 1870–1930* (University of Chicago Press, 1980); and Rosemary Stevens, *In Sickness and in Wealth* (Johns Hopkins University Press, 1999).

58. See Paul Brown, "Band Aids by the Boxcar," *Forbes* 128, August 31, 1981.

59. National Center for Health Statistics, *Hospitals, Beds, and Occupancy Rates: United States 1975–2008* (2010). For a journalistic account, "Major Move against the Tide," *Forbes* 121, January 9, 1978, p. 127.

60. Roger Rapoport, "A Candle for St. Greed's," *Harper's* 245, December 1972, p. 71.

61. Ibid., 72.

62. Ibid., 74.

63. Ibid.

64. "Humana's Hopes," *Forbes* 120, September 1, 1977, p. 24.

65. "Adding Insult to Injury," *Forbes*, March 1, 1977.

66. Thomas Delbanco, Katherine Meyers, and Elliot Segal, "Paying the Physician's Fee," *New England Journal of Medicine* 301:24, December 13, 1979.

67. See Elliot Marshall, "Anatomy of Health Care Costs V: Blue Cross," *New Republic*, July 2, 1977.

68. Joseph Califano details his efforts in *America's Health Care Revolution* (Random House, 1986).

69. "The Corporate Attack on Rising Medical Costs," *Business Week*, August 6, 1979.

Chapter 3. Reining in the Excess

1. For details on the recommendations of the Committee on the Costs of Medical Care, see Jonathan Engel, *Doctors and Reformers* (University of South Carolina Press, 2002); Alan Derickson, *Health Security for All* (Johns Hopkins University Press, 2005); and Milton Roemer, "I. S. Falk, the CCMC, and the Drive for National Health Insurance," *American Journal of Public Health* 75:8, August 1985.

2. "Current Status of Group Medical Practice in the United States," *Public Health Reports* 92:5, September–October 1977.

3. Arnold Relman, "Faculty Practice Plans," *New England Journal of Medicine* 304:5, January 29, 1981. Notably, the community clinics experienced high rates of physician turnover and rampant professional dissatisfaction. See Robert Pantell, Terry Reilly, and Matthew Liang, "Analysis of the Reasons for High Turnover of Clinicians in Neighborhood Health Centers," *Public Health Reports* 95:4, July–August 1980.

4. See Karl Singer, "Relative Costs of HMOs and Fee for Service," *New England Journal of Medicine* 299:15, October 12, 1978, p. 837.

5. See Joseph Dorsey, "HMOs and the Cost of Medical Care," *New England Journal of Medicine* 298:24, June 15, 1978. Also Joseph Dorsey, "Factors Impacting Hospital Utilization," *Proceedings of the Medical Directors Education Conference* 1:1, Group Health Association of America, 1976.

6. William Rosenberg, "Cost Effectiveness of PSRO," *New England Journal of Medicine* 300:6, February 8, 1979, p. 324. Also, see Harold Luft's important study, "How Do Health Maintenance Organizations Achieve Their 'Savings,'" *New England Journal of Medicine* 298:24, June 15, 1978.

7. Joseph Califano, "National Health Care Planning: The Health Maintenance Organization," *Vital Speeches*, October 27, 1977.

8. See Luft, "How Do HMOs Achieve Their 'Savings,'" 1342. Luft explicitly mentions the possibility that HMOs are achieving their savings in part by

withholding necessary or beneficial treatments. At the time he wrote, few rigorous outcomes studies were being performed, and thus no medical watcher really knew whether HMO members were suffering as a result of HMO policies regarding referrals and hospital admissions.

9. Robert Claiborne, an established science and medicine writer, attributed physician resistance to "AMA indoctrination," which continued through the 1990s. See Claiborne, "Why We Can't Afford National Health Insurance," *Saturday Review* 15, May 13, 1978, p 16.

10. Alain Enthoven, "Shattuck Lecture: Cutting Cost without Cutting the Quality of Care," *New England Journal of Medicine* 298:22, June 1, 1978, p. 1234.

11. Alain Enthoven, "Consumer-Choice Health Plan," parts I and II, *New England Journal of Medicine* 298:13, March 30, 1978.

12. Eli Ginzberg, "The Competitive Solution: Two Views," *New England Journal of Medicine* 303:19, November 6, 1980, p. 1113.

13. Ibid., 1115.

14. See, for example, Eli Ginzberg, "Paradoxes and Trends: An Economist Looks at Health Care," *New England Journal of Medicine* 296:14, April 7, 1977. Ginzberg writes, "The future of American medicine will in considerable measure be shaped by the expectations of the American people about the potential of health care to improve the quality of their lives" (816).

15. Bertha Bryant, "Issues on the Distribution of Health Care: Some Lessons from Canada," *Public Health Reports* 96:5, September–October 1981.

16. Quoted in John Iglehart, "Canada's Health Care System (II of III)," *New England Journal of Medicine* 315:22, September 18, 1986, p. 779. For a more comprehensive exposition of Evans's views, see Robert Evans and Noralou P. Roos, "What Is Right about the Canadian Health Care System?," *Milbank Quarterly* 77:3, 1999.

17. Ibid., 781.

18. Researchers did not agree on the source of the savings. See, for example, M. A. Baltzan, "Administrative Waste in US Healthcare," *New England Journal of Medicine* 315:16, October 16, 1986, p. 1034.

19. John Iglehart, "Canada's Health are System (I of III)," *New England Journal of Medicine* 315:3, July 17, 1986, p. 203.

20. R. Klein, *The Politics of the National Health Service* (Longman Group, 1983), 152, as quoted in John Iglehart, "The British National Health Service under the Conservatives (Part II)," *New England Journal of Medicine* 310:1, January 5, 1984.

21. See John Lister, "Private Medical Practice and the National Health Service," *New England Journal of Medicine* 311:16, October 18, 1984. Also, John Lister, "The British Medical Scene since 1980," *New England Journal of Medicine* 308:9, March 31, 1983. For comparative treatment of the historical development of healthcare in the United Kingdom and the United States, see Daniel Fox, *Health Policies, Health Politics* (Princeton University Press, 1986).

22. Iglehart, "The British National Health Service under the Conservatives (Part II)," 63.

23. Thomas Ballantine, "The Role of Government in Health-Care Delivery in the 1980s," *Vital Speeches*, February 15, 1980; John Tupper, "A New American Revolution," *Vital Speeches*, March 12, 1979.

24. Saul Gilson, "Is Cost the Physician's Business?," *New England Journal of Medicine* 296:18, p. 1071.

25. Michael DeBakey and Lois DeBakey, "Big Government and Hospital Care: Prescription for Disaster," *Reader's Digest*, July 1980, pp. 192, 194.

26. Eliot Marshall, "AMA vs. HMOs," *New Republic*, October 29, 1977, p. 10.

27. "Cost Containment: A Statement by the American Surgical Association," *New England Journal of Medicine* 301:5, August 2, 1979.

28. See Stephen Solomon, "How One Hospital Broke Its Inflation Fever," *Fortune* 99, June 18, 1979. Hopkins's success was built on budgetary decentralization and Taylorism—the close study of industrial processes designed to break complex tasks down into their components and then streamline the subtasks. Although Hopkins was successful, its nursing staff bore the brunt of the scrutiny and reorganization and was ultimately downsized. Twenty years later, most hospital administrators were using similar staff reduction techniques to control costs, albeit often at the expense of nursing job satisfaction.

29. See "Fair Test," *Scientific American* 231:50, November 1974, for a description of an IOM report endorsing HMOs.

30. John Burnum, "The Physicians as a Double Agent," *New England Journal of Medicine* 297:5, August 4, 1977, p. 278.

31. David Haymes, "Physicians and Health-Care Costs," *New England Journal of Medicine* 305:6, p. 349.

32. A nice overview of the reformist ferment of the time can be found in Richard Margolis, "National Health Insurance: The Dream Whose Time Has Come?," *New York Times*, January 9, 1977.

33. Quoted in Marjorie Sun, "New Ethics Code Is Major Break from Past," *Science*, 209, August 15, 1980, p. 790.

Chapter 4. The Lure of Profits

1. Rosemary Stevens, "Past Is Prologue," *Society* 23, July–August 1986, p. 32.

2. The literature on the history of US hospitals in rich. See, among others, Rosemary Stevens, *In Sickness and in Health* (Johns Hopkins University Press, 1999); Charles Rosenberg, *The Care of Strangers* (Johns Hopkins University Press, 1995); and David Rosner, *A Once Charitable Enterprise* (Princeton University Press, 1982).

3. Geraldine Dallek, "Hospital Care for Profit," *Society*, July–August 1986, p. 54.

4. John Bedrosian, "The Health Care Industry: Facing the Realities of the Eighties," *Vital Speeches*, May 6, 1981.

5. Dallek, "Hospital Care for Profit." Also Barbara Culliton, "For-Profit Hospitals Loom Large on Health Care Scene," *Science* 233, August 29, 1986; and J. M. Watt, Robert Derzon, et al., "The Comparative Economic Performance of Investor-Owned Chain and Not-for-Profit Hospitals," *New England Journal of Medicine* 314:2, January 9, 1986.

6. Dallek, "Hospital Care for Profit," 57.

7. Ellyn Spragins, "Marketing a High-Powered Pitch to Cure Hospitals' Ills," *Business Week*, September 2, 1985, p. 60.

8. Anne Fisher, "The New Game in Health Care: Who Will Profit," *Fortune* 111, March 4, 1985.

9. See Ronald Henderson, "Cooperation or Conflict: The Changing Physician-Hospital Relationship," *Vital Speeches*, June 10, 1982.

10. Donald Robinson, "Investor-Owned Hospitals: Rx for Success," *Reader's Digest*, April 1983, p. 83.

11. The IOM study is referenced in Culliton, "For-Profit Hospitals Loom Large." The staffing ratios statistics can be found in L. S. Lewin, R. A. Derzon, and R. Margulies, "Investor-Owned and Nonprofits Differ in Economic Performance," *Hospitals* 55:13, 1981.

12. Eli Ginzberg, "The Moneterization of Medical Care," *New England Journal of Medicine* 310:18, May 3, 1984.

13. See John Iglehart, "Report of the Ninth Duke University Medical Center Private Sector Conference," *New England Journal of Medicine* 311:3, January 19, 1984.

14. Fisher, "The New Game," 139. Also, "Why Private Hospitals Are Checking into the Chains," *Business Week*, November 7, 1983; and Richard Greene and Thomas Baker, "Paging Adam Smith," *Forbes* 127, April 13, 1981.

15. Michael Lerner, Mary Hager, et al., "New War on Health Costs," *Newsweek*, May 9, 1983; also John Bedrosian, "The Health Care Industry: Facing the Realities of the Eighties," *Vital Speeches*, May 6, 1981.

16. William Reed, Karen Cawley, and Ron Anderson, "The Effect of a Public Hospital's Transfer Policy on Patient Care," *New England Journal of Medicine* 315:22, November 27, 1986.

17. Jack Hadley, Ross Mullner, and Judith Feder, "The Financially Distressed Hospital," *New England Journal of Medicine* 307:20, November 11, 1982; also Robert Hughes and Philip Lee, "Public Prospects," *American Hospital*, July August 1986.

18. The problem was particularly acute in California, where the Medi-Cal "county option" had allowed counties to maintain their own public hospitals. As this option was dropped, county hospitals lost Medi-Cal patients to the privates and suffered accordingly. See Timothy Noah, "The Medi-Cal Diet,"

New Republic, June 13, 1981. For an interesting take on this problem, see Toby Cohen, "The Medicaid Class Struggle," *Nation,* February 21, 1981.

19. Steven Waldman, "The Other AIDS Crisis: Who Pays for Treatment?," *Washington Monthly* 17, January 1986, pp. 25–31.

20. Stephen Soumerai, Jerry Avorn, et al., "Payment Restrictions for Prescription Drugs under Medicaid," *New England Journal of Medicine* 317:9, August 27, 1987.

21. Jack Mayer, "About Men," *New York Times Magazine,* October 19, 1986, p. 96.

22. Kevin O'Rourke, "Investor-Owned Catholic Teaching Hospitals," *New England Journal of Medicine* 313:20, November 14, 1985, p. 1297.

23. See Richard O'Brien and Michael Haller, "Investor-Owned or Nonprofit? Issues and Implications for Academic and Ethical Values in a Catholic Teaching Hospital," *New England Journal of Medicine* 313:3, January 18, 1985. Also P. J. Farley, "Who Are the Underinsured?," *Milbank Quarterly* 63, 1985; and Brad Gray, *The New Health Care for Profit* (National Academies Press, 1983).

24. F. M. Scherer, "Pricing, Profits, and Technological Progress in the Pharmaceutical Industry," *Journal of Economic Perspectives* 7:3, Summer 1993, p. 98. For a contemporary reporting account, see Dan Moreau, "As Mighty Merck Turns 100, R&D Is the Rx for Growth," *Kiplinger's Personal Finance Magazine* 45:10, October 1, 1991.

25. Jane Cutaia, "Drug Profits Seem to Be on Steroids," *Business Week,* January 9, 1989.

26. Scherer, "Pricing, Profits," 97–100. For a liberal critique, Arthur Rowse, "Medication Inflation," *Progressive,* October 1990.

27. Raymond Woosley, "Prescription Drugs," *Issues in Science and Technology,* Spring 1944.

28. A. Kippen, "Doctored Results," *Washington Monthly* 22, October 1990.

29. J. Avorn, M. Chen, and R. Hartley, "Scientific versus Commercial Sources of Influence on the Prescribing of Physicians, *American Journal of Medicine* 73, 1982. For a more populist account, see "Pushing Drugs to Doctors," *Consumer Reports,* February 1992.

30. The physician was M. D. Rawlins. Quoted in Eugene Bricker, "Industrial Marketing and Medical Ethics," *New England Journal of Medicine* 320:25, June 22, 1989, p. 1691.

31. David Kessler, "Drug Promotion and Scientific Exchange," *New England Journal of Medicine* 325:3, June 18, 1991.

32. Ibid.

33. John Beary, "Prescription Drugs," *Issues in Science and Technology,* Summer 1994, pp. 6–7; Joseph Weber, "A Culture That Just Keeps Dishing Up Success," *Business Week,* Innovation Issue, 1989. Also Joseph Weber, "Merck Needs More Gold from the White Coats," *Business Week,* March 8, 1991.

34. Roy Vagelos, "Are Prescription Drug Prices High?," *Science* 252, May 24, 1991.

35. See Mark Field, "The Soviet Pharmaceutical System: The Pluralistic Approach to Drug Research," *Proceedings of the PMA Research and Development Section Seminar*, 1977, as cited in Gerald Mossinghoff, "Cost of Drug Advertising," *New England Journal of Medicine* 319:12, September 22, 1988, p. 798.

36. Tabitha Powledge, "Gene Pharming," *Technology Review* 95:6, August–September 1992; also Gene Bylinsky "Biotech Firms Tackle the Giants," *Fortune* 124:4, August 12, 1991; Ann Gibbons, "Biotech Pipeline: Bottleneck Ahead," *Science* 254, October 18, 1991.

37. John Iglehart, "The FDA and Its Problems," *New England Journal of Medicine* 325:3, July 18, 1991.

Chapter 5. Efforts to Rationalize

1. Abigail Trafford, "Are Medicare, Medicaid Going Belly Up?," *US News* 93, September 6, 1982.

2. Statement of Paul Ginzburg (CBO) to the Subcommittee on Health, Committee on Ways and Means, June 15, 1982.

3. Phillip Keisling, "Protection from Catastrophe: Medicare Reform We Really Need," *Washington Monthly*, November 1983, p. 40.

4. John Iglehart, "Medicare's Uncertain Future," *New England Journal of Medicine* 306:21, May 27, 1982.

5. See Paul Starr, "The Laisse-Faire Elixir," *New Republic*, April 18, 1983.

6. Quoted in John Iglehart, "The Administration Responds to the Cost Spiral," *New England Journal of Medicine* 305:22, November 26, 1981, p. 1364. On alternatives for structural reform being floated at the time, see John Goodman, "Why Not Medical IRAs? (Since the Future of Medicare Is Grim)," *Forbes* 70, February 11, 1985.

7. New Jersey called its program the Standard Hospital Accounting and Rate Evaluation System (SHARE) and, interestingly, never actually used the term DRG in its enabling legislation. See J. Wasserman, *DRG Evaluation* 1, Health Research and Educational Trust of New Jersey, 1982.

8. For details, see Steven Sheingold, "An Analysis of the Impacts of a DRG-Specific Price Blending Option for Medicare's PPs," Congressional Budget Office, December 20, 1984.

9. Helen Smits and Rita Watson, "DRGs and the Future of Surgical Practice," *New England Journal of Medicine* 311:25, December 20, 1984.

10. "Sick System," *Scientific American* 253, September 1985. Also, Gerard Anderson and Earl Steinberg, "To Buy or Not to Buy: Technology Acquisition under Prospective Payment," *New England Journal of Medicine* 311:3, July 19, 1984.

11. See Vicky Cahan and Irene Pave, "Do Medicare's Watchdocs Need a Shorter Leash?," *Business Week*, February 17, 1986.

12. William Schwartz and Daniel Mendelson, "Hospital Cost Containment in the 1980s: Hard Lessons Learned and Prospects for the 1990s," *New England Journal of Medicine* 324:15, April 11, 1991.

13. For example, Mount San Rafael Hospital reported a decline in Medicare patient days from 7,111 in 1983 to 2,933 in 1985. See Ron Scherer, Linda Lanier, et al., "Why Are You Discharging Her?," *US News* 27, February 17, 1986. Also Steven Chapman, "Off the Respirator: Medicare's Road to Recovery," *New Republic*, June 16, 1986.

14. R. F. Coulam and G. L. Gaumer, "Medicare's Prospective Payment System: A Critical Appraisal," *Health Care Financing Review* supplement, 1991. Also K. L. Kahn, L. V. Rubenstein, et al., "The Effects of the DRG-Based Prospective Payment System on Quality of Care for Hospitalized Medicare Patients," *Journal of the American Medical Association* 264, 1990. See also, Judith Feder, Jack Hadley, et al., "How Did Medicare's Prospective Payment System Affect Hospitals?," *New England Journal of Medicine* 317:14, October 1, 1987.

15. Dale Schumacher, M. Jo Naerow, et al., "Prospective Payment for Psychiatry: Feasibility and Impact," *New England Journal of Medicine* 315:21, November 20, 1986.

16. "Statement of Nancy Gordon before the Subcommittee on Health, Committee on Finance, US Senate," April 7, 1987. The Prospective Payment Commission found hospitals' length of stay creeping up a few years later, as well as discharged patients festering for longer periods in nursing homes. See Prospective Payment Commission, *Medicare Prospective Payment and the American Health Care System* (GPO, 1988).

17. John Iglehart, "Second Thoughts about HMOs for Medicare Patients," *New England Journal of Medicine* 316:23, June 4, 1987. Also, CBO, *Containing Medical Care Costs through Market Forces*, May 1983, pp. 8–21.

18. John Iglehart, "Moment of Truth for the Teaching Hospitals," *New England Journal of Medicine* 307:2, July 8, 1982.

19. See S. D. Horn, "Measuring the Severity of Illness across Institutions," *American Journal of Public Health* 73, 1983. For a good case to the opposite, see Stanley Bergen and Amy Roth, "Prospective Payment and the University Hospital," *New England Journal of Medicine* 310:5, February 2, 1984.

20. G. Witkin and D. Friedman, "Health Care Fraud," *US News* 112, February 24, 1992.

21. See Rita Ricardo-Campbell, "Economics and Health," *Vital Speeches*, February 5, 1986.

22. Joan Hamilton, "The Prognosis on Health Care: Critical, and Getting Worse," *Business Week*, January 9, 1989.

23. Julia Flynn Siler and Thane Peterson, "Hospital, Heal Thyself," *Business Week*, August 27, 1990.

24. For details on Medicare premiums to different types of hospitals, and for specific rate increases under OBRA 1989/1990, see CBO, *Rural Hospitals and*

Medicare's Prospective Payment System, December 1991; CBO, *Medicare's Disproportionate Share Adjustment for Hospitals,* May 1990; CBO, "Setting Medicare's
Indirect Teaching Adjustment for Hospitals," *CBO Papers,* May 1989. The premium to the teaching hospitals rose to 12 percent for each 0.1 percent rise in the
ratio of interns and residents to beds.

25. Carl Schramm and Jon Gabel, "Sounding Board: Prospective Payment,"
New England Journal of Medicine 318:25, June 23, 1988.

26. Steven Schroeder and Joel Cantor, "On Squeezing Balloons," *New
England Journal of Medicine* 325:15, October 10, 1991. Also Henry Aaron, "Prospective Payment: The Next Big Policy Disappointment," *Health Affairs* 3, 1984,
pp. 3102–7.

27. Carol McCarthy, "DRGs—Five Years Later," *New England Journal of
Medicine* 318:25, June 23, 1988, p. 1683.

28. Ibid., 1685.

29. CBO, "Rising Health Care Cost: Causes, Implications, and Strategies,"
April 1991.

30. Susan Garland, "Terminating the Medical Arms Race," *Business Week,*
April 29, 1991, p. 69.

31. Lawrence Malkin, "A Tale of Two Eyes," *New Republic,* September 4,
1989.

32. S. Hackman and R. Howard, "Confronting the Crisis in Health Care,"
Technology Review, July 1989, p. 34. See also, William Gold, "The Effect of the
Medicare Prospective Payment System on the Adoption of New Technology,"
New England Journal of Medicine 322:18, May 3, 1990.

33. James Todd, "The American Health Care System," *Vital Speeches,* October
5, 1989.

34. Gregory Goyert, Sidney Bottoms, et al., "The Physician Factor in Cesarean Birth Rates," *New England Journal of Medicine* 320:11, March 16, 1989.

35. "Wasted Health Care Dollars," *Consumer Reports,* July 1992.

36. Ibid. For a more detailed account of these regional differences, see the
Dartmouth Atlas of Health Care (www.dartmouthatlas.org), replete with maps
showing prevalence of various procedures throughout New England.

37. Christopher Georges, "Scalpel, Please," *Washington Monthly* 25, Sep-
tember 1993. Also, Norman Levinsky, "Recruiting for Primary Care," *New
England Journal of Medicine* 328:9, March 4, 1993; and Gwendolyn Kelly, "Is
There a Family Doctor in the House?," *Business Week,* November 2, 1992.

38. "Wasted Health Care Dollars," *Consumer Reports,* July 1992, p. 444. Also
Anthony Robbins, "How to Control U.S. Health Costs," *Scientific American* 261,
December 1989.

39. A. W. Astin, *The American Freshman: 25 Year Trend* (University of California Press, 1991); also, D. H. Fundenstein, *Medical Students, Medical Schools,
and Society during Five Eras* (Ballinger, 1978).

40. Allan Kolker, "Why Are Today's Medical Students Choosing High-Technology Specialties over Internal Medicine?," *New England Journal of Medicine* 318:7, February 18, 1988, p. 454.

41. Robert Petersdorf, "Primary Care Applicants—They Get No Respect," *New England Journal of Medicine* 326:6, February 6, 1992.

42. Michael Nupuff, "Where Have All the Primary Care Applicants Gone?," *New England Journal of Medicine* 326:26, June 25, 1992, p. 1778.

43. Timothy Johnson, "Restoring Trust between Patient and Doctor," *New England Journal of Medicine* 322:3, January 18, 1990, p. 197.

44. Mark Grunwald, "Primary Care Medicine in Canada," *New England Journal of Medicine* 327:15, October 8, 1992.

45. Jon Hamilton, "What'll It Cost, Doc?," *American Health*, April 1989.

46. John Iglehart, "The Struggle over Physician-Payment Reform," *New England Journal of Medicine* 325:11, September 12, 1991.

47. The CBO conducted extensive analysis of the potential effects of RBRVS as well as competing payment systems and concluded that adopting the system would cut Medicare disbursements by 5 percent. See CBO (Christensen and Harrison), *Comparison of Current Congressional Proposals for Changing Medicare's System for Paying Physicians*, October 1989.

48. "Unbundled Services and 'Code Creep,'" *Consumer Reports* 54, June 1989.

49. David Hemenway, Alice Killen, et al., "Physicians' Responses to Financial Incentives," *New England Journal of Medicine* 322:15, April 12, 1990.

50. Allan Hillman, "Financial Incentives for Physicians in HMOs," *New England Journal of Medicine* 317:27, December 31, 1987. Also, D. Freund and E. Neuschler, "Overview of Medicaid Capitation and Case-Management Initiatives," *Health Care Financing Review*, Supplement, 1986, pp. 21–30.

51. Alan Hillman, Mark Pauly, and Joseph Kerstein, "How Do Financial Incentives Affect Physicians' Clinical Decisions?," *New England Journal of Medicine* 321:2, July 13, 1989.

52. Douglas Levinson, "Toward Full Disclosure of Referral Restrictions and Financial Incentives by Prepaid Health Plans," *New England Journal of Medicine* 317:27, December 31, 1987, p. 1730.

53. Sanford Marcus, "Trade Unionism for Doctors: An Idea Whose Time Has Come," *New England Journal of Medicine* 311:23, December 6, 1984.

54. Philip Alper, "The New Language of Hospital Management," *New England Journal of Medicine* 311:19, November 8, 1984, p. 1250.

55. Jack Fincher, "New Machines May Soon Replace the Doctor's Black Bag," *Smithsonian* 14, January 1984. Also, see William Kissick's prescient speech at the Philadelphia College of Physicians, "Health Care in the 80s," *Vital Speeches*, September 26, 1985.

56. Isadore Rosenfeld, "A Doctor Defends His Calling," *New York Times Magazine*, November 15, 1981, p. 126.

57. Louis Richman, "Health Benefits Comes under the Knife," *Fortune* 107, May 2, 1983.

58. Albert Siu, Frank Sonnenberg, et al., "Inappropriate Use of Hospitals in a Randomized Trial of Health Insurance Plans," *New England Journal of Medicine* 315:20, November 13, 1986.

59. See, for example, Alan Sager, "Opiate of the Managers," *Society*, July–August 1986, p. 66.

60. Richman, "Health Benefits Comes under the Knife," 95.

61. For a detailed description of the Chrysler program see Joseph Califano Jr., "American Health Care: Who Lives? Who Dies? Who Pays?," *Current*, November 1986.

62. Healthcare inflation in Rochester between 1980 and 1984 was 55 percent, versus 87 percent nationally.

63. Erik Gunn, "Cutting Costs, Not Care: Rochester Hospitals Try Cooperation Instead of Competition," *Washington Monthly* 18, June 1986.

64. GAO, "Physician Cost-Containment Training Can Reduce Medical Costs," HRD-82-36, February 4, 1982.

65. It is worth noting that Hawaii, being geographically isolated, was better able to impose payment restriction on local physicians. See M. Holoweiko, "Health Care Reform: What Does Hawaii Have to Teach?," *Medical Economics*, February 3, 1992. Also, S. A. Goldberger, "The Politics of Universal Access: The Massachusetts Health Security Act of 1988," *Journal of Health Politics, Policy and Law* 15, 1990.

66. The mechanism was devised by Robert Kaplan, a professor at UC San Diego, using a "quality-of-well-being" scale. Kaplan's team made use of phone surveys to elicit opinions about comparable levels of suffering from different ailments. See Virginia Morell, "Listing to Starboard: The Oregon Formula," *Science* 249, August 3, 1990.

67. E. M. Reingold, "Oregon's Value Judgment," *Time* 138, November 25, 1991.

68. Quoted in William Bennett, "The Oregon Medicaid Controversy," *New England Journal of Medicine* 327:9, August 27, 1992, p. 642.

69. Bear in mind that all might have died, regardless. The transplants that were denied payment were those with the greatest costs and lowest success rates.

70. "Rationing Health," *Nation*, April 12, 1993, p. 470.

71. H. Gilbert Welch and Eric Larson, "Dealing with Limited Resources," *New England Journal of Medicine* 319:3 July 21, 1988.

72. John Kitzhaber, "Who'll Live? Who'll Die? Who'll Pay?," *Oregonian*, November 29, 1987, p. B6, quoted in Welch and Larson, "Dealing with Limited Resources," 172.

73. See Joseph Shapiro, "To Ration or Not to Ration?," *US News* 113, August 10, 1992.

Chapter 6. HillaryCare

1. Quoted in Paula Dwyer and Susan Garland, "A Roar of Discontent: Voters Want Health Care Reform Now," *Business Week*, November 25, 1991, p. 28.

2. Only 22 percent of Americans would be willing to pay more than an additional $200 in taxes to fund such a program! R. Blendon and K. Donelan, "The Public and Emerging Debate over National Health Insurance," *New England Journal of Medicine* 323:3, July 19, 1990.

3. T. Morganthau and M. Hager, "Cutting through the Gobbledygook," *Newsweek* 119, February 3, 1992.

4. See Eli Ginzberg, "Where Are We and Where Should We Be Going?," *New England Journal of Medicine* 327:18, October 29, 1992, p. 1310.

5. Samuel Levey and James Hill, "National Health Insurance: The Triumph of Equivocation," *New England Journal of Medicine* 321:25, December 21, 1989, p. 1753. See also "Getting Well," *Commonweal*, March 27, 1992. The most comprehensive treatment of the politics surrounding the Clinton health reform effort can be found in Theda Skocpol, *Boomerang: Clinton's Health Security Effort and the Turn against Government in US Politics* (Norton, 1996).

6. See John Hess, "The Catastrophic Health Care Fiasco," *Nation*, May 21, 1990; and John Iglehart, "Medicare's New Benefits: 'Catastrophic' Health Insurance," *New England Journal of Medicine* 320:5, February 2, 1989.

7. Medicare did not cover nursing home care. Medicaid did, but only after the beneficiary spent their assets down to poverty levels, eroding the savings of most middle-class couples along the way.

8. Peter Ferrara, "The Catastrophic Health Care Fiasco," *Consumer's Research*, February 1990.

9. "Catastrophic Politics," *National Review*, November 24, 1989, p. 13. Also, "Medicare's Catastrophe?," *US News* 106, January 23, 89.

10. M. Stanton Evans tried to get the White House senior staff to address the issue in 1989. He wrote of the experience, "From the President's expression, body language, and lack of response to these remarks, I might as well have been discussing binomial theorem or the mineral heritage of Zimbabwe." Quoted in Fred Barnes, "Rude Health," *New Republic*, December 2, 1991, p. 9.

11. See ibid.

12. The Bush plan also stopped the cessation of insurance benefits after a job loss and capped tort awards in malpractice cases.

13. Michael Kinsley, "Quack," *New Republic*, March 2, 1992, p. 4. See the tepid defense of the Bush plan written by the secretary of Health and Human Services, Louis Sullivan, in "The Bush Administration's Health Care Plan," *New England Journal of Medicine* 327:11, September 10, 1992.

14. The National Leadership Coalition was composed of various corporations and unions including Chrysler, International Paper, and Lockheed. A number of congressional Democratic leaders also signed onto these plans.

15. Thomas Bodenheimer, "The Way to Real Health Security," *Nation*, December 16, 1991. Also, John Schwartz and Mary Hager, "Start the Revolution with Me," *Newsweek* 120, December 14, 1992; and A. Toufexis and B. Dolan, "A Call for Radical Surgery," *Time* 135, May 7, 1990.

16. These numbers were consistent with GAO estimates.

17. David Himmelstein and Steffie Woolhandler, "A National Health Program for the United States," *New England Journal of Medicine* 320:2, June 12, 1989.

18. I find this argument unpersuasive, given that the burden would fall equally across a sector. Each firm would be required to raise prices to accommodate their new labor costs, leaving no one firm any less competitive than previously.

19. David Caplan, "Two Plans for Universal Health Insurance," *New England Journal of Medicine* 321:2, July 13, 1989, p. 115.

20. Roy Poses, Bruce Hillner, et al., "Two Plans for Universal Health Insurance," *New England Journal of Medicine* 321:2, July 13, 1989, p. 115.

21. Henry Aaron and William Schwartz, "Rationing Health Care: The Choice before Us," *Science* 247, January 26, 1990.

22. See, for example, Daniel Howley, "Cost Effectiveness and Medicare Coverage," *New England Journal of Medicine* 322:11, March 15, 1990. Also, Arnold Relman, "Don't Ration Health Care," *Consumer's Research* 73, December 1990. At least one notable ethicist suggested that people were ethically obligated to "die cheaply," in an effort to preserve resources for the living. See Paul Menzel, *Strong Medicine: The Ethical Rationing of Health Care* (Oxford University Press, 1990). The quote is from Ron Hamel, "Cost and Choice: The Ethics of Rationing Health Care," *Christian Century*, May 1, 1991, p. 489.

23. Bill Clinton, "The Clinton Health Plan," *New England Journal of Medicine* 327:11, September 10, 1992, p. 805.

24. Clinton had already implemented a program called ElderChoices in Arkansas to be used as a template for long-term care provision.

25. Representatives Richard Gephardt (D-MO) and Pete Stark (D-CA) both pushed for a single-payer model. See Vicente Navarro, "Swaying the Health Care Task Force," *Nation*, September 6, 1993, as well as John Hubner, "The Abandoned Father of Health Care Reform," *New York Times Magazine*, July 18, 1993.

26. Many analyses were written of managed competition. See, among others, Duncan Neuhauser, "Enthoven's 'Health Plan,'" *New England Journal of Medicine* 303:19, November 6, 1980; Alain Enthoven and Richard Kronick, "A Consumer-Choice Health Plan for the 1990s," *New England Journal of Medicine* 320:2, January 12, 1989; and CBO, *Managed Competition and Its Potential to Reduce Health Spending*, May 1993. For a broader history of the Clinton effort, written shortly after, see Jacob Hacker, *The Road to Nowhere: The Genesis of President Clinton's Plan for Health Security* (Princeton University Press, 1997).

27. Enthoven and Kronick, "A Consumer-Choice Health Plan," 96.

28. Joyce Nelson, "Dr. Rockefeller Will See You Now," *Canadian Forum*, February 1995.

29. Theodore Marmor, "Strong Medicine," *Lear's*, February 1993, p. 20. For a more detailed exposition of his slant on health reform at the time, see Marmor, *Understanding Health Care Reform* (Yale University Press, 1994).

30. Michael Kramer, "Pulling the Plug," *Time* 142:14, October 4, 1993; also Arnold Relman, "Controlling Costs by Managing Competition: Would It Work?," *New England Journal of Medicine* 328:2, January 14, 1993.

31. Robert Dreyfuss, "The Big Idea," *Mother Jones*, May–June 1993, p. 18.

32. Art Levine and Ken Silverstein, "How the Drug Lobby Cut Cost Controls," *Nation*, December 13, 1993.

33. Steve Waldman and Bob Cohn, "Health-Lobby Mania," *Newsweek* 122:1, July 5, 1993.

34. V. Kemper and V. Novak, "What's Blocking Health Care Reform?," *Common Cause Magazine* 18, January–March 1992.

35. Ibid.

36. William Greider, "Bill and Hillary Will See You Now," *Rolling Stone*, April 29, 1993.

37. "Health Reform at Risk," *Commonweal*, July 16, 1993.

38. Susan Headden and Penny Loeb, "Money, Congress, and Health Care," *US News* 114:20, May 24, 1993.

39. Quoted in David Segal and Jennifer Elsea, "Mr. Break-It," *Washington Monthly* 25:5, May 1993.

40. The best objective description of the HAS's provisions and potential economic effects is found in the substantial CBO report, *An Analysis of the Administration's Health Proposal* (GPO), February 1994.

41. Robert Shapiro, "Bitter Pill," *New Republic*, August 16, 1993, p. 23. Marilyn Moon, an economist at the Urban Institute, was similarly skeptical of the Clinton plan's potential for saving money, estimating that managed competition would save no more than 1.6 percent of all health costs. See Susan Fitzgerald and Mark Jaffe, "What Could Hillary Learn from Canada and Germany?," *Washington Monthly* 26:3, March 1994.

42. David Frum, "What to Do About Health Care," *Commentary*, June 1995, p. 29.

43. William Niskanen, "Government-Managed Health Care," *Vital Speeches*, November 11, 1993, p. 212.

44. James Todd, "Right Sizing Health Reform," *Vital Speeches*, October 4, 1993, p. 146.

45. Quoted in Ann Dowd and Suneel Ratan, "Companies Hate the Health Plan," *Fortune* 128:14, November 29, 1993.

46. Malcolm Forbes, "Creating a Crisis," *Forbes* 152:7, September 27, 1993. See also Michael Novak, "It Hurts Too Much," *Forbes* 152:11, November 8, 1993.

47. John Goodman, "Health Care: Market Incentives," *Vital Speeches*, March 15, 1994.

48. Peter Samuel, "Health-Reform Politics," *National Review*, May 24, 1993, p. 37.

49. Marcia Berss, "Mayo's Dilemma," *Forbes* 152:10, October 25, 1993.

50. Quoted in Rick Tetzeli, "Managed Care Faces the Hillary Factor," *Fortune* 127:8, April 19, 1993.

51. Christopher Georges and Mike Bach, "Bad Forms," *Washington Monthly* 25:4, April 1993.

52. David Himmelstein and Steffie Woolhandler, "The American Health Care System—Medicare," *New England Journal of Medicine* 328:24, June 17, 1993, p. 1789.

53. See Christopher Koller, "Good Plan, Major Flaw," *Commonweal*, January 14, 1994. Also, Joe White, "Small Business versus Doctors," *Brookings Review* 12:3, Summer 1994.

54. Quoted in William Greider, "Rx Now, Pay Later," *Rolling Stone*, November 25, 1993.

55. Robert Samuelson, "Don't Be Afraid of the Health Debate," *Newsweek* 122:17, October 25, 1993.

56. Quoted in William May, "The Ethical Foundations of Health Care Reform," *Christian Century*, June 1, 1994, p. 575.

57. Robin Toner, "On Language: Streamlining the Ungainly," *New York Times Magazine*, July 25, 1993.

58. Margaret Carlson, "Harry and Louise," *Time* 143:10, March 7, 1994.

59. Jacob Weissberg, "Cooperman," *New Republic*, November 22, 1993. Also editorial, "For the Cooper Plan," *New Republic*, December 6, 1993.

60. Quoted in George Church and Janice Castro, "Are You Ready for the Cure?," *Time* 141:21, May 24, 1993.

61. Quoted in Susan Headden, "The Little Lobby That Could," *US News* 117:10, September 12, 1994.

62. "Catholic Bishops on Health Care Reform," *Christian Century* 110, May 12, 1993, p. 513.

63. "Religion and Health Care," *Christian Century* 110, June 30, 1993.

64. Paul Starr, "For the Clinton Plan," *New Republic*, December 6, 1993.

65. Walter Zelman, "The Horse's Mouth," *New Republic*, October 11, 1993, p. 15.

66. Marcia Angell, "Fixing Medicare," *New England Journal of Medicine* 337:3, July 17, 1997.

67. R. Riegelman, "Medical Student Myopia Syndrome," *American Journal of Preventive Medicine* 7, 1991. The quote is from Stephen Havas, Sallie Rixey, et al., "The University of Maryland Experience in Integrating Preventive Medicine into the Clinical Medicine Curriculum," *Public Health Reports* 108:3, May–June 1993, p. 333.

68. The statistic is for 1993. In coming years, hospital closures would drive occupancy rates above 90 percent.

69. Jack Hadley and Stephen Zuckerman, *Determinants of Hospital Costs: Outputs, Inputs, and Regulation in the 1980s* (Urban Institute Press, 1991).

70. James Todd, "Reform of the Health Care System and Professional Liability," *New England Journal of Medicine* 329:23, December 2, 1993, p. 1733.

71. Gregory Curtis, "A Healthy Practice," *Texas Monthly* 22:2, February 1994.

72. Hacker, *Road to Nowhere*, 152.

Chapter 7. Managing Care

1. Elizabeth McCaughey, "No Exit," *New Republic*, February 7, 1994. McCaughey leveraged her brief celebrity into a spot on the New York gubernatorial ticket. She served as lieutenant governor of New York from 1995 to 1999, when Governor George Pataki dropped her from his administration.

2. Statistics from Susan Brink and Nancy Shute, "Are HMOs the Right Prescription?," *US News* 123:14, October 13, 1997; and Christine Gorman, William Dowell, et al., "Playing the HMO Game," *Time* 152:2, July 13, 1998.

3. Gregg Easterbrook, "Healing the Great Divide," *US News* 123:14, October 13, 1997.

4. Joe Selby, Bruce Fireman, and Bix Swain, "Effect of Copayment on Use of the Emergency Department in a Health Maintenance Organization," *New England Journal of Medicine* 334:10, March 7, 1996.

5. Paul Feldstein, "Private Cost Containment: The Effects of Utilization Review Programs on Health Care Use and Expenditures," *New England Journal of Medicine* 318:20, May 19, 1988. For a longer discussion, see CBO Staff Memorandum, *The Effects of Managed Care on Use and Cost of Health Services*, June 1992, particularly pp. 8–12.

6. Janet Firshein, "Blow for US Physician-Hospital Organizations," *Lancet* 346, September 23, 1995.

7. Bruce Barron, "The Sick Business," *New Republic* 217:26, December 29, 1997.

8. Susan Dentzer, "Inside the World of Managed Care," *US News* 120:15, April 15, 1996, p. 56.

9. David Noonan, "An Ailing Profession," *Newsweek* 136:13, September 25, 2000, p. 32.

10. US GAO, *Managed Care: Explicit Gag Clauses Not Found in HMO Contracts, But Physician Concerns Remain*, GAO/HEHS-97-175, August 1997. Notably, the GAO did find many examples of clauses barring physicians from disparaging the managed care company, and physicians admitted that fear of being dropped from a managed care contract might induce them to withhold information and treatment recommendations from patients.

11. James Robinson and Lawrence Casalino, "The Growth of Medical Groups Paid through Capitation in California," *New England Journal of Medicine* 333:25, December 21, 1995.

12. Susan Brink, "How Your HMO Could Hurt You," *US News* 120:2, January 15, 1996. Also Thomas Bodenheimer, "The HMO Backlash—Righteous or Reactionary," *New England Journal of Medicine* 335:21, November 21, 1996, as well as K. Swartz and T. Brennan, "Integrated Health Care, Capitated Payment, and Quality: The Role of Regulation," *Annals of Internal Medicine* 124, 1996.

13. Philip Caper, "Commentary on Managed Care," *Public Health Reports* 110, November–December 1995, p. 682.

14. Eugene Helsel, "Physicians and Managed Care," *New England Journal of Medicine* 332:17, April 27, 1995, p. 1174; James Reinertsen, review of George Anders, *Health Against Wealth*, in *New England Journal of Medicine* 336:7, February 13, 1997, p. 517; Charles Peck and Michael Eleff, "Corporate Managed Care," *New England Journal of Medicine* 334:16, April 18, 1996, p. 1061.

15. See Lawrence Goodrich, "New Referee on Health Care," *Christian Science Monitor* 90:2, November 26, 1997. Also, Marcia Angell, "Patients' Rights Bills and Other Futile Gestures," *New England Journal of Medicine* 342:22, June 1, 2000.

16. Katherine Biele, "States Push to Legislate Manage Health Care," *Christian Science Monitor* 90:66, March 3, 1998.

17. Maria Angell, "Quality and the Medical Marketplace—Following Elephants," *New England Journal of Medicine* 335:12, September 19, 1996, p. 883.

18. Harold Eist, "Managed Care and Mental Health," *New England Journal of Medicine* 335:1, July 4, 1996, p. 56.

19. Steven Simon, Richard Pan, et al., "Views of Managed Care," *New England Journal of Medicine* 340:12, March 25, 1999.

20. Lila Larimore Anastas, "When Managed Care Means Mediocre Care," *Newsweek* 134:7, August 16, 1999, p. 10.

21. Susan Reid, "Miss Treatment: Is Managed Care Unfair to Women?," *New Republic* 217:26, December 29, 1997.

22. See James Robinson, "The Curious Conversion of Empire Blue Cross," *Health Affairs* 22:4, July–August 2003.

23. "Direct Access to Specialists Is Increasing," *Southern Medical Journal* 90, March 1997, supplement.

24. Pamela Sherrid, "Managed Care Not So Managed," *US News* 123:20, November 24, 1997.

25. Marc Rivo and David Kindig, "A Report Card on the Physician Work Force in the United States," *New England Journal of Medicine* 333:14, April 4, 1996. Also, "Dealing with Job Dissatisfaction in Medicine," *Lancet* 357, May 5, 2001; and Jodie Morse, "Unionizing the ER," *Time* 154:1, July 5, 1999.

26. "Doctoring the Truth," *New Republic* 221:20, November 15, 1999; John Hayes and Howard Rudnitsky, "M.D. Inc.," *Forbes* 156:6, September 11, 1995.

27. Doug Podolosky, "If Your Doctor Can Do the Job, Why Go to the Hospital at All?," *US News* 117, July 18, 1994; Karen Southwick, "McDocs for the Rich," *Forbes* 168:3, August 6, 2001.

28. Neil Caesar, "That Sigh of Relief May Be Premature," *Southern Medical Journal* 90:1, January 1997, supplement, p. 2.

29. Matt Walsh, "Ronald Vessey Threw in the Towel," *Forbes* 154, July 4, 1994.

30. Laurence Linn, Virginia Clark, and Arlene Fink, "Physician and Patient Satisfaction as Factors Related to the Organization of Internal Medicine Group Practices," *Medical Care* 23:10, October 1985.

31. For more on the development of hospitalists, see Kevin O'Leary and Mark Williams, "The Evolution and Future of Hospital Medicine," *Mt. Sinai Journal of Medicine* 75:5, October 2008.

32. Susan Brink, "The Hospitalist," *US News* 125:4, July 27, 1998.

33. Karen Gianni, "Doctor Discontent," and David Squillacote, "Doctor Discontent," both correspondence in *New England Journal of Medicine* 340:8, February 25, 1999, pp. 650–52.

34. Kevin Grumbach, Dennis Osmond, et al., "Primary Care Physicians' Experience of Financial Incentives in Managed-Care Systems," *New England Journal of Medicine* 339:21, November 19, 1998.

35. David Asch and Peter Ubel, "Rationing by Any Other Name," *New England Journal of Medicine* 336:23, June 5, 1997, p. 1668.

36. Bernard Lown, "Restoring Care to Health Care," *Christian Science Monitor* 91:67, March 4, 1999, p. 11.

37. John Collins, "Reproductive Technology—The Price of Progress," *New England Journal of Medicine* 331:4, July 28, 1994.

38. Jerome Kassirer, "Managed Care and the Morality of the Marketplace," *New England Journal of Medicine* 333:1, July 6, 1995, p. 51. Malpractice was also an issue, with malpractice awards tripling between 1994 and 2000, leading many neurosurgeons and obstetricians to increase their use of defensive procedures such as cesarean sections. See GAO, *Medical Malpractice Insurance*, GAO-03-702, June 2003. For descriptions of excessive awards, see A. R. Localio, A. G. Lawthers, et al., "Relationship between Malpractice Claims and Cesarean Delivery," *Journal of the American Medical Association* 269, 1993.

39. "California Hospital under Fire for Seeking Healthier Patients," *Modern Healthcare*, August 21, 1995, as quoted in David Himmelstein and Steffie Woolhandler, "Extreme Risk—The New Corporate Proposition for Physicians," *New England Journal of Medicine* 333:25, December 21, 1995, p. 1707.

40. Ibid., 1706.

41. Louis Vernacchio, "Depersonalizing the Medical Student," *America* 172, February 25, 1995. The Cassell quote is from Eric Cassell, *Doctoring: The Nature of Primary Care Medicine* (Oxford University Press, 1997), 46.

42. The psychologist was Judith Hall of Northeastern University. Survey results are presented in "How Is Your Doctor Treating You?," *Consumer Reports*, February 1995.

43. Bernard Barber, "Compassion in Medicine: Toward New Definitions and New Institutions," *New England Journal of Medicine* 295:17, October 21, 1976, p. 939.

44. Debra Roter, Judith Hall, and Yutaka Aoki, "Physician Gender Effects in Medical Communication," *Journal of the American Medical Association* 288:6, August 14, 2002.

45. John Iglehart, "Academic Medical Centers Enter the Market: The Case of Philadelphia," *New England Journal of Medicine* 333:15, October 12, 1995.

46. Jonathan Cohn, "Sick," *New Republic* 224:22, May 28, 2001.

47. From Alan Sager, quoted in George Church, "Teaching Hospitals in Crisis," *Time* 146:3, July 17, 1995, p. 40.

48. Nancy Shute, "Code Blue: Crisis in the ER," *US News* 131:9, September 10, 2001.

49. Karen Kim and Edward Muir, "Drive-By Deliveries," *Public Health Reports* 112, July–August 1997.

50. Suzanne Gordon, "Is There a Nurse in the House?," *Nation*, February 13, 1995, p. 202.

51. Ibid.

52. James Kunen, "The New Hands-Off Nursing," *Time* 148, September 30, 1996.

53. Robert Sherrill, "The Madness of the Market," *Nation*, January 9, 1995.

54. Notably, Mount Sinai and NYU Hospitals in Manhattan found that they could not work constructively together and quickly dissolved the merger.

55. The quote is from Bruce Vladeck, then a professor at Mt. Sinai, quoted in Pamela Sherrid, "Why Dr. Kildare Stuck to Medicine," *US News* 127, July 12, 1999, p. 2. The insight is brilliant. Patients with the deepest loyalty to a particular practice were generally those who used the practice most because they were saddled with the most intractable chronic health issues.

56. See Jack Needleman, "Nonprofit to For-Profit Conversions," *Public Health Reports* 114, March–April 1999.

57. G. J. Young, K. R. Desai, and C. V. Lukas, "Does the Sale of Nonprofit Hospitals Threaten Health Care for the Poor?," *Health Affairs* 16:1, 1997. Stuart Altman and David Shactman disagreed. See *The Conversion of Hospitals from Not-for-Profit to For-Profit Status*, presented to the Council on the Economic Impact of Health System Change, Washington DC, September 26, 1996.

58. Elaine Silverman, Jonathan Skinner, and Elliot Fisher, "The Association between for-Profit Hospital Ownership and Increased Medicare Spending," *New England Journal of Medicine* 341:6, August 5, 1999.

59. Phyllis Berman and Bernard Condon, "Columbia Health versus Managed Care," *Forbes* 157:11, June 3, 1996.

60. See Jerome Kassirer, "Our Ailing Public Hospitals," *New England Journal of Medicine* 333:20, November 16, 1995.

61. A. Dobson, K. Coleman, and Richard Mechanic, "Analysis of Teaching Hospital Costs," Lewin/VHI, 1994. See also Donald Taylor, David Whellan, and Frank Sloan, "Effects of Admission to a Teaching Hospital on the Cost and Quality of Care for Medicare Beneficiaries," *New England Journal of Medicine* 340:4, January 28, 1999. Also, Daniel Greenberg, "USA Faces the Strains Put on Academic Health Centers," *Lancet* 350, July 19, 1997.

62. Cited in Avery Comarow, "Your Medical School May Be Suffering from Ill Health," *US News* 128:14, April 10, 2000.

63. John Iglehart, "Rapid Changes for Academic Medical Centers," *New England Journal of Medicine* 331:20, November 7, 1994, p. 1393.

64. H. Loft, J. Bunder, and Alain Enthoven, "Should Operations Be Regionalized?," *New England Journal of Medicine* 301:25, December 20, 1979.

65. Edward Hannan, "The Relation between Volume and Outcome in Health Care," *New England Journal of Medicine* 340:21, May 27, 1999.

66. Jersey Chen, Martha Radford, et al., "Do 'America's Best Hospitals' Perform Better for Acute Myocardial Infarction?," *New England Journal of Medicine* 340:4, January 28, 1999.

67. Daniel Greenberg, "Rapid Rise for US Health Care Costs, Again," *Lancet* 351, May 30, 1998.

68. GAO, *Employment-Based Health Insurance*, GAO/HEHS 97-35, GPO, February 1997.

69. D. Rowland, J. Feder, and P. Keenan, "The Problem of the Uninsured: It's Real and Getting Worse," in S. Altman, Uwe Reinhardt, and A. Shields, eds., *The Future US Healthcare System: Who Will Care for the Poor and Uninsured?* (Health Administration Press, 1998).

70. Medicaid managed care was allowed through either 1915b program waivers, 1115 demonstration waivers, or BBA 1932 provisions. See GAO, *Medicaid Managed Care*, GAO/HEHS-99-118, September 1999.

Chapter 8. Quantity and Quality

1. Examples drawn from Marc Kirscher, Elizabeth Marincola, and Elizabeth Teisberg, "The Role of Biomedical Research in Health Care Reform," *Science* 266, October 1994.

2. Michael Gianturco, "Surgeon's Helper," *Forbes* 155:5, February 27, 1995.

3. Both quotes are from Christopher Anderson, "Can Researchers Help to Lower Costs?," *Science* 261, July 23, 1993.

4. Ibid., 416.

5. "Just How Tainted Has Medicine Become?," *Lancet* 359, April 6, 2002. See also Helen Epstein's damning story about Roche's financing of the efficacy research for Tamiflu, which was purported to be effective against various

virulent strains of flu in the early 2000s. Epstein, "Flu Warning: Beware the Drug Companies!," *New York Review of Books*, May 12, 2011.

6. "Drug Company Influence on Medical Education in the USA," *Lancet* 356, September 2, 2000.

7. Quotes from Lainie Friedman-Ross and John Norton, "Is Academic Medicine for Sale?" (correspondence), *New England Journal of Medicine* 343:7, August 17, 2000, p. 508.

8. Thomas Ruane, "Is Academic Medicine for Sale?" (correspondence), *New England Journal of Medicine* 343:7, August 17, 2000, p. 510.

9. T. Bodenheimer, "Uneasy Alliance: Clinical Investigators and the Pharmaceutical Industry," *New England Journal of Medicine* 342:20, May 18, 2000.

10. Marcia Angell, "Is Academic Medicine for Sale?" (correspondence), *New England Journal of Medicine* 342:20, May 18, 2000, p. 1518.

11. "How the Industries Stack Up," *Fortune*, April 17, 2000.

12. The stipulation about informing consumers of potentially harmful side effects led to the bizarre pattern of listing the "quiet voiceover" in which the effects were quickly enumerated by an announcer in a low tone while evocative pictures showed on the screen.

13. Alexandra Marks, "A Harder Look at Prescription Drug Ads," *Christian Science Monitor* 93:95, April 11, 2001. See also the Government Accountability Office's lengthy report, *Prescription Drugs: FDA Oversight of Direct-to-Consumer Advertising Has Limits*, GAO-03-177, October 2002. The GAO estimated that 8.5 million consumers, annually, received a prescription from their physician in response to a direct-to-consumer ad (p. 4).

14. Joseph Shapiro and Stacey Schultz, "Prescriptions: How Your Doctor Makes the Choice," *US News* 130:7, February 19, 2001, p. 58.

15. Marks, "A Harder Look," 1.

16. For more on the social history of pharmaceutical use, see Elizabeth Watkins's excellent study on hormone replacement therapy and the US conception of aging: *The Estrogen Elixir* (Johns Hopkins University Press, 2010). For a broader overview on the impulse to "medicalize" previously undiagnosed conditions, see Peter Conrad, *The Medicalization of Society* (Johns Hopkins University Press, 2007).

17. Jonathan Skinner, Elliot Fisher, and John Wennberg, "The Efficiency of Medicare," NBER Working Paper 8395, July 2001.

18. A. Berg, "Variations among Family Physicians' Management Strategies for Lower Urinary Tract Infection in Women," *Journal of the American Board of Family Practitioners* 4, 1991.

19. Michael Millenson, "What Doctors Don't Know," *Washington Monthly* 30:12, December 1998.

20. Institute of Medicine, *Medicare: A Strategy for Quality Assurance*, ed. Kathleen Lohr (National Academies Press, 1990).

21. Mark Chassin, Edward Hannan, and Barbara DeBuono, "Benefits and Hazards of Reporting Medical Outcomes Publicly," *New England Journal of Medicine* 334:6, February 8, 1996.

22. In 2013, Michael Hochman published the wonderfully user-friendly *50 Studies Every Doctor Should Know* (Oxford University Press). The mere existence of such an anthology was hardly conceivable a generation earlier.

23. Patricia Howard and Edward Ellerbeck, "Optimizing Beta-Blocker Use after Myocardial Infarction," *American Family Physician* 62:8, October 15, 2000.

24. Atul Gawande wrote of "docking for mediocrity" (the obverse of paying for quality) but noted the profession's resistance to the sort of outside grading that pay-for-performance would require. See Gawande, "The Bell Curve," *New Yorker* 80:38, December 6, 2004.

25. See David Atkins, Kenneth Fink, and Jean Slutsky, "Better Information for Better Healthcare," *Annals of Internal Medicine* 142:12, June 21, 2005.

26. Institute of Medicine, *To Err Is Human: Building a Safer Health System* (National Academies Press, 1999).

27. Quoted in Robert Langreth, "Fixing Hospitals," *Forbes* 175:13, June 20, 2005, p. 72.

Chapter 9. Ethical Wrangling

1. The literature on Quinlan is vast. See "Should Karen Quinlan Be Allowed to Die?," *Christianity Today*, October 10, 1975, p. 41.

2. Amitai Etzioni, "Life, Dying, Death: Ethics and Open Decisions," *Science News*, August 17, 1974, p. 109. For a longer exposition of Etzioni's views, see *Genetic Fix* (Macmillan, 1973).

3. Matt Clark, Mariana Gosnell, et al., "A New Doctor's Dilemma," *Newsweek* 31, March 3, 1975, p. 125.

4. Horace Freeland Judson, "Fearful of Science," *Harper's* 250, March 1975, p. 32.

5. See Constance Holden, "Ethics: Biomedical Advances Confront Politicians, as Well as Professionals, with New Issues," *Science* 175, January 7, 1972.

6. See James Jones, *Bad Blood* (Free Press, 1993), for a detailed account of the Tuskegee experiments. Also, Seward Hiltner, "The Tuskegee Syphilis Study under Review," *Christian Century* 90, November 28, 1972; and Allan Brandt, "Racism and Research: The Case of the Tuskeegee Syphilis Study," in Judith Leavitt and Ronald Numbers, eds., *Sickness and Health in America* (University of Wisconsin Press, 1985).

7. Paul Lowinger, "Psychosurgery," *New Republic*, April 13, 1974. For details on the Willowbrook experiments, see David and Sheila Rothman, *The Willowbrook Wars: A Decade of Struggle for Social Justice* (Harper and Row, 1984).

8. The standard reference in the field is Ruth Faden and Tom Beauchamp, *A History and Theory of Informed Consent* (Oxford University Press, 1986). See, in particular, chapter 10 on manipulation and coercion of research subjects.

9. Jessica Mitford, "Experiments Behind Bars," *Atlantic* 231, January 1973, p. 65.

10. In addition to Faden and Beauchamp, see Franklin Miller, *The Ethics of Consent: Theory and Practice* (Oxford University Press, 2009), and Alan Wertheimer, *Exploitation* (Princeton University Press, 1999). Wertheimer's work is particularly accessible to the lay reader, using such examples as college athletes and surrogate mothers to illustrate the tricky issues surrounding consent.

11. George Silver, "Medicine: The Calculated Risks," *Nation*, January 27, 1969, p. 117. For a slightly different emphasis, see Henry Beecher, "Projection for the Investigator and His Subject Is Necessary," *Science* 164, June 13, 1969.

12. Steve Callahan, interview with Edmund Pellegrino, from "The Right to Die: Should a Doctor Decide?," *US News*, November 3, 1975, p. 53.

13. See Gina Kolata, "Withholding Medical Treatment," *Science* 205:31, August 31, 1979, p. 883.

14. Ibid.

15. Quoted in Robert Weir, "The Government and Selective Non-Treatment of Handicapped Infants," *New England Journal of Medicine* 309:11, September 15, 1983, p. 662.

16. Ibid.

17. Marcia Angell, "Handicapped Children: Baby Doe and Uncle Sam," *New England Journal of Medicine* 309:11, September 15, 1983, p. 659.

18. Ward Casscells, "Heart Transplantation," *New England Journal of Medicine* 315:21, November 20, 1986.

19. Dana Seiden, "Diminishing Resources; Critical Choices," *Commonweal* 112, March 8, 1985, p. 139.

20. Koop worked to establish patient-care review committees at hospitals around the country, which would include an assigned patient advocate whose job included the obligation to inform authorities at DHHS if she observed noncompliance with the dictate to treat all handicapped persons. Beth Spring, "Surgeon General Koop and the Fight for the Newborn," *Christianity Today* 28, March 16, 1984, p. 37.

21. Lester Thurow, "The Ethical Costs of Health Care," *Harper's*, April 1985, p. 23.

22. "When Lawyers Second Guess Doctors," *US News* 96, February 13, 1984, p. 46.

23. Victor Fuchs, "The 'Rationing' of Medical Care," *New England Journal of Medicine* 311:24, December 13, 1984, p. 1572.

24. John Paris and Andrew Varga, "Care of the Hopelessly Ill," *America*, September 22, 1984, p. 142.

25. Norman Daniel, "Why Saying No to Patients in the United States Is So Hard," *New England Journal of Medicine* 314:21, May 22, 1986, p. 1383.

26. George Annas, "Nancy Cruzan and the Right to Die," *New England Journal of Medicine* 323:10, September 6, 1990, p. 671.

27. The case prompted several dozen bioethicists to draft a response at the second annual Conference of Bioethicists in Lutsen, Minnesota, July 1, 1990. The full text, titled, *Bioethicists' Statement on the U.S. Supreme Court's Cruzan Decision*, can be downloaded from PubMed.gov.

28. Jerry Buckley, "How Doctors Decide Who Shall Live and Who Shall Die," *US News* 108, January 22, 1990, pp. 50–58.

29. Lisa Belkin, "The High Cost of Living," *New York Times Magazine*, January 31, 1993.

30. Stephen Lammers, "Tragedies and Medical Choices," *Christian Century*, September 8, 1993, pp. 845–46. Lammers noted that at the time of the procedure, there was not a single surviving individual of such an effort to separate conjoined twins in which the twins had a faulty heart.

31. Albert Rosenfeld, "Tough Cases, Tough Choices," *New York Magazine*, January 9, 1989, p. 34.

32. AMA, Council on Ethical and Judicial Affairs, "Ethical Issues in Managed Care," *Journal of the American Medical Association* 273, 1995.

33. R. Koepp and S. H. Miles, "Comment on the AMA Report, 'Ethical Issues in Managed Care,'" *Journal of Clinical Ethics* 6, 1995; M. A. Hall and R. A. Berenson, "Ethical Practice in Managed Care: A Dose of Realism," *Annals of Internal Medicine* 128, 1995.

34. Joseph Shapiro, "Who Cares How High Her IQ Really Is?," *US News* 119:10, September 11, 1995.

35. Peter Neumann, Soheyla Gharib, and Milton Weinstein, "The Cost of a Successful Delivery with In Vitro Fertilization," *New England Journal of Medicine* 331:4, July 29, 1994.

36. Jean Seligmann and Karen Springen, "Is It More Human Not to Operate?," *Newsweek* 122:8, August 23, 1993.

37. Ezekiel Emanuel and Linda Emanuel, "The Economics of Dying," *New England Journal of Medicine* 330:8, February 24, 1994.

38. See Eric Lindblom, "Where There's a Living Will," *Washington Monthly* 27, November 1995.

39. Emanuel and Emanuel, "Economics of Dying," 541.

40. Anne Dye, Peggy Rodebush, and Geri Hempel, "Hospice and End-of-Life Care," in David Plocher and Patricia Metzger, eds., *The Case Manager's Training Manuel* (Aspen, 2001).

41. P. J. van der Waal, Wal van der Waal, et al. "Physician Assisted Suicide and Other Medical Practices Involving the End of Life in the Netherlands," *New England Journal of Medicine* 335:22, November 28, 1996.

42. Matt Clark, Susan Agrest, et al., "A Right to Die?," *Newsweek*, November 3, 1975, p. 59. See also Katherine Bouton, "Painful Decisions," *New York Times Magazine*, August 5, 1990.

43. Stewart King, "Death and Dignity: The Case of Diane," *New England Journal of Medicine* 325:9, August 29, 1991, p. 658.

44. Quoted in Kathleen Foley, "Competent Care for the Dying Instead of PAS," *New England Journal of Medicine* 336:1, January 2, 1997, p. 54.

45. David Schiedermayer, "Oregon and the Death of Dignity," *Christianity Today*, February 6, 1995, p. 18.

46. Marcia Angell, "The Supreme Court and Physician Assisted Suicide: The Ultimate Right," *New England Journal of Medicine* 336:1, January 2, 1997.

Chapter 10. Medicare and Medicaid

1. The trust fund consisted of overpayments made into the system while Baby Boomers were in their prime working years. As they retired, they would draw down the trust fund. Scholarly work on underfunding the trust fund dates back to Paul Ginsburg and Malcolm Curtis, "Prospects for Medicare's Hospital Insurance Trust Fund," *Health Affairs* 2, February 1983. See also Gail Wilensky and Joseph Newhouse, "Medicare: What's Right? What's Wrong? What's Next?," *Health Affairs* 18, January 1999; and Richard Foster, "The Financial Status of Medicare," *Public Health Reports* 113, March–April 1998.

2. Phillip Longman, "The Insatiable Entitlement," *Washington Monthly* 27:4, April 1995.

3. For an insightful discussion of managing expectations for medical outcomes in elderly populations, see Atul Gawande, *Being Mortal* (Metropolitan Books, 2014).

4. Dan Crippen, "Medicare's Payments to Physicians," statement before the Committee on Ways and Means, US House of Representatives, February 28, 2002.

5. "Medicare under Siege," *Consumer Reports*, September 1994.

6. Jerald McClendon, Robert Politzer, et al., "Downsizing the Physicians Workforce," *Public Health Reports* 112, May–June 1997.

7. Council on Graduate Medical Education, *Recommendations to Improve Access to Health Care through Physician Workforce Reform* (HHS, 1994). See also Pew Health Professions Commission, *Critical Challenges: Revitalizing the Health Professions for the Twenty-First Century* (UCSF Center for Health Professions, 1995).

8. Jay Noren, "A National Physician Workforce Policy," *Public Health Reports* 112, May–June 1997. Of note, a dissenting view argued that prolonged life expectancy, more intensive use of medical services and tests, and increasing use of medicine by rural populations would negate any surplus in the physician workforce. See William Schwartz, Frank Sloan, and Daniel Mendelson, "Why There Will Be Little or No Physician Surplus between Now and the Year 2000," *New England Journal of Medicine* 318:14, April 4, 1988.

9. See Uwe Reinhardt, "Planning the Nation's Health Workforce: Let the Market In," *Inquiry* 31, 1994. Also, Daniel Greenberg, "Prescription for Doctor Glut Targets Foreign Graduates," *Lancet* 347, February 3, 1996.

10. Sara Collins, "Desperate for Doctors," *US News* 115:11, September 20, 1993.

11. Many of these fifteen states limited prescriptions to non-addictive drugs.

12. Jeane Knudtsen and Jean Rasch, "Nurse Practitioners in Primary Care," *New England Journal of Medicine* 330:21, May 26, 1994.

13. Office of Technology Assessment, *Health Care in Rural America*, Washington, September 1990. Also, Eric Larson, Gary Hart, and Jeffrey Humel, "Rural Physician Assistants: A Survey of Graduates of MEDEX Northwest," *Public Health Reports* 109:2, March–April 1994.

14. David Rubin, "Nurse Practitioners in Primary Care," correspondence, *New England Journal of Medicine* 330:21, May 26, 1994.

15. Abigail Zuger, "Nurse Practitioners in Primary Care," correspondence, *New England Journal of Medicine* 330:21, May 26, 1994.

16. William Scanlon, "Nursing Workforce: Recruitment and Retention of Nurses and Nurse's Aides Is a Growing Concern," statement before the Committee on Health, Education, Labor, and Pensions, US Senate, GAO-01-750T, May 17, 2001.

17. Ibid.

18. Michael Kinsley, "The Best Way to Fix Medicare," *Time* 146:10, September 5, 1995, p. 24.

19. Quoted in Trudy Lieberman, "How the GOP Made Medicare," *Nation*, November 6, 1995, p. 536.

20. Ibid.

21. "Medicare Supplement Insurance," *Consumer Reports*, June 1984, p. 350.

22. See Einer Elhauge, "Medi-Choice," *New Republic*, November 13, 1995. Also, Ed Rubenstein, "How Not to Cut," *National Review*, July 31, 1995; and Michael Kinsley, "Been There, Done That," *New Republic* 315:15, October 9, 1995.

23. J. E. Ware, et al., "Differences in 4-Year Health Outcomes for Elderly and Poor, Chronically Ill Patients in HMO and Fee-for-Service Systems," *Journal of the American Medical Association* 276:13, October 2, 1996.

24. See GAO, *Medicare+Choice*, GAO/HEHS-00-183, September 2000.

25. New Jersey, Maryland, Pennsylvania, Illinois, Rhode Island, Connecticut, and New York all had pharmacy assistance programs by 1995. All capped eligibility at just above federal poverty limits. See S. B. Soumerai, D. Ross-Degnan, et al., "A Critical Analysis of Studies of State Drug Reimbursement Policies," *Milbank Quarterly* 71:2, 1993.

26. Dan Crippen, "A CBO Analysis of the Administration's Prescription Drug Proposal," presented to the Subcommittee on Health, Committee on Ways and Means, May 11, 2000.

27. "Medscam," *Mother Jones* 20, March–April 1995, p. 26.

28. Chester Robinson, Thomas Hoyer, and Thomas Ault, "Encouraging Medical Device Innovation," *Public Health Reports* 111, September–October 1996.

29. The nation's Medicaid and Medicare beneficiaries filed over four billion claims in 1995.

30. "Medscam," 28. See also Paul Van de Water, "Fraud, Waste, and Abuse in Medicare," statement before the Committee on Finance, US Senate, July 31, 1995.

31. The figure is only for outpatient prescription drugs. Inpatient drugs were covered under Medicare Part A benefits.

32. Figures are from CBO, "Issues in Designing a Prescription Drug Benefit for Medicare," October 2002.

33. Daniel Greenberg, "Congress Glumly Moves toward Medicare Drug Benefit," *Lancet* 361, June 28, 2003, p. 2216.

34. Part B premiums covered less than one-fourth of the cost of the Part B program.

35. The White House plan was described at length in the administration's *Mid-Session Review* from June 2000 but was never introduced into Congress.

36. CBO, *A Detailed Description of CBO's Cost Estimate for the Medicare Prescription Drug Benefit*, July 2004. See also Douglas Holz-Eakin to Bill Thomas, February 9, 2005, downloadable from www.cbo.gov.

37. To this point, the CBO estimated in 2007 that the government could achieve scant savings by negotiating bulk prices for Medicare drugs. See Peter Orszag to Ron Wyden, April 10, 2007, downloadable from www.cbo.gov.

38. The states were New Jersey, Maryland, Pennsylvania, Illinois, Rhode Island, Connecticut, and New York. Notably, these states were among the nation's wealthiest and could better afford to shoulder the full cost of the programs than could poorer states. See Stephen Soumerai and Dennis Ross-Degnan, "Inadequate Prescription-Drug Coverage for Medicare Enrollees," *New England Journal of Medicine* 340:9, March 4, 1999.

39. Jonathan Cohn, "Shrug Coverage," *New Republic* 234:3, January 30, 2006, p. 6.

40. Ibid.

41. Sara Rosenbaum and Joel Teitelbaum, "Implementing the Medicare Part D Prescription Drug Benefit Program," *Public Health Reports* 120, July–August 2005. Also CBO, *Spending Patterns for Prescription Drugs under Medicare Part D*, December 2011.

42. See GAO, "Extent of Dental Disease in Children Has Not Decreased and Millions Are Estimated to Have Untreated Tooth Decay," GAO-08-1121, September 2008.

43. Charles Baum and Christopher Ruhm, *Age, Socioeconomic Status and Obesity Growth*, NBER Working Paper No. 13289, August 2007. See also CBO, *Growing Disparities in Life Expectancy*, April 17, 2008.

44. Henrie Treadwell and Marguerite Ro, "Poverty, Race, and the Invisible

Men," *American Journal of Public Health* 98 (supp.), September 2008, p. 143. For statistics on black/white disparities in cardiovascular disease, see Lewis Kuller, "Not Genes, Not Medical Care, but How People Live," *Public Health Reports* 110, September–October 1995.

45. Christine Gorman, "A Racial Gap," *Time* 154:17, October 25, 1999.

46. E. D. Peterson, S. M. Wright, et al., "Racial Variation in Cardiac Procedure Use and Survival Following Acute Myocardial Infarction in the Department of Veterans Affairs," *Journal of the American Medical Association* 271, 1994. Also, Jack Geiger, "Race and Health Care: An American Dilemma?," *New England Journal of Medicine* 335:11, September 12, 1996.

47. R. S. Morrison, S. Wallenstein, et al., "We Don't Carry That: Failure of Pharmacies in Predominantly Nonwhite Neighborhoods to Stock Opioid Analgesics," *New England Journal of Medicine* 342, 2000.

48. Rachel Johnson, Debra Roter, et al., "Patient Race/Ethnicity and Quality of Patient-Physician Communication," *American Journal of Public Health* 94:12, December 2004.

49. Robert Steinbrook, "Diversity in Medicine," *New England Journal of Medicine* 334:20, May 16, 1996.

50. Vera Thurmond and Darrell Kirch, "Impact of Minority Physicians on Health Care," *Southern Medical Journal* 91:11, November 1998.

51. Ibid.

52. Bruce Shulman suggests that the *Bakke* case ultimately increased racial diversity in higher education by drawing the attention of university leaders to the issue. See Shulman, *The Seventies: The Great Shift in American Culture, Society, and Politics* (Simon and Schuster, 2001), 68–70.

53. Robert Levine, James Foster, et al., "Black-White Inequalities in Mortality and Life Expectancy, 1933–1999," *Public Health Reports* 116, September–October 2001.

54. Ibid.

55. Congress oversaw the plans through the Quality Assurance Reform Initiative and the Quality Improvement System for Managed Care, which worked to ensure that plans were not short-changing Medicaid beneficiaries. Health outcomes suggested the Medicaid beneficiaries received higher quality care in managed care than in traditional fee-for-service medicine—a finding somewhat at odds with the general population.

56. See GAO, "Medicaid Managed Care: Access and Quality Requirements Specific to Low-Income and Other Special Needs Enrollees," GAO-05-44R, December 8, 2004.

57. The devil was in the details. States could set enrollment criteria and varied the ceiling from 140 percent of poverty to 350 percent. The federal burden ranged from 65 to 87 percent depending on the wealth of the state and the cost of providing care. By contrast, the federal burden for the Medicaid programs ranged from 50 to 76 percent.

58. See CBO, "The State Children's Health Insurance Program," May 2007.

59. "The Monster That Ate Nashville," *Economist* 374, January 22, 2005, p. 33.

Chapter 11. (Un)Affordable Care

1. Institute for Health and Socio-Economic Policy, "IHSP Hospital 200: The Nation's Most—and Least—Expensive Hospitals," December 13, 2005.

2. Recounted in Dug Garr, "Sick, and Tired of the Endless Paperwork," *Newsweek* 143:25, June 21, 2004, p. 19.

3. David Himmelstein, Deborah Thorne, Elizabeth Warren, and Steffie Woolhandler, "Illness and Injury as Contributors to Bankruptcy," February 8, 2005, unpublished paper, available on the Social Science Research Network. See also, by the same authors, "Medical Bankruptcy in the United States 2007," *American Journal of Medicine* 122:8, August 2009.

4. Quoted in Dan Frosch, "Your Money or Your Life," *Nation* 280:7, February 21, 2005, p. 13.

5. For a good summary of the planning process underlying the Affordable Care Act, see Norm Ornstein, "The Real Story of Obamacare's Birth," *Atlantic*, July 6, 2015.

6. See Lisa Cool, "Healthcare Reform's Public Option: Everything You Need to Know," CBS News, November 13, 2009.

7. Matt Cover, "Lieberman on Public Option Health Care," CBS News, November 10, 2009.

8. "Town Halls Having an Impact? White House Bends on Health Care Provision," Fox News, August 16, 2009.

9. Donald Cottler, MD, interview with the author, August 27, 2009.

10. See, for example, "PhRMA Statement on Health Care Reform," March 25, 2010, available at www.phrma.org/press-release/phrma-statement-on-health-care-reform2.

11. James Kirchick, "Why Martha Coakley Lost Ted Kennedy's Senate Seat," *New York Daily News*, January 20, 2010.

12. From the Office of the Press Secretary, White House, March 23, 2010.

13. Mitt Romney, statement, Project Vote Smart, June 7, 2012.

14. Estimates in late 2014 for states wishing to establish exchanges were $80 million on contract and staff fees to build the exchanges and lead times of 12–18 months. Moreover, patches and fixes on exchanges begun in 2013 cost tens of millions of dollars. See Stephanie Armour, "Five States' Health-Care Exchanges See Costly Fixes," *Wall Street Journal*, June 3, 2014.

15. The math is actually a bit more complicated, as a number of states created state–federal partnership in which they piggy-backed the federal exchange while managing local insurance products in whole or in part. In fall 2013, sixteen states and the District of Columbia were operating independent exchanges, and

nineteen states were relying entirely on the federal exchange. The remaining fifteen states were using the federal exchange while maintaining some control over their insurance offerings. See the Commonwealth Fund, *State Action to Establish Health Insurance Marketplaces*, http://www.commonwealthfund.org /Maps-and-Data/State-Exchange-Map.aspx (accessed November 24, 2013).

16. Dan Pfeiffer, "President Obama's Long Form Birth Certificate," White House Blog, http://www.whitehouse.gov/blog/2011/04/27/presi dent-obamas-long-form-birth-certificate.

17. Robert Pear, "Most Governors Refuse to Set Up Health Exchanges," *New York Times*, December 14, 2012.

18. The chart is from Kaiser Health News, as reprinted in Sarah Kliff, "It's Official: The Feds Will Run Most Obamacare Exchanges," *Washington Post*, February 18, 2012.

19. See Jonathan Engel, *Poor People's Medicine* (Duke University Press, 2006), for details on Medicaid expansion between 1970 and 1990. For status of Medicaid expansion under the ACA, see Advisory Board Company, *Where the States Stand on Medicaid Expansion*, http://www.advisory.com/Daily-Briefing /Resources/Primers/MedicaidMap (accessed November 24, 2013).

20. Stephanie Condon, "Senate Moves to Fix 'Donut Hole' in Drug Prices," CBS News, December 15, 2009.

21. When Americans finally realized that they would no longer have access to the inexpensive catastrophic plans, which many had purchased prior to the roll-out of the exchanges, an enterprising reporter from the *Tampa Bay Times* found thirty-seven instances in which the White House had made this precise promise. See PolitiFact.Com on "Obama: If you like your health care plan you'll be able to keep your health care plan," http://www.politifact.com/obama-like-health-care-keep/.

22. Rachel Garfield, Anthony Damico, et al., "The Coverage Gap: Uninsured Poor Adults in States That Do Not Expand Medicaid," Henry Kaiser Foundation Issue Brief, http://kff.org/health-reform/issue-brief (accessed December 3, 2014).

23. Many responsible (that is, nonpartisan) projections were created during the debate over the legislation and the ensuing three-year roll-out. See, for example, the US GAO, *Patient Protection and Affordable Care Act: Effect on Long-Term Federal Budget Outlook Largely Depends on Whether Cost Containment Sustained*, GAO-13-281, January 31, 2013. Data are ubiquitous through the think tanks and government agencies. See, for example, US GAO, *Health Care Spending: Public Payers Face Burden of Entitlement Program Growth, While All Payers Face Rising Prices and Increasing Use of Services*, GAO-07-497T, February 15, 2007.

24. See Jonathan Oberlander, "Throwing Darts: America's Elusive Search for Cost Control," *Journal of Health Politics, Policy and Law* 36:3, June 2011, pp. 477–84.

25. For a nice analysis of the political fallout from the shut-down, see Dan Balz and Scott Clement, "Major Damage to GOP after Shutdown," *Washington Post*, October 22, 2013.

26. *National Federation of Independent Business v. Sibelius*, US Supreme Court, June 28, 2012. Notably, the Court failed to uphold the law under the Commerce Clause, but turned to the taxation powers of Congress to justify the law's constitutionality. The majority opinion, written by Chief Justice John Roberts, seemed as much aimed at establishing the court's political neutrality as it was in establishing a clean precedent. Congress had assiduously avoided the word *tax* in enacting the original legislation (in an effort to avoid appearing to be fiscally expansionist) and thus was somewhat chagrinned to find the word foisted on it by a seemingly friendly court.

27. Chris Conover, "Should States Expand Medicaid?," *Forbes*, February 6, 2013. For a helpful map of states that chose to expand their Medicaid program, and four additional states that considered doing so, see Families USA, "A 50-State Look at Medicaid Expansion," http://familiesusa.org/product/50-state-look-medicaid-expansion.

28. Douglas Holtz-Eakin, "The Real Arithmetic of Health Care Reform," *New York Times*, March 21, 2010. Also, Douglas Elmendorf to the Honorable Judd Gregg, CBO correspondence, July 7, 2009. More broadly, Douglas Elmendorf, *CBO's Analysis of Major Health Care Legislation Enacted in March 2010*, March 30, 2011.

29. Steven Brill, "The Bitter Pill: Why Medical Bills Are Killing Us," *Time*, March 4, 2013.

30. Michael Cannon, "Avoiding a Health Care Disaster," Cato Institute, January 22, 2009.

31. Matthew Holt, "Critical of *Critical*," Health Care Blog, December 31, 2008, found at http://thehealthcareblog.com/blog/2008/12/31/critical-of-critical/.

32. *The Cost of Illegal Immigration to Californians*, American Federation for Immigration Reform, November 2004. See also, Stephen Wallace, Jacqueline Torres, et al., *Undocumented and Uninsured: Barriers to Effective Care for Immigrant Populations*, Commonwealth Fund, August 2013.

33. Arnold Relman, "The Health Reform We Need and Are Not Getting," *New York Review of Books*, July 2, 2009.

34. Marcia Angell, "Should Obama's Health Care Be Opposed? An Exchange," *New York Review of Books*, June 7, 2012.

35. Quoted in ibid.

36. Relman writes at length of flaws in both the ACOs and the IPAB. See Arnold Relman, "How Doctors Could Rescue Health Care," *New York Review of Books*, October 27, 2011.

37. Quoted in Jeff Madrick, "Obama and Health Care: The Straight Story," *New York Review of Books*, June 21, 2012.

38. See Lainie Rutkow and Jon Vernick, "The U.S. Constitution's Commerce

Clause, the Supreme Court, and Public Health," *Public Health Reports* 126, September–October 2011.

39. A nice exposition of the debates around the case can be found in Ezra Klein, "Unpopular Mandate," *New Yorker*, June 25, 2012.

40. See Ronald Dworkin, "Why Did Roberts Change His Mind?," *New York Review of Books* blog, July 9, 2012, available at http://www.nybooks.com/daily/2012/07/09/why-did-roberts-change-his-mind/.

41. *National Federation of Independent Business, et al., v. Sibelius, Secretary of Health and Human Services, et al.*, June 28, 2012, p. 6.

42. Andrea Sisko, Christopher Truffer, et al., "Health Spending Projections through 2018," *Health Affairs*, http://content.healthaffairs.org/content/28/2/w346.full.

43. Donald Berwick and Andrew Hackbarth, "Eliminating Waste in US Health Care," *Journal of the American Medical Association* 307:14, April 11, 2012.

44. Steve Brill published an expose of insanity in hospital pricing with a lengthy cover article in *Time* titled "Bitter Pill: Why Medical Bills Are Killing Us." The issue became the best-selling issue ever (February 20, 2013).

45. Ibid.

46. CBO, *Evidence on the Costs and Benefits of Health Information Technology*, May 2008.

47. Arnold Relman, "Health Care: The Disquieting Truth," *New York Review of Books*, September 30, 2010.

48. See CBO, *Technological Change and the Growth of Health Care Spending*, January 2008.

49. Gerard Anderson and Jane Horvath, "The Growing Burden of Chronic Disease in America," *Public Health Reports* 119, May–June 2004.

50. Sabrina Corlette, Kevin Lucia, Justin Giovannelli, and Dania Palanker, *Uncertain Future for Affordable Care Act Leads Insurers to Rethink Participation, Prices*, Urban Institute, January 2017. See also Laura Skopec, John Holohan, and Patricia Solleveld, *Health Insurance Coverage in 2014: Significant Progress, but Gaps Remain*, Urban Institute, September 2016.

51. John Holohan, Linda Blumberg, Erik Wengle, and Patricia Solleveld, *What Explains the 21 Percent Increase in 2017 Marketplace Premiums and Why Do Increases Vary across the Country?*, Urban Institute, January 2017.

52. Stacey McMorrow and John Hollahan, *The Widespread Slowdown in Health Spending Growth Implications for Future Spending Projections and the Cost of the Affordable Care Act*, Urban Institute, June 2016.

53. See the full description of the Ryan plan, with executive summary, at http://paulryan.house.gov/healthcare/.

54. Alice Rivlin, Loren Adler, and Stuart Butler, *Why Repealing the ACA Before Replacing It Won't Work, and What Might*, Brookings Institution, December 13, 2016.

55. In 2008, before the implementation of the ACA, nearly a third of people

between ages 60 and 64 trying to purchase policies on the individual market had been rejected.

Chapter 12. Afterword

1. Canada's seventeen medical schools are accredited by the Association of American Medical Colleges (AAMC) and held to the same standards as US medical schools. The AAMC does not accredit schools of osteopathic medicine, which grant the DO degree.

2. The Affordable Care Act (ACA) set standards of medical loss ratios that will cut into administrative salaries and corporate profits. For total profits, see Ezekiel Emanuel, "Less Than $26 Billion: Don't Bother," *New York Times*, November 3, 2011.

3. Return on revenues has hovered at 16 percent for the past decade. See Public Citizen, "Pharmaceuticals Rank as Most Profitable Industry Again," *Congress Watch*, April 17, 2002.

4. The current national occupancy rate is about 92 percent.

5. The best exposition on this is Steven Brill, "Bitter Pill," *Time*, April 4, 2013.

6. Jessica Glenza, "British Couple Face $200,000 Hospital Bill after Baby Born Early in New York," *Guardian*, January 1, 2015, http://www.theguardian .com/us-news/2015/jan/01/british-couple-hospital-bill-baby-born-new-york.

7. Bureau of Labor Statistics, "Occupational Outlook Handbook," http:// www.bls.gov/ooh/healthcare/physicians-and-surgeons.htm.

8. Notably, despite improvements, the VA produces disparities in outcomes along racial lines. See Amal Trivedi, Regina Grebla, et al., "Despite Improved Quality of Care in the Veterans Affairs Health System, Racial Disparity Persists for Important Clinical Outcomes," *Health Affairs* 30:4, April 2011. Literature on TriCare is extensive. For a quick overview, see *Evaluation of the TriCare Program* for the latest year. For future changes to the benefit structure of the program, see US DOD, *Final Report of the Task Force on the Future of Tricare*, December 20, 2007.

9. Paul Van de Water, "Medicare Is Not Bankrupt," from the Center on Budget and Policy Priorities, August 4, 2014, http://www.cbpp.org/files /7-12-11health.pdf.

10. For a historical perspective on the accomplishments of Medicaid, see Jonathan Engel, *Poor People's Medicine* (Duke University Press, 2006).

Index

AAMC (Association of American Medical Colleges), 26, 97, 185, 270n1
Aaron, Henry, 102, 106
AARP, 110, 177–78, 180, 199–200
abortion, 110–11, 155
Abramowitz, Kenneth, 116
abuse. *See* fraud/abuse
ACA. *See* Affordable Care Act
ACOs (accountable care organizations), 205–7
ADA (Americans With Disabilities Act; 1990), 99–100
administrative complexity, 209
adverse selection, 105, 176, 180
Aetna, 111, 119, 129–30
affirmative action, 23
Affordable Care Act (ACA; "Obamacare"; 2010): administration of, 197–98; catastrophic plans eliminated by, 200, 202, 213, 267n21; conservatives' opposition to, 206; constitutionality of, 202, 206–7, 268n26; and the Consumer-Choice Health Plan, 56; co-payments and deductibles, 208, 213; cost control by, 203–4, 211; coverage expansion to age 26, 194; failures of, 207–10, 219, 221–22; healthcare costs under, 4, 192–93, 203; illegal immigrants under, 204; insurance exchanges, 195–98, 201, 266–67nn14–15; job-killing aspect of, 196–97; liberals' opposition to, 205–6; as managed competition, 192; mandatory buy-in, 195–96, 206–7, 220–21; mandatory employer provision, 196–97; and Medicaid expansion, 198–202, 220; medical loss ratios under, 270n2; planning for/passage of, 191–94; preexisting-condition coverage, 194–95; premiums, 211; prescription drug coverage, 199–200; private insurance system preserved by, 196; public plan under, 192–93; reception of, 213–14; Republican opposition to, 198, 201–2, 206–7, 211–12; revenue mechanisms of, 201, 203, 267n23; Ryan's replacement